# Data-Oriented Design

Richard Fabian

September 29, 2018

**Data oriented design** by Richard Fabian

Published by Richard Fabian

**Cover design:** Richard Fabian
**Proofreader:** Caitlin P. Ring

First published in 2018
See www.dataorienteddesign.com for updates and information.

# Contents

# Introduction

It took a lot longer than expected to be able to bring this book out, but it's been all the better for how long the ideas have been fermenting in the heads of so many developers. Many of the concepts that were fledgling assumptions have now been tested out in practice. In many cases, the following chapters are ideas that started out as simple observations and slowly evolved into solid frameworks for building software in a data-oriented manner. Some sections have remained largely unchanged from their first drafts, such as the sections on existence based processing or the arguments against the object-oriented approach, but others have been re-written a number of times, trying to distill just the right kind of information at the right pace.

The data-oriented movement has also calmed down now. It's no longer fighting to be heard, and many more people are seeing the core issues with object-oriented approaches, so the idea of data-oriented design sounds a lot less like a rage against the establishment. People who used to be all entrenched advocates of object-oriented design have moved to functional programming with languages like Clojure, or to concurrency centric languages like Go, or moved the goalposts by embracing a distributed way of developing their software, such as through service oriented architectures, or microservices. With the enterprise developer taking their leave of the monolithic object-oriented approach, the voices for object-oriented design now seem more like the zealots.

Most people come at data-oriented design from object-oriented design, and have heard of it only because of people claiming object-oriented design to be bad, or wrong, or simply not the only way of doing things. This may be the case for large-scale software, and though object-oriented code does have its place (as we shall discuss in chapter 14), it has been the cause[1] of much wasted time and effort during its relatively short life in our passionate industry of software development and game development in particular.

My own journey through imperative procedural programming, then object-oriented programming then finally finding, embracing, and now spreading the word of data-oriented design, all started with C++. I like to think of C++ as a go to language for the best of both worlds when you require one of the worlds to be assembly level quality of control over your instructions. The other world is the world of abstractions, the ability to create code that does more in less time. Over the years, I have learned a great deal about how C++ helps add layer upon layer of abstraction to help make less code do more, but I've also seen how the layers of various quality code can cause a cascade of errors and unmaintainable spaghetti that puts off even the most crunch hardened programmers.

I'd like to thank those who have helped in the making of this book, whether by reading early versions of this text and criticising the content or structure, or by being an inspiration or guiding light on what would truly best represent this new paradigm. You can thank the critics for the layout of the chapters and the removal of so much of the negativity that originally sat on the pages in the critique of design patterns, which are very nearly the opposite of data-oriented design. It was natural they took a beating. However, the whole chapter felt like a flame war, so it was removed.

This book is a practical guide for software developers. It is for software engineers working to create high quality prod-

---

[1]Large-Scale C++[2] is a book almost entirely dedicated to showing how object-oriented development needn't destroy the productivity of large-scale software projects

ucts across multiple platforms. It's for independent developers trying to get the most out of their chosen target hardware. In fact, it's for anyone who develops large-scale, cutting-edge software in restrictive hardware, in a competitive environment. It is a book about how to write code. It is a book written to educate developers in a coding paradigm that is future proof, unlike the style of coding we've become so accustomed to. It is a book rooted in C++, the language of choice by game developers of the last ten years, and provides practical advice on how to migrate without throwing away years of accumulated code and experience. This book is about how you can transform your development.

This book is for you because I cannot hold it back anymore. There needs to be a book on this subject, and even though I'm not the right person to write it (this is my first textbook and I have no support from a publisher or anyone with experience in writing textbooks) it's probably better it exists, so someone can criticise its content and write a better one. As an author, a programmer, a parent, a dabbler in many things, I suffer from imposter syndrome, and the idea that I could write a book that people would find useful is alien, but the reason this book is in print right now is that real people have told me the version I released for free has already helped them. Knowing some people have read that book, with its errors, incomplete sections, and sometimes, outright misinformation due to the decay over time and the problems with trying to translate experience into facts, I couldn't let it be the only resource anymore.

So here we are. More experience has shown that even though the concepts within the book are timeless, some of the ways in which the subject was taught have not survived the movement of game development towards relying much more on third party engines. Some of the concrete implementation details no longer work on current hardware, so the point of testing your work, and working out what is happening yourself, have been emphasised.

Let's make this absolutely clear here: the literal techniques that are identified in this book as ways of working with hardware to increase performance wouldn't have worked twenty years ago, and very likely, won't work in another twenty years. That is another reason why this book needed a revision before being released fully. The ideas that data-oriented design pushes are not specific to an era, they can even be used outside of programming. The ideals are timeless, but they are also rooted in their history of needing a solution to an era of game development that was suffering from a delusion of piling on more and more complexity to fight against slipping deadlines. The games industry really needed a new way to think about what it was we were really trying to do when developing games.

This updated, but technically first edition, is an attempt to make the book perennial in nature and as such has removed some of the examples and suggestions, and instead replaced them with processes that lead to the same results which can be applied without being aware of what the future holds. Where previously there were chapters on how to do a thing, there are now examples of how a thing is moved to the data-oriented style.

I say in this book, programmers are not fortune tellers. It's true. I cannot tell what the future holds for us, or what happens after I am gone, but instead I have relied on those that told the truth longer ago. I've curated the processes which haven't changed over time and apply well to data-oriented design. I've kept the core message of looking at patterns, and being investigative and realistic over architectural and abstract in your approach.

The first version was never produced in a printed form other than as a couple of handmade proof copies. This will be the first version available to buy in hard copy. Bringing this book to physical release will be committing the ideas more permanently than before, and I hope this version will be around a lot longer, hence taking more time to make sure it's a good reference. I'm still not happy with it. I don't think I ever will be. But perfect is the enemy of good, so what you have, and what you can hopefully gain insight from, is what I could do in the time I've had.

Thanks go to my reviewers, Pavel Bibergal, Alexandre "Lanedraex" Cavalcante, Stefan Hoppe, Russell Klenk, and Caitlin Ring. Without them, the book would be much less readable, and might have had as many errors as the original online version. Thanks also go to Alexandru Ene for inspiration and example code in listing 8.1.

# Chapter 1

# Data-Oriented Design

Data-oriented design has been around for decades in one form or another but was only officially given a name by Noel Llopis in his September 2009 article[1] of the same name. Whether it is, or is not a programming paradigm is seen as contentious. Many believe it can be used side by side with other programming paradigms such as object-oriented, procedural, or functional programming. In one respect they are right, data-oriented design can function alongside the other paradigms, but that does not preclude it from being a way to approach programming in the large. Other programming paradigms are known to function along-side each other to some extent as well. A Lisp programmer knows that functional programming can coexist with object-oriented programming and a C programmer is well aware that object-oriented programming can coexist with proce-dural programming. We shall ignore these comments and claim data-oriented design as another important tool; a tool just as capable of coexistence as the rest. [1]

---

[1] There are some limits, but it is not mutually exclusive with any paradigm other than maybe the logic programming languages such as Prolog. The ex-tremely declarative *"what, not how"* approach does seem to exclude thinking about the data and how it interacts with the machine.

The time was right in 2009. The hardware was ripe for a change in how to develop. Potentially very fast computers were hindered by a hardware ignorant programming paradigm. The way game programmers coded at the time made many engine programmers weep. The times have changed. Many mobile and desktop solutions now seem to need the data-oriented design approach less, not because the machines are better at mitigating an ineffective approach, but the games being designed are less demanding and less complex. The trend for mobile seems to be moving to AAA development, which should bring the return of a need for managing complexity and getting the most out of the hardware.

As we now live in a world where multi-core machines include the ones in our pockets, learning how to develop software in a less serial manner is important. Moving away from objects messaging and getting responses immediately is part of the benefits available to the data-oriented programmer. Programming, with a firm reliance on awareness of the data flow, sets you up to take the next step to GPGPU and other compute approaches. This leads to handling the workloads that bring game titles to life. The need for data-oriented design will only grow. It will grow because abstractions and serial thinking will be the bottleneck of your competitors, and those that embrace the data-oriented approach will thrive.

## 1.1   It's all about the data

Data is all we have. Data is what we need to transform in order to create a user experience. Data is what we load when we open a document. Data is the graphics on the screen, the pulses from the buttons on your gamepad, the cause of your speakers producing waves in the air, the method by which you level up and how the bad guy knew where you were so as to shoot at you. Data is how long the dynamite took to explode and how many rings you dropped when you fell on the spikes. It is the current position and velocity of every particle in the beautiful scene that ended the game which was loaded off the disc and into your life via transformations by machinery driven by decoded instructions themselves ordered by assemblers instructed by compilers fed with source-code.

No application is anything without its data. Adobe Photoshop without the images is nothing. It's nothing without the brushes, the layers, the pen pressure. Microsoft Word is nothing without the characters, the fonts, the page breaks. FL Studio is worthless without the events. Visual Studio is nothing without source. All the applications that have ever been written, have been written to output data based on some input data. The form of that data can be extremely complex, or so simple it requires no documentation at all, but all applications produce and need data. If they don't need recognisable data, then they are toys or tech demos at best.

Instructions are data too. Instructions take up memory, use up bandwidth, and can be transformed, loaded, saved and constructed. It's natural for a developer to not think of instructions as being data[2], but there is very little differentiating them on older, less protective hardware. Even though memory set aside for executables is protected from harm and modification on most contemporary hardware, this relatively new invention is still merely an invention, and the modified Harvard architecture relies on the same memory for data as it does for instructions. Instructions are therefore still data, and they are what we transform too. We take instructions and turn them into actions. The number, size, and frequency of them is something that matters. The idea that we have control over which instructions we use to solve problems leads us to optimisations. Applying our knowledge of what the data is allows us to make decisions about how the data can be treated. Knowing the outcome of instructions gives us the data to decide what instructions are necessary, which are busywork, and which can be replaced with equiv-

---

[2]unless they are a Lisp programmer

alent but less costly alternatives.

This forms the basis of the argument for a data-oriented approach to development, but leaves out one major element. All this data and the transforming of data, from strings, to images, to instructions, they all have to run on something. Sometimes that thing is quite abstract, such as a virtual machine running on unknown hardware. Sometimes that thing is concrete, such as knowing which specific CPU and GPU you have, and the memory capacity and bandwidth you have available. But in all cases, the data is not just data, but data that exists on some hardware somewhere, and it has to be transformed by that same hardware. In essence, data-oriented design is the practice of designing software by developing transformations for well-formed data where the criteria for well-formed is guided by the target hardware and the patterns and types of transforms that need to operate on it. Sometimes the data isn't well defined, and sometimes the hardware is equally evasive, but in most cases a good background of hardware appreciation can help out almost every software project.

If the ultimate result of an application is data, and all input can be represented by data, and it is recognised that all data transforms are not performed in a vacuum, then a software development methodology can be founded on these principles; the principles of understanding the data, and how to transform it given some knowledge of how a machine will do what it needs to do with data of this quantity, frequency, and its statistical qualities. Given this basis, we can build up a set of founding statements about what makes a methodology data-oriented.

## 1.2  Data is not the problem domain

The first principle: Data is not the problem domain.

For some, it would seem that data-oriented design is the antithesis of most other programming paradigms because data-oriented design is a technique that does not readily allow the problem domain to enter into the software as written in source. It does not promote the concept of an object as a mapping to the context of the user in any way, as data is intentionally and consistently without meaning. Abstraction heavy paradigms try to pretend the computer and its data do not exist at every turn, abstracting away the idea that there are bytes, or CPU pipelines, or other hardware features, and instead bringing the model of the problem into the program. They regularly bring either the model of the view into the code, or the model of the world as a context for the problem. That is, they either structure the code around attributes of the expected solution, or they structure the code around the description of the problem domain.

Meaning can be applied to data to create information. Meaning is not inherent in data. When you say 4, it means very little, but say 4 miles, or 4 eggs, it means something. When you have 3 numbers, they mean very little as a tuple, but when you name them x,y,z, you can put meaning on them as a position. When you have a list of positions in a game, they mean very little without context. Object-oriented design would likely have the positions as part of an object, and by the class name and neighbouring data (also named) you can get an idea of what that data means. Without the connected named contextualising data, the positions could be interpreted in a number of different ways, and though putting the numbers in context is good in some sense, it also blocks thinking about the positions as just sets of three numbers, which can be important for thinking of solutions to the real problems the programmers are trying to solve.

For an example of what can happen when you put data so deep inside an object that you forget its impact, consider the numerous games released, and in production, where a 2D or 3D grid system could have been used for the data layout, but for unknown reasons the developers kept with the object paradigm for each entity on the map. This isn't a singular event, and real shipping games have seen this object-centric approach commit crimes against the hardware by having hundreds of objects placed in WorldSpace at grid coordinates, rather than actually being driven by a grid. It's possible that programmers look at a grid, and see the number of elements required to fulfil the request, and are hesitant to the idea of allocating it in a single lump of memory. Consider a simple 256 by 256 tilemap requiring 65,536 tiles. An object-oriented programmer may think about those sixty-five thousand objects as being quite expensive. It might make more sense for them to allocate the objects for the tiles only when necessary, even to the point where there literally are sixty-five thousand tiles created by hand in editor, but because they were placed by hand, their necessity has been established, and they are now something to be handled, rather than something potentially worrying.

Not only is this pervasive lack of an underlying form a poor way to handle rendering and simple element placement, but it leads to much higher complexity when interpreting locality of elements. Gaining access to elements on a grid-free representation often requires jumping through hoops such as having neighbour links (which need to be kept up to date), running through the entire list of elements (inherently costly), or references to an auxiliary augmented grid object or spatial mapping system connecting to the objects which are otherwise free to move, but won't, due to the design of the game. This fake form of freedom introduced by the grid-free design presents issues with understanding the data, and has been the cause of some significant performance penalties in some titles. Thus also causing a significant waste of programmer mental resources in all.

Other than not having grids where they make sense, many modern games also seem to carry instances for each and every item in the game. An instance for each rather than a variable storing the number of items. For some games this is an optimisation, as creation and destruction of objects is a costly activity, but the trend is worrying, as these ways of storing information about the world make the world impenetrable to simple interrogation.

Many games seem to try to keep everything about the player in the player class. If the player dies in-game, they have to hang around as a dead object, otherwise, they lose access to their achievement data. This linking of what the data is, to where it resides and what it shares lifetime with, causes monolithic classes and hard to untangle relationships which frequently turn out to be the cause of bugs. I will not name any of the games, but it's not just one title, nor just one studio, but an epidemic of poor technical design that seems to infect those who use off the shelf object-oriented engines more than those who develop their own regardless of paradigm.

The data-oriented design approach doesn't build the real-world problem into the code. This could be seen as a failing of the data-oriented approach by veteran object-oriented developers, as examples of the success of object-oriented design come from being able to bring the human concepts to the machine, then in this middle ground, a solution can be written that is understandable by both human and computer. The data-oriented approach gives up some of the human readability by leaving the problem domain in the design document, bringing elements of constraints and expectations into the transforms, but stops the machine from having to handle human concepts at any data level by just that same action.

Let us consider how the problem domain becomes part of the software in programming paradigms that promote needless abstraction. In the case of objects, we tie meanings to data by associating them with their containing classes and their associated functions. In high-level abstraction, we separate actions and data by high-level concepts, which might not apply at the low level, thus reducing the likelihood the functions can be implemented efficiently.

When a class owns some data, it gives that data a context

which can sometimes limit the ability to reuse the data or understand the impact of operations upon it. Adding functions to a context can bring in further data, which quickly leads to classes containing many different pieces of data that are unrelated in themselves, but need to be in the same class because an operation required a context and the context required more data for other reasons such as for other related operations. This sounds awfully familiar, and Joe Armstrong is quoted to have said "I think the lack of reusability comes in object-oriented languages, not functional languages. Because the problem with object-oriented languages is they've got all this implicit environment that they carry around with them. You wanted a banana but what you got was a gorilla holding the banana and the entire jungle."[3] which certainly seems to resonate with the issue of contextual referencing that seems to be plaguing the object-oriented languages.

You could be forgiven for believing that it's possible to remove the connections between contexts by using interfaces or dependency injection, but the connections lie deeper than that. The contexts in the objects are often connecting different classes of data about different categories in which the object fits. Consider how this banana has many different purposes, from being a fruit, to being a colour, to being a word beginning with the letter B. We have to consider the problem presented by the idea of the banana as an instance, as well as the banana being a class of entity too. If we need to gain information about bananas from the point of view of the law on imported goods, or about its nutritional value, it's going to be different from information about how many we are currently stocking. We were lucky to start with the banana. If we talk about the gorilla, then we have information about the individual gorilla, the gorillas in the zoo or jungle, and the class of gorilla too. This is three different layers of abstraction about something which we might give one name. At least with a banana, each individual doesn't have much in the way of important data. We see this kind of contextual linkage all the time in the real world, and we manage the

---

[3]From Peter Seibel's *Coders at Work*[3]

complexity very well in conversation, but as soon as we start putting these contexts down in hard terms we connect them together and make them brittle.

All these mixed layers of abstraction become hard to untangle as functions which operate over each context drag in random pieces of data from all over the classes meaning many data items cannot be removed as they would then be inaccessible. This can be enough to stop most programmers from attempting large-scale evolving software projects, but there is another issue caused by hiding the actions applied to the data that leads to unnecessary complexity. When you see lists and trees, arrays and maps, tables and rows, you can reason about them and their interactions and transformations. If you attempt to do the same with homes and offices, roads and commuters, coffee shops and parks, you can often get stuck in thinking about the problem domain concepts and not see the details that would provide clues to a better data representation or a different algorithmic approach.

There are very few computer science algorithms that cannot be reused on primitive data types, but when you introduce new classes with their own internal layouts of data, that don't follow clearly in the patterns of existing data-structures, then you won't be able to fully utilise those algorithms, and might not even be able to see how they would apply. Putting data structures inside your object designs might make sense from what they are, but they often make little sense from the perspective of data manipulation.

When we consider the data from the data-oriented design point of view, data is mere facts that can be interpreted in whatever way necessary to get the output data in the format it needs to be. We only care about what transforms we do, and where the data ends up. In practice, when you discard meanings from data, you also reduce the chance of tangling the facts with their contexts, and thus you also reduce the likelihood of mixing unrelated data just for the sake of an operation or two.

## 1.3   Data and statistics

The second principle: Data is the type, frequency, quantity, shape, and probability.

The second statement is that data is not just the structure. A common misconception about data-oriented design is that it's all about cache misses. Even if it was all about making sure you never missed the cache, and it was all about structuring your classes so the hot and cold data was split apart, it would be a generally useful addition to your programming toolkit, but data-oriented design is about all aspects of the data. To write a book on how to avoid cache misses, you need more than just some tips on how to organise your structures, you need a grounding in what is really happening inside your computer when it is running your program. Teaching that in a book is also impossible as it would only apply to one generation of hardware, and one generation of programming languages, however, data-oriented design is not rooted in just one language and just some unusual hardware, even though the language to best benefit from it is C++, and the hardware to benefit the approach the most is anything with unbalanced bottlenecks. The schema of the data is important, but the values and how the data is transformed are as important, if not more so. It is not enough to have some photographs of a cheetah to determine how fast it can run. You need to see it in the wild and understand the true costs of being slow.

The data-oriented design model is centred around data. It pivots on live data, real data, data that is also information. Object-oriented design is centred around the problem definition. Objects are not real things but abstract representations of the context in which the problem will be solved. The objects manipulate the data needed to represent them without any consideration for the hardware or the real-world data patterns or quantities. This is why object-oriented design allows you to quickly build up first versions of applications, allowing you to put the first version of the design document or problem definition directly into the code, and make a quick attempt at a solution.

Data-oriented design takes a different approach to the problem, instead of assuming we know nothing about the hardware, it assumes we know little about the true nature of our problem, and makes the schema of the data a second-class citizen. Anyone who has written a sizeable piece of software may recognise that the technical structure and the design for a project often changes so much that there is barely any section from the first draft remaining unchanged in the final implementation. Data-oriented design avoids wasting resources by never assuming the design needs to exist anywhere other than in a document. It makes progress by providing a solution to the current problem through some high-level code controlling sequences of events and specifying schema in which to give temporary meaning to the data.

Data-oriented design takes its cues from the data which is seen or expected. Instead of planning for all eventualities, or planning to make things adaptable, there is a preference for using the most probable input to direct the choice of algorithm. Instead of planning to be extendable, it plans to be simple and replaceable, and get the job done. Extendable can be added later, with the safety net of unit tests to ensure it remains working as it did while it was simple. Luckily, there is a way to make your data layout extendable without requiring much thought, by utilising techniques developed many years ago for working with databases.

Database technology took a great turn for the positive when the relational model was introduced. In the paper *Out of the Tar Pit*[4], Functional Relational Programming takes it a step further when it references the idea of using relational model data-structures with functional transforms.

These are well defined, and much literature on how to adapt their form to match your requirements is available.

## 1.4   Data can change

Data-oriented design is current. It is not a representation of the history of a problem or a solution that has been brought up to date, nor is it the future, with generic solutions made up to handle whatever will come along. Holding onto the past will interfere with flexibility, and looking to the future is generally fruitless as programmers are not fortune tellers. It's the opinion of the author, that future-proof systems rarely are. Object-oriented design starts to show its weaknesses when designs change in the real-world.

Object-oriented design is known to handle changes to underlying implementation details very well, as these are the expected changes, the obvious changes, and the ones often cited in introductions to object-oriented design. However, real world changes such as change of user's needs, changes to input format, quantity, frequency, and the route by which the information will travel, are not handled with grace. It was introduced in *On the Criteria To Be Used in Decomposing Systems into Modules*[5] that the modularisation approach used by many at the time was rather like that of a production line, where elements of the implementation are caught up in the stages of the proposed solution. These stages themselves would be identified with a current interpretation of the problem. In the original document, the solution was to introduce a data hiding approach to modularisation, and though it was an improvement, in the later book *Software Pioneers: Contributions to Software Engineering*[6], D. L. Parnas revisits the issue and reminds us that even though initial software development can be faster when making structural decisions based on business facts, it lays a burden on maintenance and evolutionary development. Object-oriented design approaches suffer from this inertia inherent in keeping the problem domain coupled with the implementation. As mentioned, the problem domain, when introduced into the implementation, can help with making decisions quickly, as you can immediately see the impact the implementation will have on getting closer to the goal of solving or working with the problem in its current form. The problem with object-oriented design lies in the inevitability of change at a higher level.

Designs change for multiple reasons, occasionally including times when they actually haven't. A misunderstanding of a design, or a misinterpretation of a design, will cause as much change in the implementation as a literal request for change of design. A data-oriented approach to code design considers the change in design through the lens of understanding the change in the meaning of the data. The data-oriented approach to design also allows for change to the code when the source of data changes, unlike the encapsulated internal state manipulations of the object-oriented approach. In general, data-oriented design handles change better as pieces of data and transforms can be more simply coupled and decoupled than objects can be mutated and reused.

The reason this is so, comes from linking the intention, or the aspect, to the data. When lumping data and functions in with concepts of objects, you find the objects are the schema of the data. The aspect of the data is linked to that object, which means it's hard to think of the data from another point of view. The use case of the data, and the real-world or design, are now linked to the data layout through a singular vision implied by the object definition. If you link your data layout to the union of the required data for your expected manipulations, and your data manipulations are linked by aspects of your data, then you make it hard to unlink data related by aspect. The difficulty comes when different aspects need different subsets of the data, and they overlap. When they overlap, they create a larger and larger set of values that need to travel around the system as one unit. It's common to refactor a class out into two or more classes, or give ownership of data to a different class. This is what is meant by tying data to an aspect. It is tied to the lens through which the data has purpose, but with static typed objects that purpose is predefined, a union of multiple purposes, and sometimes carries around defunct relationships. Some purposes may no longer required by the design. Unfortunately, it's easier to see when a relationship needs to exist, than when it doesn't, and that leads to more connections, not fewer, over time.

If you link your operations by related data, such as when you put methods on a class, you make it hard to unlink your operations when the data changes or splits, and you make it hard to split data when an operation requires the data to be together for its own purposes. If you keep your data in one place, operations in another place, and keep the aspects and roles of data intrinsic from how the operations and transforms are applied to the data, then you will find that many times when refactoring would have been large and difficult in object-oriented code, the task now becomes trivial or non-existent. With this benefit comes a cost of keeping tabs on what data is required for each operation, and the potential danger of de-synchronisation. This consideration can lead to keeping some cold code in an object-oriented style where objects are responsible for maintaining internal consistency over efficiency and mutability. Examples of places where object-oriented design is far superior to data-oriented can be that of driver layers for systems or hardware. Even though Vulkan and OpenGL are object-oriented, the granularity of the objects is large and linked to stable concepts in their space, just like the object-oriented approach of the FILE type or handle, in open, close, read, and write operations in filesystems.

A big misunderstanding for many new to the data-oriented design paradigm, a concept brought over from abstraction based development, is that we can design a static library or set of templates to provide generic solutions to everything presented in this book as a data-oriented solution. Much like with domain driven design, data-oriented design is product and work-flow specific. You learn how to do data-oriented design, not how to add it to your project. The fundamental truth is that data, though it can be generic by type, is not generic in how it is used. The values are different and often contain patterns we can turn to our advantage. The idea that data can be generic is a false claim that data-oriented design attempts to rectify. The transforms applied to data can be generic to some extent, but the order and selection of operations are literally the solution to the problem. Source code is the recipe for conversion of data from one form into another. There cannot be a library of templates for understanding and leveraging patterns in the data, and that's what drives a successful data-oriented design. It's true we can build algorithms to find patterns in data, otherwise, how would it be possible to do compression, but the patterns we think about when it comes to data-oriented design are higher level, domain-specific, and not simple frequency mappings.

Our run-time benefits from specialisation through performance tricks that sometimes make the code harder to read, but it is frequently discouraged as being not object-oriented, or being too hard-coded. It can be better to hard-code a transform than to pretend it's not hard-coded by wrapping it in a generic container and using less direct algorithms on it. Using existing templates like this provides a benefit of an increase in readability for those who already know the library, and potentially fewer bugs if the functionality was in some way generic. But, if the functionality was not well mapped to the existing generic solution, writing it with a function template and then extending will make the code harder to understand. Hiding the fact that the technique had been changed subtly will introduced false assumptions. Hard-coding a new algorithm is a better choice as long as it has sufficient tests, and is objectively new. Tests will also be easier to write if you constrain yourself to the facts about concrete data and only test with real, but simple data for your problem, and not generic types on generic data.

## 1.5   How is data formed?

The games we write have a lot of data, in a lot of different formats. We have textures in multiple formats for multiple platforms. There are animations, usually optimised for different skeletons or types of playback. There are sounds, lights, and scripts. Don't forget meshes, they consist of multiple buffers of attributes. Only a very small proportion of meshes are old fixed function type with vertices containing positions, UVs, and normals. The data in game development is hard to box, and getting harder to pin down as more ideas which were previously considered impossible have now become commonplace. This is why we spend a lot of time working on editors and tool-chains, so we can take the free-form output from designers and artists and find a way to put it into our engines. Without our tool-chains, editors, viewers, and tweaking tools, there would be no way we could produce a game with the time we have. The object-oriented approach provides a good way to wrap our heads around all these different formats of data. It gives a centralised view of where each type of data belongs and classifies it by what can be done to it. This makes it very easy to add and use data quickly, but implementing all these different wrapper objects takes time. Adding new functionality to these objects can sometimes require large amounts of refactoring as occasionally objects are classified in such a way that they don't allow for new features to exist. For example, in many old engines, textures were always 1,2, or 4 bytes per pixel. With the advent of floating point textures, all that code required a minor refactoring. In the past, it was not possible to read a texture from the vertex shader, so when texture based skinning came along, many engine programmers had to refactor their render update. They had to allow for a vertex shader texture upload because it might be necessary when uploading transforms for rendering a skinned mesh. When the PlayStation2 came along, or an engine first used shaders, the very idea of what made a material had to change. In the move from small 3D environments to large open worlds with level of detail caused many engineers to start thinking about what it meant for something to need rendering. When newer hardware became more picky about alignment, other hard to inject changes had to be made. In many engines, mesh data is optimised for rendering, but when you have to do mesh ray casting to see where bullets have hit, or for doing IK, or physics, then you need multiple representations of an entity. At this point, the object-oriented approach starts to look cobbled together as there are fewer objects that represent real things, and more objects used as containers so programmers can think in larger building blocks. These blocks hinder though, as they become the only blocks used in thought, and stop potential mental connections from happening. We went from 2D sprites to 3D meshes, following the format of the hardware provider, to custom data streams and compute units turning the streams into rendered triangles. Wave data, to banks, to envelope controlled grain tables and slews of layered sounds. Tilemaps, to portals and rooms, to streamed, multiple levels of detail chunks of world, to hybrid mesh palette, props, and unique stitching assets. From flipbook to Euler angle sequences, to quaternions and spherical interpolated animations, to animation trees and behaviour mapping/trees. Change is the only constant.

All these types of data are pretty common if you've worked in games at all, and many engines do provide an abstraction to these more fundamental types. When a new type of data becomes heavily used it is promoted into engines as a core type. We normally consider the trade-off of new types being handled as special cases until they become ubiquitous to be one of usability vs performance. We don't want to provide free access to the lesser understood elements of game development. People who are not, or can not, invest time in finding out how best to use new features, are discouraged from using them. The object-oriented game development way to do that is to not provide objects which represent them, and instead only offer the features to people who know how to utilise the more advanced tools.

Apart from the objects representing digital assets, there are also objects for internal game logic. For every game, there are objects which only exist to further the game-play. Collectable card games have a lot of textures, but they also have a great deal of rules, card stats, player decks, match records, with many objects to represent the current state of play. All of these objects are completely custom designed for one game. There may be sequels, but unless it's primarily a re-skin, it will use quite different game logic in many places, and therefore require different data, which would imply different methods on the now guaranteed to be internally different objects.

Game data is complex. Any first layout of the data is inspired by the game's initial design. Once development is underway, the layout needs to keep up with whichever way the game evolves. Object-oriented techniques offer a quick way to implement any given design, are very quick at implementing each singular design in turn, but don't offer a clean or graceful way to migrate from one data schema to the next. There are hacks, such as those used in version based asset handlers, or in frameworks backed by update systems and conversion scripts, but normally, game developers change the tool-chain and the engine at the same time, do a full re-export of all the assets, then commit to the next version all in one go. This can be quite a painful experience if it has to happen over multiple sites at the same time, or if you have a lot of assets, or if you are trying to provide engine support for more than one title, and only one wants to change to the new revision. An example of an object-oriented approach that handles migration of design with some grace is the Django framework, but the reason it handles the migration well is that the objects would appear to be views into data models, not the data itself.

There have not yet been any successful efforts to build a

generic game asset solution. This may be because all games differ in so many subtle ways that if you did provide a generic solution, it wouldn't be a game solution, just a new language. There is no solution to be found in trying to provide all the possible types of object a game can use. But, there is a solution if we go back to thinking about a game as merely running a set of computations on some data. The closest we can get in 2018 is the FBX format, with some dependence on the current standard shader languages. The current solutions appear to have excess baggage which does not seem easy to remove. Due to the need to be generic, many details are lost through abstractions and strategies to present data in a non-confrontational way.

# 1.6 What can provide a computational framework for such complex data?

Game developers are notorious for thinking about game development from either a low level all out performance perspective or from a very high-level gameplay and interaction perspective. This may have come about because of the widening gap between the amount of code that has to be high performance, and the amount of code to make the game complete. Object-oriented techniques provide good coverage of the high-level aspect, so the high-level programmers are content with their tools. The performance specialists have been finding ways of doing more with the hardware, so much so that a lot of the time content creators think they don't have a part in the optimisation process. There has never been much of a middle ground in game development, which is probably the primary reason why the structure and performance techniques employed by big-iron companies didn't seem useful. The secondary reason could be that game developers don't normally develop systems and applications which have decade-long maintenance expectations[4] and therefore are less likely to be concerned about why their code should be encapsulated and protected or at least well documented. When game development was first flourishing into larger studios in the late 1990's, academic or corporate software engineering practices were seen as suspicious because wherever they were employed, there was a dramatic drop in game performance, and whenever any prospective employees came from those industries, they failed to impress. As games machines became more like the standard micro-computers, and standard micro-computers drew closer in design to the mainframes of old, the more apparent it became that some of those standard professional software engineering practices could be useful. Now the scale of games has grown to match the hardware, but the games industry has stopped looking at where those non-game development practices led. As an industry, we should be looking to where others have gone before us, and the closest set of academic and professional development techniques seem to be grounded in simulation and high volume data analysis. We still have industry-specific challenges such as the problems of high frequency highly heterogeneous transformational requirements that we experience in sufficiently voluminous AI environments, and we have the issue of user proximity in networked environments, such as the problems faced by MMOs when they have location-based events, and bandwidth starts to hit $n^2$ issues as everyone is trying to message everyone else.

With each successive generation, the number of developer hours to create a game has grown, which is why project management and software engineering practices have become standardised at the larger games companies. There was a time when game developers were seen as cutting-edge programmers, inventing new technology as the need arises, but with the advent of less adventurous hardware (most notably in the x86 based recent 8[th]generations), there has been a shift away from ingenious coding practices, and towards a

---

[4]people at Blizzard Entertainment, Inc. likely have something to say about this

standardised process. This means game development can be
tuned to ensure the release date will coincide with market-
ing dates. There will always be an element of randomness
in high profile game development. There will always be an
element of innovation that virtually guarantees you will not
be able to predict how long the project, or at least one part
of the project, will take. Even if data-oriented design isn't
needed to make your game go faster, it can be used to make
your game development schedule more regular.

Part of the difficulty in adding new and innovative features to a game is the data layout. If you need to change the
data layout for a game, it will need objects to be redesigned
or extended in order to work within the existing framework.
If there is no new data, then a feature might require that
previously separate systems suddenly be able to talk to each
other quite intimately. This coupling can often cause system-
wide confusion with additional temporal coupling and corner
cases so obscure they can only be reproduced one time in
a million. These odds might sound fine to some developers,
but if you're expecting to sell five to fifty million copies of your
game, at one in a million, that's five to fifty people who will
experience the problem, can take a video of your game be-
having oddly, post it on the YouTube, and call your company
rubbish, or your developers lazy, because they hadn't fixed
an obvious bug. Worse, what if the one in a million issue
was a way to circumvent in-app-purchases, and was reproducible if you knew what to do and the steps start spreading
on Twitter, or maybe created an economy-destroying influx
of resources in a live MMO universe[5]. In the past, if you had
sold five to fifty million copies of your game, you wouldn't
care, but with the advent of free-to-play games, five million
players might be considered a good start, and poor reviews
coming in will curb the growth. IAP circumventions will kill
your income, and economy destruction will end you.

---

[5]The webcomic and anecdotes site The-Trenches did a sequence of strips in a webcomic on this, and pointed out
many of the issues with trying to fix it once it has gone live
http://www.trenchescomic.com/comic/post/apocalypse

Big iron developers had these same concerns back in the 1970's. Their software had to be built to high standards because their programs would frequently be working on data concerned with real money transactions. They needed to write business logic that operated on the data, but most important of all, they had to make sure the data was updated through a provably careful set of operations in order to maintain its integrity. Database technology grew from the need to process stored data, to do complex analysis on it, to store and update it, and be able to guarantee it was valid at all times. To do this, the ACID test was used to ensure atomicity, consistency, isolation, and durability. Atomicity was the test to ensure all transactions would either complete or do nothing. It could be very bad for a database to update only one account in a financial transaction. There could be money lost or created if a transaction was not atomic. Consistency was added to ensure all the resultant state changes which should happen during a transaction do happen, that is, all triggers which should fire, do fire, even if the triggers cause triggers recursively, with no limit. This would be highly important if an account should be blocked after it has triggered a form of fraud detection. If a trigger has not fired, then the company using the database could risk being liable for even more than if they had stopped the account when they first detected fraud. Isolation is concerned with ensuring all transactions which occur cannot cause any other transactions to differ in behaviour. Normally this means that if two transactions appear to work on the same data, they have to queue up and not try to operate at the same time. Although this is generally good, it does cause concurrency problems. Finally, durability. This was the second most important element of the four, as it has always been important to ensure that once a transaction has completed, it remains so. In database terminology, durability meant the transaction would be guaranteed to have been stored in such a way that it would survive server crashes or power outages. This was important for networked computers where it would be important to know what transactions had definitely happened when a server crashed or a connection dropped.

Modern networked games also have to worry about highly important data like this. With non-free downloadable content, consumers care about consistency. With consumable downloadable content, users care a great deal about every transaction. To provide much of the functionality required of the database ACID test, game developers have gone back to looking at how databases were designed to cope with these strict requirements and found reference to staged commits, idempotent functions, techniques for concurrent development, and a vast literature base on how to design tables for a database.

# 1.7 Conclusions and takeaways

We've talked about data-oriented design being a way to think about and lay out your data and to make decisions about your architecture. We have two principles that can drive many of the decisions we need to make when doing data-oriented design. To finish the chapter, there are some takeaways you can use immediately to begin your journey.

Consider how your data is being influenced by what it's called. Consider the possibility that the proximity of other data can influence the meaning of your data, and in doing so, trap it in a model that inhibits flexibility. For the consideration of the first principle, *data is not the problem domain*, it's worth thinking about the following items.

- What is tying your data together, is it a concept or implied meaning?
- Is your data layout defined by a single interpretation from a single point of view?
- Think about how the data could be reinterpreted and cut along those lines.
- What is it about the data that makes it uniquely important?

You are not targeting an unknown device with unknowable characteristics. Know your data, and know your target hardware. To some extent, understand how much each stream of data matters, and who is consuming it. Understand the cost and potential value of improvements. Access patterns matter, as you cannot hit the cache if you're accessing things in a burst, then not touching them again for a whole cycle of the application. For the consideration of the second principle, *data is the type, frequency, quantity, shape, and probability*, it's worth thinking about the following items.

- What is the smallest unit of memory on your target platform?[6]
- When you read data, how much of it are you using?
- How often do you need the data? Is it once, or a thousand times a frame?
- How do you access the data? At random, or in a burst?
- Are you always modifying the data, or just reading it? Are you modifying all of it?
- Who does the data matter to, and what about it matters?
- Find out the quality constraints of your solutions, in terms of bandwidth and latency.
- What information do you have that isn't in the data per se? What is implicit?

---

[6]On most machines in 2018, the smallest unit of memory is 64 byte aligned lump called a cache line.

# Chapter 2

# Relational Databases

In order to lay your data out better, it's useful to have an understanding of the methods available to convert your existing structures into something linear. The problems we face when applying data-oriented approaches to existing code and data layouts usually stem from the complexity of state inherent in data-hiding or encapsulating programming paradigms. These paradigms hide away internal state so you don't have to think about it, but they hinder when it comes to reconfiguring data layouts. This is not because they don't abstract enough to allow changes to the underlying structure without impacting the correctness of the code that uses it, but instead because they have connected and given meaning to the structure of the data. That type of coupling can be hard to remove.

In this chapter, we go over some of the pertinent parts of the relational model, relational database technology, and normalisation, as these are examples of converting highly complex data structures and relationships into very clean collections of linear storable data entries.

You certainly don't have to move your data to a database style to do data-oriented design, but there are many places where you will wish you had a simple array to work with, and this chapter will help you by giving you an example of how you can migrate from a web of connected complex objects to a simpler to reason about relational model of arrays.

## 2.1   Complex state

When you think about the data present in most software, it has some qualities of complexity or interconnectedness. When it comes to game development, there are many ways in which the game entities interact, and many ways in which their attached resources will need to feed through different stages of processes to achieve the audio, visual and sometimes haptic feedback necessary to fully immerse the player. For many programmers brought up on object-oriented design, the idea of reducing the types of structure available down to just simple arrays, is virtually unthinkable. It's very hard to go from working with objects, classes, templates, and methods on encapsulated data to a world where you only have access to linear containers.

In *A Relational Model of Data for Large Shared Data Banks*[7], Edgar F. Codd proposed the relational model to handle the current and future needs of agents interacting with data. He proposed a solution to structuring data for insert, update, delete, and query operations. His proposal claimed to reduce the need to maintain a deep understanding of how the data was laid out to use it well. His proposal also claimed to reduce the likelihood of introducing internal inconsistencies.

The relational model provided a framework, and in *Further Normalization of the Data Base Relational Model.*[8], Edgar F. Codd introduced the fundamental terms of normalisation we use to this day in a systematic approach to reducing the most complex of interconnected state information to linear lists of unique independent tuples.

## 2.2  What can provide a computational framework for complex data?

Databases store highly complex data in a structured way and provide a language for transforming and generating reports based on that data. The language, SQL, invented in the 1970's by Donald D. Chamberlin and Raymond F. Boyce at IBM, provides a method by which it is possible to store computable data while also maintaining data relationships following in the form of the relational model. Games don't have simple computable data, they have classes and objects. They have guns, swords, cars, gems, daily events, textures, sounds, and achievements. It is very easy to conclude that database technology doesn't work for the object-oriented approach game developers use.

The data relationships in games can be highly complex, it would seem at first glance that it doesn't neatly fit into database rows. A CD collection easily fits in a database, with your albums neatly arranged in a single table. But, many game objects won't fit into rows of columns. For the uninitiated, it can be hard to find the right table columns to describe a level file. Trying to find the right columns to describe a car in a racing game can be a puzzle. Do you need a column for each wheel? Do you need a column for each collision primitive, or just a column for the collision mesh?

An obvious answer could be that game data doesn't fit neatly into the database way of thinking. However, that's only because we've not normalised the data. To show how you can convert from a network model, or hierarchical model to what we need, we will work through these normalisation steps. We'll start with a level file as we find out how these decades-old techniques can provide a very useful insight into what game data is really doing.

We shall discover that everything we do is already in a

database, but it wasn't obvious to us because of how we
store our data. The structure of any data is a trade-off between performance, readability, maintenance, future proof-
ing, extendibility, and reuse. For example, the most flexible
database in common use is your filesystem. It has one table with two columns. A primary key of the file path, and a
string for the data. This simple database system is the perfect fit for a completely future proof system. There's nothing
that can't be stored in a file. The more complex the tables
get, the less future proof, and the less maintainable, but
the higher the performance and readability. For example, a
file has no documentation of its own, but the schema of a
database could be all that is required to understand a sufficiently well-designed database. That's how games don't even
appear to have databases. They are so complex, for the sake
of performance, they have forgotten they are merely a data
transform. This sliding scale of complexity affects scalability
too, which is why some people have moved towards NoSQL
databases, and document store types of data storage. These
systems are more like a filesystem where the documents are
accessed by name, and have fewer limits on how they are
structured. This has been good for horizontal scalability, as
it's simpler to add more hardware when you don't have to
keep your data consistent across multiple tables that might
be on different machines. There may come a day when memory is so tightly tied to the closest physical CPU, or when
memory chips themselves get more processing power, or running 100 SoCs inside your desktop rig is more effective than
a single monolithic CPU, that moving to document store at
the high-level could be beneficial inside your app, but for
now, there do not seem to be any benefits in that processing
model for tasks on local hardware.

We're not going to go into the details of the lowest level
of how we utilise large data primitives such as meshes, textures, sounds and such. For now, think of these raw assets
(sounds, textures, vertex buffers, etc.) as primitives, much
like the integers, floating point numbers, strings and boolean
values we shall be working with. We do this because the re-

lational model calls for atomicity when working with data. What is and is not atomic has been debated without an absolute answer becoming clear, but for the intents of developing software intended for human consumption, the granularity can be rooted in considering the data from the perspective of human perception. There are existing APIs that present strings in various ways depending on how they are used, for example the difference between human-readable strings (usually UTF-8) and ASCII strings for debugging. Adding sounds, textures, and meshes to this seems quite natural once you realise all these things are resources which if cut into smaller pieces begin to lose what it is that makes them what they are. For example, half of a sentence is a lot less useful than a whole one, and loses integrity by disassociation. A slice of a sentence is clearly not reusable in any meaningful way with another random slice of a different sentence. Even subtitles are split along meaningful boundaries, and it's this idea of meaningful boundary that gives us the our definition of atomicity for software developed for humans. To this end, when working with your data, when you're normalising, try to stay at the level of nouns, the nameable pieces. A whole song can be an atom, but so is a single tick sound of a clock. A whole page of text is an atom, but so is the player's gamer-tag.

## 2.3   Normalising your data

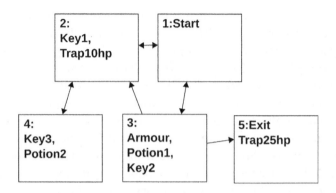

Figure 2.1: Visual representation of the setup script

We're going to work with a level file for a game where you hunt for keys to unlock doors in order to get to the exit room. The level file is a sequence of script calls which create and configure a collection of different game objects which represent a playable level of the game, and the relationships between those objects. First, we'll assume it contains rooms (some trapped, some not), with doors leading to other rooms which can be locked. It will also contain a set of pickups, some let the player unlock doors, some affect the player's stats (like health potions and armour), and all the rooms have lovely textured meshes, as do all the pickups. One of the rooms is marked as the exit, and one has a player start point.

In this setup script (Listing 2.1) we load some resources, create some pickup prototypes, build up a few rooms, add some instances to the rooms, and then link things together. Here we also see a standard solution to the problem of things which reference each other. We create the rooms before we connect them to each other because before they exist we can't. When we create entities in C++, we assume they are

```
1   // create rooms, pickups, and other things.
2   Mesh msh_room = LoadMesh( "roommesh" );
3   Mesh msh_roomstart = LoadMesh( "roommeshstart" );
4   Mesh msh_roomtrapped = LoadMesh( "roommeshtrapped" );
5   Mesh msh_key = LoadMesh( "keymesh" );
6   Mesh msh_pot = LoadMesh( "potionmesh" );
7   Mesh msh_arm = LoadMesh( "armourmesh" );
8   // ...
9   Texture tex_room = LoadTexture( "roomtexture" );
10  Texture tex_roomstart = LoadTexture( "roomtexturestart" );
11  Texture tex_roomtrapped = LoadTexture( "roomtexturetrapped" );
12  Texture tex_key = LoadTexture( "keytexture" );
13  Texture tex_pot = LoadTexture( "potiontexture" );
14  Texture tex_arm = LoadTexture( "armourtexture" );
15
16  Anim anim_keybob = LoadAnim( "keybobanim" );
17  // ...
18  PickupID k1 = CreatePickup( TYPE_KEY, msh_key, tex_key,
        TintColourCopper, anim_keybob );
19  PickupID k2 = CreatePickup( TYPE_KEY, msh_key, tex_key,
        TintColourSilver, anim_keybob );
20  PickupID k3 = CreatePickup( TYPE_KEY, msh_key, tex_key,
        TintColourGold, anim_keybob );
21  PickupID p1 = CreatePickup( TYPE_POTION, msh_pot, tex_pot,
        TintColourGreen );
22  PickupID p2 = CreatePickup( TYPE_POTION, msh_pot, tex_pot,
        TintColourPurple );
23  PickupID a1 = CreatePickup( TYPE_ARMOUR, msh_arm, tex_arm );
24  // ...
25  Room r1 = CreateRoom( WorldPos(0,0), msh_roomstart, tex_roomstart
        );
26  Room r2 = CreateRoom( WorldPos(-20,0), msh_roomtrapped,
        tex_roomtrapped, HPDamage(10) );
27  Room r3 = CreateRoom( WorldPos(-10,20), msh_room, tex_room );
28  Room r4 = CreateRoom( WorldPos(-30,20), msh_room, tex_room );
29  Room r5 = CreateRoom( WorldPos(20,10), msh_roomtrapped,
        tex_roomtrapped, HPDamage(25) );
30  // ...
31  AddDoor( r1, r2 );
32  AddDoor( r1, r3, k1 );
33  SetRoomAsSpecial( r1, E_STARTINGROOM, WorldPos(1,1) );
34  //
35  AddPickup( r2, k1, WorldPos(-18,2));
36  AddDoor( r2, r1 );
37  AddDoor( r2, r4, k2 );
38  // ...
39  AddPickup( r3, k2, WorldPos(-8,12));
40  AddPickup( r3, p1, WorldPos(-7,13));
41  AddPickup( r3, a1, WorldPos(-8,14));
42  AddDoor( r3, r1 );
43  AddDoor( r3, r2 );
44  AddDoor( r3, r5, k3 );
45  // ...
46  AddDoor( r4, r2 );
47  AddPickup( r4, k3, WorldPos(-28,14));
48  AddPickup( r4, p2, WorldPos(-27,13));
49  // ...
50  SetRoomAsSpecial( r5, E_EXITROOM );
```

Listing 2.1: A setup script

bound to memory, and the only efficient way to reference them is through pointers, but we cannot know where they exist in memory before we allocate them, and we cannot allocate them before filling them out with their data as the allocation and initialisation are bound to each other through the 'new' mechanism. This means we have difficulty describing relationships between objects before they exist and have to stagger the creation of content into phases of setting up and connecting things together.

To bring this setup script into a usable database-like format, or relational model, we will need to normalise it. When putting things in a relational model of any sort, it needs to be in tables. In the first step you take all the data and put it into a very messy, but hopefully complete, table design. In our case we take the form of the data from the object creation script and fit it into a table. The asset loading can be directly translated into tables, as can be seen in table 2.1

Meshes

| MeshID | MeshName |
| --- | --- |
| msh_rm | "roommesh" |
| msh_rmstart | "roommeshstart" |
| msh_rmtrap | "roommeshtrapped" |
| msh_key | "keymesh" |
| msh_pot | "potionmesh" |
| msh_arm | "armourmesh" |

Textures

| TextureID | TextureName |
| --- | --- |
| tex_rm | "roomtexture" |
| tex_rmstart | "roomtexturestart" |
| tex_rmtrapped | "roomtexturetrapped" |
| tex_key | "keytexture" |
| tex_pot | "potiontexture" |
| tex_arm | "armourtexture" |

Animations

| AnimID | AnimName |
| --- | --- |
| anim_keybob | "keybobanim" |

Table 2.1: Initial tables created by converting asset load calls

Primed with this data, it's now possible for us to create the Pickups. We convert the calls to CreatePickup into the

tables in table 2.2. Notice that there was a pickup which
did not specify a colour tint, and this means we need to use
a NULL to represent not giving details about that aspect of
the row. The same applies to animations. Only keys had
animations, so there needs to be NULL entries for all non-
key rows.

Pickups

| **PickupID** | MeshID | TextureID | PickupType | ColourTint | Anim |
|---|---|---|---|---|---|
| k1 | msh_key | tex_key | KEY | Copper | anim_keybob |
| k2 | msh_key | tex_key | KEY | Silver | anim_keybob |
| k3 | msh_key | tex_key | KEY | Gold | anim_keybob |
| p1 | msh_pot | tex_pot | POTION | Green | NULL |
| p2 | msh_pot | tex_pot | POTION | Purple | NULL |
| a1 | msh_arm | tex_arm | ARMOUR | NULL | NULL |

Table 2.2: Initial tables created by converting CreatePickup
calls

Once we have loaded the assets and have created the
pickup prototypes, we move onto creating a table for rooms.
We need to invent attributes as necessary using NULL everywhere that an instance doesn't have that attribute. We
convert the calls to CreateRoom, AddDoor, SetRoomAsSpe-
cial, and AddPickup, to columns in the Rooms table. See
table 2.3 for one way to build up a table that represents all
those setup function calls.

Rooms

| **RoomID** | MeshID | TextureID | WorldPos | Pickups | ... |
|---|---|---|---|---|---|
| r1 | msh_rmstart | tex_rmstart | 0, 0 | NULL | ... |
| r2 | msh_rmtrap | tex_rmtrap | -20,10 | k1 | ... |
| r3 | msh_rm | tex_rm | -10,20 | k2,p1,a1 | ... |
| r4 | msh_rm | tex_rm | -30,20 | k3,p2 | ... |
| r5 | msh_rmtrap | tex_rmtrap | 20,10 | NULL | ... |

| ... | DoorsTo | Locked | IsStart | IsEnd | |
|---|---|---|---|---|---|
| ... | NULL | r2,r3 | r3 with k1 | true WorldPos(1,1) | false |
| ... | 10HP | r1,r4 | r4 with k2 | false | false |
| ... | NULL | r1,r2,r5 | r5 with k3 | false | false |
| ... | NULL | r2 | | false | false |
| ... | 25HP | NULL | | false | true |

Table 2.3: Initial table created by converting CreateRoom
and other calls.

Once we have taken the construction script and generated these first tables, we find the tables contain a lot of NULLs. The NULLs in the rows replace the optional content of the objects. If an object instance doesn't have a certain attribute then we replace those features with NULLs. There are also elements which contain more than one item of data. Having multiple doors per room is tricky to handle in this table. How would you figure out what doors it had? The same goes for whether the door is locked, and whether there are any pickups. The first stage in normalising is going to be reducing the number of elements in each cell to 1, and increasing it to 1 where it's currently NULL.

## 2.4  Normalisation

Back when SQL was first created there were only three well-defined stages of data normalisation. There are many more now, including six numbered normal forms. To get the most out of a database, it is important to know most of them, or at least get a feel for why they exist. They teach you about data dependency and can hint at reinterpretations of your data layout. For game structures, BCNF (Boyce-Codd normal form is explained later) is probably as far as you normally would need to take your methodical process. Beyond that, you might wish to normalise your data for hot/cold access patterns, but that kind of normalisation is not part of the standard literature on database normalisation. If you're interested in more than this book covers on the subject, a very good read, and one which introduces the phrase "The key, the whole key, and nothing but the key." is the article *A Simple Guide to Five Normal Forms in Relational Database Theory*[9] by William Kent.

If a table is in first normal form, then every cell contains one and only one atomic value. That is, no arrays of values, and no NULL entries. First normal form also requires every row be distinct. For those unaware of what a primary key is, we shall discuss that first.

## 2.4.1 Primary keys

All tables are made up of rows and columns. In a database, each row must be unique. This constraint has important consequences. When you have normalised your data, it becomes clear why duplicate rows don't make sense, but for now, from a computer programming point of view, consider tables to be more like sets, where the whole row is the set value. This is very close to reality, as sets are also not ordered, and a database table is not ordered either. There is always some differentiation between rows, even if a database management system (DBMS) has to rely on hidden row ID values. It is better to not rely on this as databases work more efficiently when the way in which they are used matches their design. All tables need a key. The key is often used to order the sorting of the table in physical media, to help optimise queries. For this reason, the key needs to be unique, but as small as possible. You can think of the key as the key in a map or dictionary. Because of the uniqueness rule, every table has an implicit key because the table can use the combination of all the columns at once to identify each row uniquely. That is, the key, or the unique lookup, which is the primary key for a table, can be defined as the totality of the whole row. If the row is unique, then the primary key is unique. Normally, we try to avoid using the whole row as the primary key, but sometimes, it's actually our only choice. We will come across examples of that later.

For example, in the mesh table, the combination of meshID and filename is guaranteed to be unique. However, currently it's only guaranteed to be unique because we have presumed that the meshID is unique. If it was the same mesh, loaded from the same file, it could still have a different meshID. The same can be said for the textureID and filename in the textures table. From the table 2.2 it's possible to see how we could use the type, mesh, texture, tint and animation to uniquely define each Pickup prototype.

Now consider rooms. If you use all the columns other

than the RoomID of the room table, you will find the combination can be used to uniquely define the room. If you consider an alternative, where a row had the same combination
of values making up the room, it would in fact be describing
the same room. From this, it can be claimed that the RoomID is being used as an alias for the rest of the data. We have
stuck the RoomID in the table, but where did it come from?
To start with, it came from the setup script. The script had
a RoomID, but we didn't need it at that stage. We needed it
for the destination of the doors. In another situation, where
nothing connected logically to the room, we would not need
a RoomID as we would not need an alias to it.

A primary key must be unique. RoomID is an example of
a primary key because it uniquely describes the room. It is
an alias in this sense as it contains no data in and of itself,
but merely acts as a handle. In some cases the primary key
is information too, which again, we will meet later.

As a bit of an aside, the idea that a row in a database
is also the key can be a core concept worth spending time
thinking about. If a database table is a set, when you insert a record, you're actually just asking that one particular
combination of data is being recorded as existing. It is as if
a database table is a very sparse set from an extremely large
domain of possible values. This can be useful because you
may notice that under some circumstances, the set of possible values isn't very large, and your table can be more easily
defined as a bit set. As an example, consider a table which
lists the players in an MMO that are online right now. For
an MMO that shards its servers, there can be limits in the
early thousands for the number of unique players on each
server. In that case, it may be easier to store the currently
online players as a bit set. If there are at most 10,000 players
online, and only 1000 players online at any one time, then
the bitset representation would take up 1.25kb of memory,
whereas storing the online players as a list of IDs, would require at least 2kb of data if their IDs were shrunk to shorts,
or 4kb if they had 32bit IDs to keep them unique across

multiple servers. The other benefit in this case is the performance of queries into the data. To quickly access the ID in the list, you need it to remain sorted. The best case then is $\mathcal{O}(\log n)$. In the bitset variant, it's $\mathcal{O}(1)$.

Going back to the asset table, an important and useful detail when we talk about the meshID and mesh filename is that even though there could be two different meshIDs pointing at the same file, most programmers would intuitively understand that a single meshID was unlikely to point at two different mesh files. Because of this asymmetry, you can deduce, the column that seems more likely to be unique will also be the column you can use as the primary key. We'll choose the meshID as it is easier to manipulate and is unlikely to have more than one meaning or usage, but remember, we could have chosen the filename and gone without the meshID altogether.

If we settle on TextureID, PickupID, and RoomID as the primary keys for those tables, we can then look at continuing on to first normal form. We're using t1, m2, r3, etc. to show typesafe ID values, but in reality, these can all be simple integers. The idea here is to remain readable, but it also shows that each type can have unique IDs for that type, but have common IDs with another. For example, a room may have an integer ID value of 0, but so may a texture. It can be beneficial to have IDs which are unique across types, as that can help debugging, and using the top few bits in that case can be helpful. If you're unlikely to have more than a million entities per class of entity, then you have enough bits to handle over a thousand distinct classes.

## 2.4.2 1$^{st}$ Normal Form

First normal form can be described as making sure the tables are not sparse. We require that there be no NULL pointers and that there be no arrays of data in each element of data. This can be performed as a process of moving the re-

peats and all the optional content to other tables. Anywhere
there is a NULL, it implies optional content. Our first fix is
going to be the Pickups table, it has optional ColourTint and
Animation elements. We invent a new table PickupTint, and
use the primary key of the Pickup as the primary key of the
new table. We also invent a new table PickupAnim. Table
2.4 shows the result of the transformation, and note we no
longer have any NULL entries.

Pickups

| **PickupID** | MeshID | TextureID | PickupType |
|---|---|---|---|
| k1 | msh_key | tex_key | KEY |
| k2 | msh_key | tex_key | KEY |
| k3 | msh_key | tex_key | KEY |
| p1 | msh_mpot | tex_pot | POTION |
| p2 | msh_mpot | tex_pot | POTION |
| a1 | msh_marm | tex_arm | ARMOUR |

PickupTints

| **PickupID** | ColourTint |
|---|---|
| k1 | Copper |
| k2 | Silver |
| k3 | Gold |
| p1 | Green |
| p2 | Purple |

PickupAnims

| **PickupID** | Anim |
|---|---|
| k1 | anim_keybob |
| k2 | anim_keybob |
| k3 | anim_keybob |

Table 2.4: Pickups in 1NF

Two things become evident at this point, firstly that normalisation appears to create more tables and fewer columns
in each table, secondly that there are only rows for things
which matter. The former is worrisome, as it means more
memory usage. The latter is interesting as when using an
object-oriented approach, we allow objects to optionally have
attributes. Optional attributes cause us to check they are
not NULL before continuing. If we store data like this, then
we know everything is not NULL. Moving away from having
to do a null check at all will make your code more concise,

and you have less state to consider when trying to reason about your systems.

Let's move onto the Rooms table. In there we saw single elements that contained multiple atomic values. We need to remove all elements from this table that do not conform to the rules of first normal form. First, we remove reference to the pickups, as they had various quantities of elements, from none to many. Then we must consider the traps, as even though there was only ever one trap, there wasn't always a trap. Finally, we must strip out the doors, as even though every room has a door, they often had more than one. Remember that the rule is one and only one entry in every meeting of row and column. In table 2.5 it shows how we only keep columns that are in a one to one relationship with the RoomID.

Rooms

| **RoomID** | MeshID | TextureID | WorldPos | IsStart | IsExit |
|------------|--------|-----------|----------|---------|--------|
| r1 | msh_rmstart | tex_rmstart | 0,0 | true | false |
| r2 | msh_rmtrap | tex_rmtrap | -20,0 | false | false |
| r3 | msh_rm | tex_rm | -10,20 | false | false |
| r4 | msh_rm | tex_rm | -30,20 | false | false |
| r5 | msh_rmtrap | tex_rmtrap | 20,10 | false | true |

Table 2.5: Rooms table now in 1NF

Now we will make new tables for Pickups, Doors, and Traps. In table 2.6 we see many decisions made to satisfy the first normal form. We have split out the array like elements into separate rows. Note the use of multiple rows to specify the numerous pickups all in the same room. We see that doors now need two tables. The first table to identify where the doors are, and where they lead. The second table seems to do the same, but doesn't cover all doors, only the ones that are locked. What's actually happening here is a need to identify doors by their primary key in the locked doors table. If you look at the Doors table, you can immediately tell that neither column is a candidate for the primary key, as neither contain only unique values. What is unique though is the combination of values, so the primary key is made up of both columns. In the table LockedDoors, From-

Room and ToRoom are being used as a lookup into the Doors table. This is often called a foreign key, meaning that there exists a table for which these columns directly map to that table's primary key. In this case, the primary key is made up of two columns, so the LockedDoors table has a large foreign key and a small bit of extra detail about that entry in the foreign table.

PickupInstances

| RoomID | PickupID |
|--------|----------|
| r2     | k1       |
| r3     | k2       |
| r3     | a1       |
| r3     | p1       |
| r4     | k3       |
| r4     | p2       |

Doors

| FromRoom | ToRoom |
|----------|--------|
| r1       | r2     |
| r1       | r3     |
| r2       | r1     |
| r2       | r4     |
| r3       | r1     |
| r3       | r2     |
| r3       | r5     |
| r4       | r2     |

LockedDoors

| FromRoom | ToRoom | LockedWith |
|----------|--------|------------|
| r1       | r3     | k1         |
| r2       | r4     | k2         |
| r3       | r5     | k3         |

Traps

| RoomID | Trapped |
|--------|---------|
| r2     | 10hp    |
| r5     | 25hp    |

Table 2.6: Additional tables to support 1NF rooms

Laying out the data in this way takes less space in larger projects as the number of NULL entries or arrays would have only increased with increased complexity of the level file. By laying out the data this way, we can add new features without having to revisit the original objects. For example, if we wanted to add monsters, normally we would not only have to add a new object for the monsters, but also add them to the room objects. In this format, all we need to do is add a new table such as in table 2.7.

Monsters

| **MonsterID** | Attack | HitPoints | StartRoom |
|---|---|---|---|
| M1 | 2 | 5 | r3 |
| M2 | 2 | 5 | r4 |

Table 2.7: Adding monsters

And now we have information about the monster and what room it starts in without touching any of the original level data.

### 2.4.3  2$^{nd}$ Normal Form

Second normal form is about trying to pull out columns that don't depend on only a part of the primary key. This can be caused by having a table that requires a compound primary key, and some attributes of the row only being dependent on part of that compound key. An example might be where you have weapons defined by quality and type, and the table looks like that in table 2.8, what you can see is that the primary key must be compound, as there are no columns with unique values here.

Weapons

| **WeaponType** | **WeaponQuality** | WeaponDamage | WeaponDamageType |
|---|---|---|---|
| Sword | Rusty | 2d4 | Slashing |
| Sword | Average | 2d6 | Slashing |
| Sword | Masterwork | 2d8 | Slashing |
| Lance | Average | 2d6 | Piercing |
| Lance | Masterwork | 3d6 | Piercing |
| Hammer | Rusty | 2d4 | Crushing |
| Hammer | Average | 2d4+4 | Crushing |

Table 2.8: Weapons in 1NF

It makes sense for us looking at the table that the primary key should be the compound of WeaponType and Weapon-Quality, as it's a fairly obvious move for us to want to look up damage amount and damage type values based on what weapon we're using. It's also possible to notice that the DamageType does not depend on the WeaponQuality, and in fact only depends on the WeaponType. That's what we mean about depending on part of the key. Even though each weapon is defined in 1NF, the type of damage being dealt currently relies on too little of the primary key to allow this table to remain in 2NF. We split the table out in table 2.9 to remove the column that only relies on WeaponType. If we found a weapon that changed DamageType based on quality, then we would put the table back the way it was. An example might be the *badly damaged morningstar*, which no longer does piercing damage, but only bludgeons.

Weapons

| **WeaponType** | **WeaponQuality** | WeaponDamage |
| --- | --- | --- |
| Sword | Rusty | 2d4 |
| Sword | Average | 2d6 |
| Sword | Masterwork | 2d8 |
| Lance | Average | 2d6 |
| Lance | Masterwork | 3d6 |
| Hammer | Rusty | 2d4 |
| Hammer | Average | 2d4+4 |

WeaponDamageTypes

| **WeaponType** | WeaponDamageType |
| --- | --- |
| Sword | Slashing |
| Lance | Piercing |
| Hammer | Crushing |

Table 2.9: Weapons in 2NF

When considering second normal form for our level data, it's worth understanding some shortcuts we made in moving to first normal form. Firstly, we didn't necessarily need to move to having a PickupID, but instead could have referenced the pickup prototype by PickupType and TintColour, but that was cumbersome, and would have introduced a NULL as a requirement as the armour doesn't have a tint.

Table 2.10 shows how this may have looked, but the complications with making this connect to the rooms was the deciding factor for introducing a PickupID. Without the pickup ID, the only way to put the pickups in rooms was to have two tables. One table for pickups with tints, and another for pickups without tints. This is not absurd, but it doesn't seem clean in this particular situation. There will be cases where this would be the right approach.

Pickups

| MeshID | TextureID | PickupType | ColourTint |
|--------|-----------|------------|------------|
| mkey | tkey | KEY | Copper |
| mkey | tkey | KEY | Silver |
| mkey | tkey | KEY | Gold |
| mpot | tpot | POTION | Green |
| mpot | tpot | POTION | Purple |
| marm | tarm | ARMOUR | NULL |

Normalising to 1NF:

Pickups 1NF

| PickupType | MeshID | TextureID |
|------------|--------|-----------|
| KEY | mkey | tkey |
| POTION | mpot | tpot |
| ARMOUR | marm | tarm |

TintedPickups 1NF

| PickupType | ColourTint |
|------------|------------|
| KEY | Copper |
| KEY | Silver |
| KEY | Gold |
| POTION | Green |
| POTION | Purple |

Table 2.10: An alternative 0NF and 1NF for Pickups

If we now revisit the Pickup table from before, with the knowledge that the PickupID is an alias for the combination of PickupType and ColourTint, then we can apply the same transform we see when moving to 1NF in the alternative form. That is, of moving MeshID and TextureID to their own table, and depending only on PickupType, not the compound key of PickupType and ColourTint.

In table 2.11, the assets elements now rely on the whole

of their compound key, not just part of it.

Pickups

| **PickupID** | PickupType |
|--------------|------------|
| k1 | KEY |
| k2 | KEY |
| k3 | KEY |
| p1 | POTION |
| p2 | POTION |
| a1 | ARMOUR |

PickupTints

| **PickupID** | ColourTint |
|--------------|------------|
| k1 | Copper |
| k2 | Silver |
| k3 | Gold |
| p1 | Green |
| p2 | Purple |

PickupAssets

| **PickupType** | MeshID | TextureID |
|----------------|--------|-----------|
| KEY | msh_key | tex_key |
| POTION | msh_pot | tex_pot |
| ARMOUR | msh_arm | tex_arm |

PickupAnims

| **PickupType** | AnimID |
|----------------|--------|
| KEY | key_bob |

Table 2.11: Pickups in 2NF

We can't apply the same normalisation of table data to the Room table. The Room table's RoomID is an alias for the whole row, possibly, or just the WorldPos, but in both cases, it's possible to see a correlation between the MeshID, TextureID, and the value of IsStart. The problem is that it also relies on the existence of entries in an external table. If we take the table as it is, the MeshID and TextureID do not directly rely on anything other than the RoomID in this form.

## 2.4.4  3$^{rd}$ Normal Form

When considering further normalisation, we first have to remove any transitive dependencies. By this we mean any dependencies on the primary key only via another column in the row. We can do a quick scan of the current tables and see all resources references refer to pairs of MeshID and TextureID values. Anything that uses a MeshID will use the matching TextureID. This means we can pull out one or the other from all the tables that use them, and look them up via a table of pairs. We shall arbitrarily choose to use the TextureID as the main lookup, and slim down to one table for meshes and textures.

TexturesAndMeshes

| TextureID | TextureName | MeshName |
|---|---|---|
| tex_room | "roomtexture" | "roommesh" |
| tex_roomstart | "roomtexturestart" | "roommeshstart" |
| tex_roomtrap | "roomtexturetrapped" | "roommeshtrapped" |
| tex_key | "keytexture" | "keymesh" |
| tex_pot | "potiontexture" | "potionmesh" |
| tex_arm | "armourtexture" | "armourmesh" |

Table 2.12: Assets in 3NF

## 2.4.5  Boyce-Codd Normal Form

The assets used for a room are based on whether it is trapped, or it's the starting room. This is a functional dependency, not a direct one, so we have to introduce a new column to describe that aspect, and it's going to require generating intermediate data to drive the value query, but it makes real the lack of direct link between the room and the assets. The rooms can be trapped, and can be starting rooms, and the assets connected to the room depend on those attributes, not the room itself. This is why Boyce-Codd Normal Form, or BCNF, can be thought of as the functionally dependent normalisation stage.

Rooms

| RoomID | WorldPos | IsStart | IsExit |
|--------|----------|---------|--------|
| r1 | 0,0 | true | false |
| r2 | -20,10 | false | false |
| r3 | -10,20 | false | false |
| r4 | -30,20 | false | false |
| r5 | 20,10 | false | true |

Rooms

| IsStart | HasTrap | TextureID |
|---------|---------|-----------|
| true | false | tex_rmstart |
| false | false | tex_rm |
| false | true | tex_rmtrap |

Table 2.13: Rooms table now in BCNF

## 2.4.6  Domain Key / Knowledge

Domain key normal form is normally thought of as the last normal form, but for developing efficient data structures, it's one of the things best studied early and often. The term *domain knowledge* is preferable when writing code as it makes more immediate sense and encourages use outside of keys and tables. Domain knowledge is the idea that data depends on other data, but only given information about the domain in which it resides. Domain knowledge can be as simple as awareness of a colloquialism for something, such as knowing that a certain number of degrees Celsius or Fahrenheit is hot, or whether some SI unit relates to a man-made concept such as 100m/s being rather quick.

An example of where domain knowledge can help with catching issues can be with putting human interpretations of values into asserts. Consider an assert for catching physics systems blowups. What is a valid expected range of values for acceleration? Multiply it by ten, and you have a check for when everything goes a bit crazy.

Some applications avoid the traditional inaccurate and erratic countdown timer, and resort to human-readable forms such as *in a few minutes* or *time to grab a coffee*, however domain knowledge isn't just about presenting a human interpretation of data. For example things such as the speed of sound, of light, speed limits and average speed of traffic on a given road network, psychoacoustic properties, the boiling point of water, and how long it takes a human to react to any given visual input. All these facts may be useful in some way, but can only be put into an application if the programmer adds it specifically as procedural domain knowledge or as an attribute of a specific instance.

Looking at our level data, one thing we can guess at is the asset filenames based on the basic name. The textures and meshes share a common format, so moving away from storing the full filenames could give us a Domain Knowledge normalised form.

AssetLookupTable

| **AssetID** | StubbedName |
|---|---|
| ast_room | "room%s" |
| ast_roomstart | "room%sstart" |
| ast_roomtrap | "room%strapped" |
| ast_key | "key%s" |
| ast_pot | "potion%s" |
| ast_arm | "armour%s" |

Table 2.14: Assets in DKNF

Domain knowledge is useful because it allows us to lose some otherwise unnecessarily stored data. It is a compiler's job to analyse the produced output of code (the abstract syntax tree) to then provide itself with data upon which it can infer and use its domain knowledge about what operations can be omitted, reordered, or transformed to produce faster or cheaper assembly. It's our job to do the same for elements the compiler can't know about, such as the chance that someone in the middle of a fight is going to be able to hear a coin drop in another room.

Domain knowledge is what leads to inventions such as JPEG and MP3. Thinking about what is possible, what is possible to perceive, and what can possibly be affected by user actions, can reduce the amount of work done by an application, and can reduce its complexity. When you jump in a game with physics, we don't move the world down by fractions of a nanometre to represent the opposite reaction caused by the forces applied.

## 2.4.7  Reflections

What we see here as we normalise our data is a tendency to split data by dependency. Looking at many third party engines and APIs, you can see some parallels with the results of these normalisations. It's unlikely that the people involved in the design and evolution of these engines took their data and applied database normalisation techniques, but sometimes the separations between object and components of objects can be obvious enough that you don't need a formal technique in order to realise some positive structural changes.

In some games, the entity object is not just an object that can be anything, but is instead a specific subset of the types of entity involved in the game. For example, in one game there might be a class for the player character, and one for each major type of enemy character, and another for vehicles. The player may have different attributes to other entities, such as lacking AI controls, or having player controls, or having regenerating health, or having ammo. This object-oriented approach puts a line, invisible to the user, but intrusive to the developer, between classes of object and their instances. It is intrusive because when classes touch, they have to adapt to each other. When they don't reside in the same hierarchy, they have to work through abstraction layers to message each other. The amount of code required to bridge these gaps can be small, but they always introduce complexity.

When developing software, this usually manifests as time spent writing out templated code that can operate on multiple classes rather than refactoring the classes involved into more discrete components. This could be considered wasted time as the likelihood of other operations needing to operate on all the objects is greater than zero, and the effort to refactor into components is usually similar to the effort to create a working templated operation.

Without classes to define boundaries, the table-based approach levels the playing field for data to be manipulated together. In all cases on our journey through normalising the level data, we have made it so changes to the design require fewer changes to the data, and made it so data changes are less likely to cause the state to become inconsistent. In many cases, it would seem we have added complexity when it wasn't necessary, and that's up to experimentation and experience to help you decide how far to go.

## 2.5 Operations

When you use objects, you call methods on them, so how do you unlock a door in this table-based approach? Actions are always going to be insert, delete, or updates. These were clearly specified in Edgar F. Codd's works, and they are all you need to manipulate a relational model.

In a real database, finding what mesh to load, or whether a door is locked would normally require a join between tables. A real database would also attempt to optimise the join by changing the sequence of operations until it had made the smallest possible expected workload. We can do better than that because we can take absolute charge of how we look at and request data from our tables. To find out if a door is locked, we don't need to join tables, we know we can look up into the locked doors table directly. Just because the data is laid out like a database, doesn't mean we have to use a query language to access it.

When it comes to operations that change state, it's best to try to stick to the kind of operation you would normally

```
 1   typedef std::pair<int,int> Door;
 2   typedef std::vector<Door> DoorVector
 3   DoorVector gDoors;
 4   int gDoors_firstClosedDoor = 0;
 5
 6   AddClosedDoor( Door d ) {
 7     gDoors.push_back();
 8   }
 9   AddOpenDoor( Door d ) {
10     gDoors.insert( gDoors.begin() + gDoors_firstClosedDoor, d );
11     gDoors_firstClosedDoor += 1;
12   }
```

Listing 2.2: Abusing the ordered nature of a vector

find in a DBMS, as doing unexpected operations brings unexpected state complexity. For example, imagine you have a
table of doors that are open, and a table of doors that are
closed. Moving a door from one table might be considered
wasteful, so you may consider changing the representation
to a single table, but with all closed doors at one end, and
all open at the other. By having both tables represented
as a single table, and having the *isClosed* attribute defined
implicitly by a cut-off point in the array, such as in listing
2.2, leads to the table being somewhat ordered. This type
of memory optimisation comes at a price. Introducing order
into a table makes the whole table inherently less parallelisable to operations, so beware the additional complexity introduced by making changes like this, and document them
well.

Unlocking a door can be a delete. A door is locked because
there is an entry in the LockedDoors table that matches the
Door you are interested in. Unlocking a door is a delete if
door matches, and you have the right key.

The player inventory would be a table with just PickupIDs.
This is the idea that *"the primary key is also the data"* mentioned much earlier. If the player enters a room and picks up
a Pickup, then the entry matching the room is deleted while
the inventory is updated to include the new PickupID.

Databases have the concept of triggers, whereupon operations on a table can cause cascades of further operations. In the case of picking up a key, we would want a trigger on insert into the inventory that joined the new PickupID with the LockedDoors table. For each matching row there, delete it, and now the door is unlocked.

## 2.6 Summing up

At this point we can see it is perfectly reasonable to store any highly complex data structures in a database format, even game data with its high interconnectedness and rapid design changing criteria.

Games have lots of state, and the relational model provides a strong structure to hold both static information, and mutable state. The strong structure leads to similar solutions to similar problems in practise, and similar solutions have similar processing. You can expect algorithms and techniques to be more reusable while working with tables, as the data layout is less surprising.

If you're looking for a way to convert your interconnected complicated objects into a simpler flatter memory layout, you could do worse than approach the conversion with normalisation in mind.

A database approach to data storage has some other useful side-effects. It provides an easier route to allowing old executables to run off new data, and it allows new executables to more easily run with old data. This can be vital when working with other people who might need to run an earlier or later version. We saw that sometimes adding new features required nothing more than adding a new table, or a new column to an existing table. That's a non-intrusive modification if you are using a database style of storage, but a significant change if you're adding a new member to a class.

## 2.7   Stream Processing

Now we realise that all the game data and game runtime can be implemented in a database-like approach, we can also see that all game data can be implemented as streams. Our persistent storage is a database, our runtime data is in the same format as it was on disk, what do we benefit from this? Databases can be thought of as collections of rows, or collections of columns, but it's also possible to think about the tables as sets. The set is the set of all possible permutations of the attributes.

For most applications, using a bitset to represent a table would be wasteful, as the set size quickly grows out of scope of any hardware, but it can be interesting to note what this means from a processing point of view. Processing a set, transforming it into another set, can be thought of as traversing the set and producing the output set, but the interesting attribute of a set is that it is unordered. An unordered list can be trivially parallel processed. There are massive benefits to be had by taking advantage of this trivialisation of parallelism wherever possible, and we normally cannot get near this because of the data layout of the object-oriented approaches.

Coming at this from another angle, graphics cards vendors have been pushing in this direction for many years, and we now need to think in this way for game logic too. We can process lots of data quickly as long as we utilise stream processing or set processing as much as possible and use random access processing as little as possible. Stream processing in this case means to process data without writing to variables external to the process. This means not allowing things like global accumulators, or accessing global memory not set as a source for the process. This ensures the processes or transforms are trivially parallelisable.

When you prepare a primitive render for a graphics card, you set up constants such as the transform matrix, the texture binding, any lighting values, or which shader you want to run. When you come to run the shader, each vertex and pixel may have its own scratchpad of local variables, but they never write to globals or refer to a global scratchpad. The concept of shared memory in general purpose GPU code, such as CUDA and OpenCL, allows the use of a kind of managed cache. None of the GPGPU techniques offer access to global memory, and thus maintain a clear separation of domains and continue to guarantee no side-effects caused by any kernels being run outside of their own sandboxed shared memory. By enforcing this lack of side-effects, we can guarantee trivial parallelism because the order of operations are assured to be irrelevant. If a shader was allowed to write to globals, there would be locking, or it would become an inherently serial operation. Neither of these are good for massive core count devices like graphics cards, so that has been a self imposed limit and an important factor in their design. Adding shared memory to the mix starts to inject some potential locking into the process, and hence is explicitly only used when writing compute shaders.

Doing all processing this way, without globals / global scratchpads, gives you the rigidity of intention to highly parallelise your processing and make it easier to think about the system, inspect it, debug it, and extend it or interrupt it to hook in new features. If you know the order doesn't matter, it's very easy to rerun any tests or transforms that have caused bad state.

## 2.8 Why does database technology matter?

As mentioned at the start of the chapter, the relational model is currently a very good fit for developing non-sparse data layouts that are manipulable with very little complicated state management required once the tables have been designed. However, the only constant is change. That which is current, regularly becomes the old way, and for widely scaled systems, the relational model no longer provides all features required.

After the emergence of NoSQL solutions for handling even larger workloads, and various large companies' work on creating solutions to distribute computing power, there have been advances in techniques to process enormous data-sets. There have been advances in how to keep databases current, distributed, and consistent (within tolerance). Databases now regularly include NULL entries, to the point where there are far more NULL entries than there are values, and these highly sparse databases need a different solution for processing. Many large calculations and processes now run via a technique called map-reduce, and distributing workloads has become commonplace enough that people have to be reminded they don't always need a cluster to add up some numbers.

What's become clear over the last decade is that most of the high-level data processing techniques which are proving to be useful are a combination of hardware-aware data manipulation layers being used by functional programming style high-level algorithms. As the hardware in your PC becomes more and more like the internet itself, these techniques will begin to dominate on personal hardware, whether it be personal computers, phones, or whatever the next generation brings. Data-oriented design was inspired by a realisation that the hardware had moved on to the point where the techniques we used to use to defend against latency from CPU to hard drive, now apply to memory. In the future, if we raise processing power by the utilisation of hoards of isolated unreliable computation units, then the techniques for distributing computing across servers that we're developing in this era, will apply to the desktops of the next.

# Chapter 3

# Existential Processing

If you saw there weren't any apples in stock, would you still haggle over their price?

Existential processing attempts to provide a way to remove unnecessary querying about whether or not to process your data. In most software, there are checks for NULL and queries to make sure the objects are in a valid state before work is started. What if you could always guarantee your pointers were not null? What if you were able to trust that your objects were in a valid state, and should always be processed?

In this chapter, a dynamic runtime polymorphism technique is shown that can work with the data-oriented design methodology. It is not the only way to implement data-oriented design friendly runtime polymorphism, but was the first solution discovered by the author, and fits well with other game development technologies, such as components and compute shaders.

# 3.1   Complexity

When studying software engineering you may find references
to cyclomatic complexity or conditional complexity. This is
a complexity metric providing a numeric representation of
the complexity of programs and is used in analysing large-
scale software projects. Cyclomatic complexity concerns itself only with flow control. The formula, summarised for our
purposes, is one (1) plus the number of conditionals present
in the system being analysed. That means for any system
it starts at one, and for each if, while, for, and do-while, we
add one. We also add one per path in a switch statement
excluding the default case if present.

Under the hood, if we consider how a virtual call works,
that is, a lookup in a function pointer table followed by a
branch into the class method, we can see that a virtual call
is effectively just as complex as a switch statement. Counting the flow control statements is more difficult in a virtual
call because to know the complexity value, you have to know
the number of possible methods that can fulfil the request.
In the case of a virtual call, you have to count the number
of overrides to a base virtual call. If the base is pure-virtual,
then you may subtract one from the complexity. However, if
you don't have access to all the code that is running, which
can be possible in the case of dynamically loaded libraries,
then the number of different potential code paths increases
by an unknown amount. This hidden or obscured complexity is necessary to allow third party libraries to interface with
the core process, but requires a level of trust that implies
no single part of the process is ever going to be thoroughly
tested.

This kind of complexity is commonly called control flow
complexity. There is another form of complexity inherent in
software, and that is the complexity of state. In the paper
*Out of the Tar Pit* [4], it's concluded that the aspect of software
which causes the most complexity is *state*. The paper continues and presents a solution which attempts to minimise

what it calls accidental state, that is, state which is required by the software to do its job, but not directly required by the problem being solved. The solution also attempts to abolish any state introduced merely to support a programming style.

We use flow control to change state, and state changes what is executed in our programs. In most cases flow control is put in for one of two reasons: to solve the problem presented (which is equivalent to the essential state in *Out of the Tar Pit*), and to help with the implementation of the solution (which is equivalent to the accidental state).

Essential control is when we need to implement the design, a gameplay feature which has to happen when some conditions are met, such as jumping when the jump button is pressed or autosaving at a save checkpoint when the savedata is dirty, or a timer has run out.

Accidental control is non-essential to the program from the point of view of the person using it, but could be foundation work, making it critical for successful program creation. This type of control complexity is itself generally split into two forms. The first form is structural, such as to support a programming paradigm, to provide performance improvements, or to drive an algorithm. The second form is defensive programming or developer helpers such as reference counting or garbage collection. These techniques increase complexity where functions operating on the data aren't sure the data exists, or is making sure bounds are observed. In practice, you will find this kind of control complexity when using containers and other structures, control flow is going to be in the form of bounds checks and ensuring data has not gone out of scope. Garbage collection adds complexity. In many languages, there are few guarantees about how and when it will happen. This also means it can be hard to reason about object lifetimes. Because of a tendency to ignore memory allocations early in development when working with these languages, it can be very hard to fix memory leaks closer to shipping dates. Garbage collection in unmanaged languages is easier to handle, as reference counts can more easily be interrogated, but also due to the fact that unmanaged languages generally allocate less often in the first place.

## 3.2  Debugging

What classes of issues do we suffer with high complexity programs? Analysing the complexity of a system helps us understand how difficult it is to test, and in turn, how hard it is to debug. Some issues can be classified as being in an unexpected state, and then having no way forward. Others can be classified as having bad state, and then exhibiting unexpected behaviour due to reacting to this invalid data. Yet others can be classified as performance problems, not just correctness, and these issues, though somewhat disregarded by a large amount of academic literature, are costly in practice and usually come from complex dependencies of state.

For example, the complexity caused by performance techniques such as caching, are issues of complexity of state. The CPU cache is in a state, and not being aware of it, and not working with the expected state in mind, leads to issues of poor or inconsistent performance.

Much of the time, the difficulty we have in debugging comes from not fully observing all the flow control points, assuming one route has been taken when it hasn't. When programs do what they are told, and not what we mean, they will have entered into a state we had not expected or prepared for.

With runtime polymorphism using virtual calls, the likelihood of that happening can dramatically increase as we cannot be sure we know all the different ways the code can branch until we either litter the code with logging, or step through in a debugger to see where it goes at run-time.

## 3.3 Why use an if

In real-world cases of game development, the most common use of an explicit flow control statement would appear to be in the non-essential set. Where defensive programming is being practiced, many of the flow control statements are just to stop crashes. There are fail-safes for out of bounds accesses, protection from pointers being NULL, and defenses against other exceptional cases that would bring the program to a halt. It's pleasing to note, GitHub contains plenty of high quality C++ source-code that bucks this trend, preferring to work with reference types, or with value types where possible. In game development, another common form of flow control is looping. Though these are numerous, most compilers can spot them, and have good optimisations for these and do a very good job of removing condition checks that aren't necessary. The final inessential but common flow control comes from polymorphic calls, which can be helpful in implementing some of the gameplay logic, but mostly are there to entertain the do-more-with-less-code development model partially enforced in the object-oriented approach to writing games.

Essential game design originating flow control doesn't appear very often in profiles as causes of branching, as all the supporting code is run far more frequently. This can lead to an underappreciation of the effect each conditional has on the performance of the software. Code that does use a conditional to implement AI or handle character movement, or decide on when to load a level, will be calling down into systems which are full of loops and tree traversals, or bounds checks on arrays they are accessing in order to return the data upon which the game is going to produce the boolean value to finally drive the side of the if to which it will fall through. That is, when the rest of your code-base is slow, it's hard to validate writing fast code for any one task. It's hard to tell what additional costs you're adding on.

If we decide the elimination of control flow is a goal worthy of consideration, then we must begin to understand what control flow operations we can eliminate. If we begin our attempt to eliminate control flow by looking at defensive programming, we can try to keep our working set of data as a collections of arrays. This way we can guarantee none of our data will be NULL. That one step alone may eliminate many of our flow control statements. It won't get rid of loops, but as long as they are loops over data running a pure functional style transform, then there are no side-effects to worry about, and it will be easier to reason about.[1]

The inherent flow control in a virtual call is avoidable, as it is a fact that many programs were written in a non-object-oriented style. Without virtuals, we can rely on switch statements. Without those, we can rely on function pointer tables. Without those, we can have a long sequence of ifs. There are many ways to implement runtime polymorphism. It is also possible to maintain that if you don't have an explicit type, you don't need to switch on it, so if you can eradicate the object-oriented approach to solving the problem, those flow control statements go away completely.

When we get to the control flow in gameplay logic, we find there is no simple way to eradicate it. This is not a terrible thing to worry about, as the gameplay logic is as close to essential complexity as we can get when it comes to game development.

Reducing the number of conditionals, and thus reducing the cyclomatic complexity on such a scale is a benefit which cannot be overlooked, but it is one that comes with a cost. The reason we are able to get rid of the check for NULL is that we will have our data in a format that doesn't allow for NULL at all. This inflexibility will prove to be a benefit, but it requires a new way of processing our entities.

Where once we would have an object instance for an area

---

[1]Sean Parent's talks on C++ seasoning are worth watching. They talk practically about simplification and elimination of unnecessary loops and structure.

in a game, and we would interrogate it for exits that take us to other areas, now we look into a structure that only contains links between areas, and filter by the area we are in. This reversal of ownership can be a massive benefit in debugging, but can sometimes appear backward when all you want to do is find out what exits are available to get out of an area.

If you've ever worked with shopping lists or to-do lists, you'll know how much more efficient you can be when you have a definite list of things to purchase or complete. It's very easy to make a list, and adding to it is easy as well. If you're going shopping, it's very hard to think what might be missing from your house in order to get what you need. If you're the type that tries to plan meals, then a list is nigh on essential as you figure out ingredients and then tally up the number of tins of tomatoes, or other ingredients you need to last through all the meals you have planned. If you have a to-do list and a calendar, you know who is coming and what needs to be done to prepare for them. You know how many extra mouths need feeding, how much food and drink you need to buy, and how much laundry you need done to make enough beds for the visitors.

To-do lists are great because you can set an end goal and then add in subtasks that make a large and long distant goal seem more doable. Adding in estimates can provide a little urgency that is usually missing when the deadline is so far away. Many companies use software to support tracking of tasks, and this software often comes with features allowing the producers to determine critical paths, expected developer hours required, and sometimes even the balance of skills required to complete a project. Not using this kind of software is often a sign that a company isn't overly concerned with efficiency, or waste. If you're concerned about efficiency and waste in your program, lists of tasks seem like a good way to start analysing where the costs are coming from. If you keep track of these lists by logging them, you can look at the data and see the general shape of the processing your software is performing. Without this, it can be difficult to tell where the real bottlenecks are, as it might not be the processing that is the problem, but the requirement to process data itself which has gotten out of hand.

When your program is running, if you don't give it homogeneous lists to work with, but instead let it do whatever comes up next, it will be inefficient and have irregular or lumpy frame timings. Inefficiency of hardware utilisation often comes from unpredictable processing. In the case of large arrays of pointers to heterogeneous classes all being called with an update() function, you can hit high amounts of data dependency which leads to misses in both data and instruction caches. See chapter 14 for more details on why.

Slowness also comes from not being able to see how much work needs to be done, and therefore not being able to prioritise or scale the work to fit what is possible within the given time-frame. Without a to-do list, and an ability to estimate the amount of time each task will take, it is difficult to decide the best course of action to take in order to reduce overhead while maintaining feedback to the user.

Object-oriented programming works very well when there are few patterns in the way the program runs. When either the program is working with only a small amount of data, or when the data is incredibly heterogeneous, to the point that there are as many classes of things as there are things.

Irregular frame timings can often be blamed on not being able to act on distant goals ahead of time. If you, as a developer, know you have to load the assets for a new island when a player ventures into the seas around it, the streaming system can be told to drag in any data necessary. This could also be for a room and the rooms beyond. It could be for a cave or dungeon when the player is within sight of the entrance. We consider this kind of preemptive streaming of data to be a special case and invent systems to provide this level of forethought. Relying on humans, or even level-designers, to link these together is prone to error. In many cases, there are chains of dependencies that can be missed without an automated check. The reason we cannot make systems self-aware enough to preload themselves is that we don't have a common language to describe temporal dependencies.

In many games, we stream things in with explicit triggers, but there is often no such system for many of the other game elements. It's virtually unheard of for an AI to pathfind to some goal because there might soon be a need to head that way. The closest would be for the developer to pre-populate a navigation map so coarse grain pathing can be completed swiftly.

There's also the problem of depth of preemptive work. Consider the problem of a small room, built as a separate asset, a waiting room with two doors near each other, both leading to large, but different maps. When the player gets near the door to the waiting room in map A, that little room can be preemptively streamed in. However, in many engines, map B won't be streamed in, as the locality of map B to map A is hidden behind the logical layer of the waiting room.

It's also not commonplace to find a physics system doing look ahead to see if a collision has happened in the future in order to start doing further work. It might be possible to do a more complex breakup simulation if it were more aware.

If you let your game generate to-do lists, shopping lists, distant goals, and allow for preventative measures by forward-thinking, then you can simplify your task as a coder into prioritising goals and effects, or writing code that generates priorities at runtime. You can start to think about how to chain those dependencies to solve the waiting room problem. You can begin to preempt all types of processing.

## 3.4   Types of processing

Existential processing is related to to-do lists.  When you process every element in a homogeneous set of data, you know you are processing every element the same way.  You are running the same instructions for every element in that set.  There is no definite requirement for the output in this specification, however, it usually comes down to one of three types of operation: a filter, a mutation, or an emission.  A mutation is a one to one manipulation of the data, it takes incoming data and some constants that are set up before the transform, and produces one and only one element for each input element.  A filter takes incoming data, again with some constants set up before the transform, and produces one element or zero elements for each input element.  An emission is a manipulation of the incoming data that can produce multiple output elements.  Just like the other two transforms, an emission can use constants, but there is no guaranteed size of the output table; it can produce anywhere between zero and infinity elements.

A fourth, and final form, is not really a manipulation of data, but is often part of a transform pipeline, and that is the generator.  A generator takes no input data, but merely produces output based on the constants set up.  When working with compute shaders, you might come across this as a function that merely clears out an array to zero, one, or an ascending sequence.

These categories can help you decide what data structure you will use to store the elements in your arrays, and whether you even need a structure, or you should instead pipe data from one stage to another without it touching down on an intermediate buffer.

Every CPU can efficiently handle running processing kernels over homogeneous sets of data, that is, doing the same operation over and over again over contiguous data.  When there is no global state, no accumulator, it is proven

3.4. TYPES OF PROCESSING

Transforms

| | | |
|---|---|---|
| **Mutation** | $in == out$ | Handles input data. Produces one item of output for every item of input. |
| **Filter** | $in >= out$ | Handles input data. Produces up to one item of output for every item of input. |
| **Emission** | $out = \begin{cases} 0, & in = 0 \\ >= 0, & otherwise \end{cases}$ | Handles input data. Produces unknown amount of items per item of input. With no input, output is also empty. |
| **Generation** | $in = 0 \wedge out >= 0$ | Does not read data. Produces an unknown amount of items just by running. |

Table 3.1: Types of transform normally encountered

to be parallelisable. Examples can be given from existing technologies such as map-reduce and simple compute shaders, as to how to go about building real work applications within these restrictions. Stateless transforms also commit no crimes that prevent them from being used within distributed processing technologies. Erlang relies on these guarantees of being side-effect free to enable not just thread safe processing or interprocess safe processing, but distributed computing safe processing. Stateless transforms of stateful data are highly robust and deeply parallelisable.

Within the processing of each element, that is for each datum operated on by the transform kernel, it is fair to use control flow. Almost all compilers should be able to reduce simple local value branch instructions into a platform's preferred branch-free representation, such as a CMOV, or select function for a SIMD operation. When considering branches inside transforms, it's best to compare to existing implementations of stream processing such as graphics card shaders or compute kernels.

In predication, flow control statements are not ignored, but they are used instead as an indicator of how to merge two results. When the flow control is not based on a constant, a predicated if will generate code that will run both sides of the branch at the same time and discard one result based on the value of the condition. It manages this by selecting one of the results based on the condition. As mentioned before, in many CPUs there is an intrinsic for this, but all CPUs can use bit masking to effect this trick.

SIMD or single-instruction-multiple-data allows the parallel processing of data when the instructions are the same. The data is different but local. When there are no conditionals, SIMD operations are simple to implement on your transforms. In MIMD, that is multiple instructions, multiple data, every piece of data can be operated on by a different set of instructions. Each piece of data can take a different path. This is the simplest and most error-prone to code for because it's how most parallel programming is currently done. We add a thread and process some more data with a separate thread of execution. MIMD includes multi-core general purpose CPUs. It often allows shared memory access and all the synchronisation issues that come with it. It is by far the easiest to get up and running, but it is also the most prone to the kind of rare fatal error caused by complexity of state. Because the order of operations become non-deterministic, the number of different possible routes taken through the code explode super-exponentially.

## 3.5   Don't use booleans

When you study compression technology, one of the most important aspects you have to understand is the difference between data and information. There are many ways to store information in systems, from literal strings that can be parsed to declare something exists, right down to something simple like a single bit flag to show that a thing might have an attribute. Examples include the text that declares the existence of a local variable in a scripting language, or the bit field containing all the different collision types a physics mesh will respond to. Sometimes we can store even less

```
 1   struct Entity {
 2     // information about the entity position
 3     // ...
 4     // now health data in the middle of the entity
 5     float timeoflastdamage;
 6     float health;
 7     // ...
 8     // other entity information
 9   };
10   list<Entity> entities;
```

Listing 3.1: basic entity approach

information than a bit by using advanced algorithms such as arithmetic encoding, or by utilising domain knowledge. Domain knowledge normalisation applies in most game development, but it is increasingly infrequently applied, as many developers are falling foul to overzealous application of quoting premature optimisation. As information is encoded in data, and the amount of information encoded can be amplified by domain knowledge, it's important that we begin to see that the advice offered by compression techniques is: what we are really encoding is probabilities.

If we take an example, a game where the entities have health, regenerate after a while of not taking damage, can die, can shoot each other, then let's see what domain knowledge can do to reduce processing.

We assume the following domain knowledge:

- If you have full health, then you don't need to regenerate.

- Once you have been shot, it takes some time until you begin regenerating.

- Once you are dead, you cannot regenerate.

- Once you are dead you have zero health.

If we have a list for the entities such as in listing 3.1, then we see the normal problem of data potentially causing cache

```
1   void UpdateHealth( Entity *e ) {
2     TimeType timeSinceLastShot = e->timeOfLastDamage - currentTime;
3     bool isHurt = e->health < MAX_HEALTH;
4     bool isDead = e->health <= 0;
5     bool regenCanStart = timeSinceLastShot >
          TIME_BEFORE_REGENERATING;
6     // if alive, and hurt, and it's been long enough
7     if( !isDead && isHurt && regenCanStart ) {
8       e->health = min(MAX_HEALTH, e->health + tickTime * regenRate)
          ;
9     }
10  }
```

Listing 3.2: simple health regen

```
1   struct Entity {
2     // information about the entity position
3     // ...
4     // other entity information
5   };
6   struct Entitydamage {
7     float timeoflastdamage;
8     float health;
9   }
10  list<Entity> entities;
11  map<EntityRef,Entitydamage> entitydamages;
```

Listing 3.3: Existential processing style health

line utilisation issues, but aside from that, we can see how you might run an update function over the list, such as in listing 3.2, which will run for every entity in the game, every update.

We can make this better by looking at the flow control statement. The function won't run if health is at max. It won't run if the entity is dead. The regenerate function only needs to run if it has been long enough since the last damage dealt. All these things considered, regeneration isn't the common case. We should try to organise the data layout for the common case.

Let's change the structures to those in listing 3.3 and then we can run the update function over the health table rather than the entities. This means we already know, as soon as

```
void UpdateHealth() {
  for( edIter : entityDamages ) {
    EntityDamage &ed = edIter->second;
    if( ed.health <= 0 ) {
      // if dead, insert the fact that this entity is dead
      EntityRef entity = edIter->first;
      deadEntities.insert( entity );
      // if dead, discard being damaged
      discard(ed);
    } else {
      TimeType timeSinceLastShot = ed.timeOfLastShot -
          currentTime;
      bool regenCanStart = timeSinceLastShot >
          TIME_BEFORE_REGENERATING;
      if( regenCanStart )
        ed->health =ed->health + tickTime * regenRate;
      // if at max health or beyond, discard being damaged
      if( ed->health >= MAX_HEALTH )
        discard(ed);
    }
  }
}
```

Listing 3.4: every entity health regen

we are in this function, that the entity is not dead, and they are hurt.

We only add a new entityhealth element when an entity takes damage. If an entity takes damage when it already has an entityhealth element, then it can update the health rather than create a new row, also updating the time damage was last dealt. If you want to find out someone's health, then you only need to look and see if they have an entityhealth row, or if they have a row in deadEntities table. The reason this works is, an entity has an implicit boolean hidden in the row existing in the table. For the entityDamages table, that implicit boolean is the isHurt variable from the first function. For the deadEntities table, the boolean of isDead is now implicit, and also implies a health value of 0, which can reduce processing for many other systems. If you don't have to load a float and check it is less than 0, then you're saving a floating point comparison or conversion to boolean.

This eradication of booleans is nothing new, because every time you have a pointer to something you introduce a boolean of having a non-NULL value. It's the fact that we don't want to check for NULL which pushes us towards finding a different representation for the lack of existence of an object to process.

Other similar cases include weapon reloading, oxygen levels when swimming, anything which has a value that runs out, has a maximum, or has a minimum. Even things like driving speeds of cars. If they are traffic, then they will spend most of their time driving at *traffic speed* not some speed they need to calculate. If you have a group of people all heading in the same direction, then someone joining the group can be *intercepting* until they manage to, at which point they can give up their independence, and become controlled by the group. There is more on this point in chapter 5.

By moving to keeping lists of attribute state, you can introduce even more performance improvements. The first thing you can do for attributes that are linked to time is to put them in a sorted list, sorted by time of when they should be acted upon. You could put the regeneration times in a sorted list and pop entityDamage elements until you reach one that can't be moved to the active list, then run through all the active list in one go, knowing they have some damage, aren't dead, and can regen as it's been long enough.

Another aspect is updating certain attributes at different time intervals. Animals and plants react to their environment through different mechanisms. There are the very fast mechanisms such as reactions to protect us from danger. Pulling your hand away from hot things, for example. There are the slower systems too, like the rationalising parts of the brain. Some, apparently quick enough that we think of them as real-time, are the quick thinking and acting processes we consider to be the actions taken by our brains when we don't have time to think about things in detail, such as catching a ball or balancing a bicycle. There is an even slower part of the brain, the part that isn't so much reading this book, but is consuming the words, and making a model of what they mean so as to digest them. There is also the even slower systems, the ones which react to stress, chemical levels spread through the body as hormones, or just the amount of sugar you have available, or current level of hydration. An AI which can think and react on multiple time-scales is more likely to waste fewer resources, but also much less likely to act oddly, or flip-flop between their decisions. Committing to doing an update of every system every frame could land you in an impossible situation. Splitting the workload into different update rates can still be regular, but offers a chance to balance the work over multiple frames.

Another use is in state management. If an AI hears gunfire, then they can add a row to a table for when they last heard gunfire, and that can be used to determine whether they are in a heightened state of awareness. If an AI has been involved in a transaction with the player, it is important they remember what has happened as long as the player is likely to remember it. If the player has just sold an AI their +5 longsword, it's very important the shopkeeper AI still have it in stock if the player just pops out of the shop for a moment. Some games don't even keep inventory between transactions, and that can become a sore point if they accidentally sell something they need and then save their progress.

From a gameplay point of view, these extra bits of information are all about how the world and player interact. In some games, you can leave your stuff lying around forever, and it will always remain just how you left it. It's quite a feat that all the things you have dumped in the caves of some open-world role-playing games, are still hanging around precisely where you left them hours and hours ago.

The general concept of tacking on data, or patching loaded data with dynamic additional attributes, has been around for quite a while. Save games often encode the state of a dynamic world as a delta from the base state, and one of the first major uses was in fully dynamic environments, where a world is loaded, but can be destroyed or altered later. Some world generators took a procedural landscape and allowed their content creators to add patches of extra information, villages, forts, outposts, or even break out landscaping tools to drastically adjust the generated data.

## 3.6   Don't use enums quite as much

Enumerations are used to define sets of states. We could have had a state variable for the regenerating entity, one that had infullhealth, ishurt, isdead as its three states. We could have had a team index variable for the avoidance entity enumerating all the available teams. Instead, we used tables to provide all the information we needed, as there were only two teams. Any enum can be emulated with a variety of tables. All you need is one table per enumerable value. Setting the enumeration is an insert into a table or a migration from one table to another.

When using tables to replace enums, some things become more difficult: finding out the value of an enum in an entity is difficult as it requires checking all the tables which represent that state for the entity. However, the main reason for getting the value is either to do an operation based on an external state or to find out if an entity is in the right state to be considered for an operation. This is disallowed and unnecessary for the most part, as firstly, accessing external state is not valid in a pure function, and secondly, any dependent data should already be part of the table element.

If the enum is a state or type enum previously handled by a switch or virtual call, then we don't need to look up the value, instead, we change the way we think about the problem. The solution is to run transforms taking the content of each of the switch cases or virtual methods as the operation to apply to the appropriate table, the table corresponding to the original enumeration value.

If the enum is instead used to determine whether or not an entity can be operated upon, such as for reasons of compatibility, then consider an auxiliary table to represent being in a compatible state. If you're thinking about the case where you have an entity as the result of a query and need to know if it is in a certain state before deciding to commit some changes, consider that the compatibility you seek could have been part of the criteria for generating the output table in the first place, or a second filtering operation could be committed to create a table in the right form.

In conclusion, the reason why you would put an enum in table form, is to reduce control flow impact. Given this, it's when we aren't using the enumerations to control instruction flow that it's fine to leave them alone. Another possibility is when the value of the enum changes with great frequency, as moving objects from table to table has a cost too.

Examples of enumerations that make sense are keybindings, enumerations of colours, or good names for small finite sets of values. Functions that return enums, such as collision responses (none, penetrating, through). Any kind of enumeration which is actually a lookup into data of another form is good, where the enum is being used to rationalise the access to those larger or harder to remember data tables. There is also a benefit to some enums in that they will help you trap unhandled cases in switches, and to some extent, they are a self-documenting feature in most languages.

# 3.7 Prelude to polymorphism

Let's consider now how we implement polymorphism. We know we don't have to use a virtual table pointer; we could use an enum as a type variable. That variable, the member of the structure that defines at runtime what that structure should be capable of and how it is meant to react. That variable will be used to direct the choice of functions called when methods are called on the object.

When your type is defined by a member type variable, it's usual to implement virtual functions as switches based on that type, or as an array of functions. If we want to allow for runtime loaded libraries, then we would need a system to update which functions are called. The humble switch is unable to accommodate this, but the array of functions could be modified at runtime.

We have a solution, but it's not elegant, or efficient. The data is still in charge of the instructions, and we suffer the same instruction cache misses and branch mispredictions as whenever a virtual function is unexpected. However, when we don't really use enums, but instead tables that represent each possible value of an enum, it is still possible to keep compatible with dynamic library loading the same as with pointer based polymorphism, but we also gain the efficiency of a data-flow processing approach to processing heterogeneous types.

For each class, instead of a class declaration, we have a factory that produces the correct selection of table insert calls. Instead of a polymorphic method call, we utilise existential processing. Our elements in tables allow the characteristics of the class to be implicit. Creating your classes with factories can easily be extended by runtime loaded libraries. Registering a new factory should be simple as long as there is a data-driven factory method. The processing of the tables and their update() functions would also be added to the main loop.

## 3.8   Dynamic runtime polymorphism

If you create your classes by composition, and you allow the state to change by inserting and removing from tables, then you also allow yourself access to dynamic runtime polymorphism. This is a feature normally only available when dynamically responding via a switch.

Polymorphism is the ability for an instance in a program to react to a common entry point in different ways due only to the nature of the instance. In C++, compile-time polymorphism can be implemented through templates and overloading. Runtime polymorphism is the ability for a class to provide a different implementation for a common base operation with the class type unknown at compile-time. C++ handles this through virtual tables, calling the right function at runtime based on the type hidden in the virtual table pointer at the start of the memory pointed to by the `this` pointer. Dynamic runtime polymorphism is when a class can react to a common call signature in different ways based on its type, but its type can change at runtime. C++ doesn't implement this explicitly, but if a class allows the use of an internal state variable or variables, it can provide differing reactions based on the state as well as the core language runtime virtual table lookup. Other languages which define their classes more fluidly, such as Python, allow each instance to update how it responds to messages, but most of these languages have very poor general performance as the dispatch mechanism has been built on top of dynamic lookup.

Consider the code in listing 3.5, where we expect the runtime method lookup to solve the problem of not knowing the type but wanting the size. Allowing the objects to change shape during their lifetime requires some compromise. One way is to keep a type variable inside the class such as in listing 3.6, where the object acts as a container for the type variable, rather than as an instance of a specific shape.

A better way is to have a conversion function to handle each case. In listing 3.7 we see how that can be achieved.

Though this works, all the pointers to the old class are now invalid. Using handles would mitigate these worries, but add another layer of indirection in most cases, dragging down performance even further.

```
1   class shape {
2   public:
3     shape() {}
4     virtual ~shape() {}
5     virtual float getarea() const = 0;
6   };
7   class circle : public shape {
8   public:
9     circle( float diameter ) : d(diameter ) {}
10    ~circle() {}
11    float getarea() const { return d*d*pi/4; }
12    float d;
13  };
14  class square : public shape {
15  public:
16    square( float across ) : width( across ) {}
17    ~square() {}
18    float getarea() const { return width*width; }
19    float width;
20  };
21  void test() {
22    circle circle( 2.5f );
23    square square( 5.0f );
24    shape *shape1 = &circle, *shape2 = &square;
25    printf( "areas are %f and %f\n", shape1->getarea(), shape2->
          getarea() );
26  }
```

Listing 3.5: simple object-oriented shape code

```
enum shapetype { circletype, squaretype };
class mutableshape {
public:
  mutableshape( shapetype type, float argument )
    : m_type( type ), distanceacross( argument )
    {}
  ~mutableshape() {}
  float getarea() const {
    switch( m_type ) {
      case circletype: return distanceacross*distanceacross*pi/4;
      case squaretype: return distanceacross*distanceacross;
    }
  }
  void setnewtype( shapetype type ) {
    m_type = type;
  }
  shapetype m_type;
  float distanceacross;
};
void testinternaltype() {
  mutableshape shape1( circletype, 5.0f );
  mutableshape shape2( circletype, 5.0f );
  shape2.setnewtype( squaretype );
  printf( "areas are %f and %f\n", shape1.getarea(), shape2.
    getarea() );
}
```

Listing 3.6: ugly internal type code

```
square squarethecircle( const circle &circle ) {
  return square( circle.d );
}
void testconvertintype() {
  circle circle( 5.0f );
  square square = squarethecircle( circle );
}
```

Listing 3.7: convert existing class to new class

If you use existential processing techniques, your classes defined by the tables they belong to, then you can switch between tables at runtime. This allows you to change behaviour without any tricks, without the complexity of managing a union to carry all the different data around for all the states you need. If you compose your class from different attributes and abilities then need to change them post creation, you can. If you're updating tables, the fact that the pointer address of an entity has changed will mean little to you. It's normal for an entity to move around memory in table-based processing, so there are fewer surprises. Looking at it from a hardware point of view, in order to implement this form of polymorphism you need a little extra space for the reference to the entity in each of the class attributes or abilities, but you don't need a virtual table pointer to find which function to call. You can run through all entities of the same type increasing cache effectiveness, even though it provides a safe way to change type at runtime.

Via the nature of having classes defined implicitly by the tables they belong to, there is an opportunity to register a single entity with more than one table. This means that not only can a class be dynamically runtime polymorphic, but it can also be multi-faceted in the sense that it can be more than one class at a time. A single entity might react in two different ways to the same trigger call because it might be appropriate for the current state of that class.

This kind of multidimensional classing doesn't come up much in traditional gameplay code, but in rendering, there are usually a few different axes of variation such as the material, what blend mode, what kind of skinning or other vertex adjustments are going to take place on a given instance. Maybe we don't see this flexibility in gameplay code because it's not available through the natural tools of the language. It could be that we do see it, but it's what some people call entity component systems.

# 3.9 Event handling

When you wanted to listen for events in a system in the old days, you'd attach yourself to an interrupt. Sometimes you might get to poke at code that still does this, but it's normally reserved for old or microcontroller scale hardware. The idea was simple, the processor wasn't really fast enough to poll all the possible sources of information and do something about the data, but it was fast enough to be told about events and process the information as and when it arrived. Event handling in games has often been like this, register yourself as interested in an event, then get told about it when it happens. The publish and subscribe model has been around for decades, but there's no standard interface built for it in some languages and too many standards in others. As it often requires some knowledge from the problem domain to choose the most effective implementation.

Some systems want to be told about every event in the system and decide for themselves, such as Windows event handling. Some systems subscribe to very particular events but want to react to them as soon as they happen, such as handlers for the BIOS events like the keyboard interrupt. The events could be very important and dispatched directly by the action of posting the event, such as with callbacks. The events could be lazy, stuck in a queue somewhere waiting to be dispatched at some later point. The problem they are trying to solve will define the best approach.

Using your existence in a table as the registration technique makes this simpler than before and lets you register and de-register with great pace. Subscription becomes an insert, and unsubscribing a delete. It's possible to have global tables for subscribing to global events. It would also be possible to have named tables. Named tables would allow a subscriber to subscribe to events before the publisher exists.

When it comes to firing off events, you have a choice. You

can choose to fire off the transform immediately, or queue up new events until the whole transform is complete, then dispatch them all in one go. As the model becomes simpler and more usable, the opportunity for more common use leads us to new ways of implementing code traditionally done via polling.

For example: unless a player character is within the distance to activate a door, the event handler for the player's action button needn't be attached to anything door related. When the character comes within range, the character registers into the *has_pressed_action* event table with the *open_door_(X)* event result. This reduces the amount of time the CPU wastes figuring out what thing the player was trying to activate, and also helps provide state information such as on-screen displays saying *pressing Green will Open the door.*

If we allow for all tables to have triggers like those found in DBMSs, then it may be possible to register interest in changes to input mappings, and react. Hooking into low-level tables such as a *insert into a has_pressed_action table* would allow user interfaces to know to change their on-screen display to show the new prompt.

This coding style is somewhat reminiscent of aspect-oriented programming where it is easy to allow for cross-cutting concerns in the code. In aspect-oriented programming, the core code for any activities is kept clean, and any side effects or vetoes of actions are handled by other concerns hooking into the activity from outside. This keeps the core code clean at the expense of not knowing what is really going to be called when you write a line of code. How using registration tables differs is in where the reactions come from and how they are determined. Debugging can become significantly simpler as the barriers between cause and effect normally implicit in aspect-oriented programming are significantly diminished or removed, and the hard to adjust nature of object-oriented decision making can be softened to allow your code to become more dynamic without the normally associated cost of data-driven control flow.

# Chapter 4

# Component Based Objects

A component-oriented design is a good start for high-level data-oriented design. Developing with components can put you in the right frame of mind to avoid linking together concepts needlessly. Objects built this way can more easily be processed by type, instead of by instance, which can lead to them being easier to profile. Entity systems built around them are often found in game development as a way to provide data-driven functionality packs for entities, allowing for designer control over what would normally be in the realm of a programmer. Not only are component based entities better for rapid design changes, but they also stymie the chances of getting bogged down into monolithic objects, as most game designers would demand more components with new features over extending the scope of existing components. This is because most new designs need iterating on, and extending an existing component by code to introduce design changes wouldn't allow game designers to switch back and forth trying out different things as easily. It's usually more flexible to add another component as an extension or as an alternative.

A problem that comes up with talking about component-oriented development is how many different types of entity component systems there are. To help clear the ambiguity, we shall describe some different ways in which component-oriented designs work.

The first kind of component-oriented approach most people use is a compound object. There are a few engines that use them this way, and most of them use the power of their scripting language to help them achieve a flexible, and designer friendly way to edit and create objects out of components. For example, Unity's GameObject is a base entity type which can include components by adding them to that particular instance's list of components. They are all built onto the core entity object, and they refer to each other through it. This approach means every entity still tends to update via iteration over root instances, not iteration over systems.

Common dialogue around creating compound objects frequently refers to using components to make up an object directly by including them as members of the object. Though this is better than a monolithic class, it is not yet a fully component based approach. This technique uses components to make the object more readable, and potentially more reusable and robust to change. These systems are extensible enough to support large ecosystems of components shareable between projects. The *Unity Asset Store* proves the worth of components from the point of view of rapid development.

When you introduce component based entities, you have an opportunity to turn the idea of how you define an object on its head. The normal approach to defining an object in object-oriented design is to name it, then fill out the details as and when they become necessary. For example, your car object is defined as a Car, if not extending Vehicle, then at least including some data about what physics and meshes are needed, with construction arguments for wheels and body shell model assets etc, possibly changing class dependent on whether it's an AI or player car. In component-oriented design, objects aren't so rigidly defined, and don't so much become defined after they are named, as much as a definition is selected or compiled, and then tagged with a name if necessary. For example, instancing a physics component with four-wheel physics, instancing a renderable for each part (wheels, shell, suspension) adding an AI or player component to control the inputs for the physics component, all adds up to something which we can tag as a Car, or leave as is and it becomes something implicit rather than explicit and immutable.

A truly component based object is nothing more than the sum of its parts. This means the definition of a component based object is also nothing more than an inventory with some construction arguments. This object or definition agnostic approach makes refactoring and redesigning a much simpler exercise. Unity's ECS provides such a solution. In the ECS, entities are intangible and implicit, and the components are first class citizens.

## 4.1 Components in the wild

Component based approaches to development have been tried and tested. Many high-profile studios have used component driven entity systems to great success[1], and this was in part due to their developer's unspoken understanding that objects aren't a good place to store all your data and traits. For some, it was the opportunity to present the complexity of what makes up an entity through simpler pieces, so designers and modders would be able to reason about how their changes fit within the game framework. For some, it was about giving power over to performance, where components are more easily moved to a structure-of-arrays approach to processing.

---

[1] Gas Powered Games, Looking Glass Studios, Insomniac, Neversoft all used component based objects.

Gas Powered Games' Dungeon Siege Architecture is probably the earliest published document about a game company using a component based approach. If you get a chance, you should read the article[10] to see where things really kicked off. The article explains that using components means the entity type[2] doesn't need to have the ability to do anything. Instead, all the attributes and functionality come from the components of which the entity is made.

The list of reasons to move to a manager driven, component based approach are numerous, and we shall attempt to cover at least a few. We will talk about the benefits of clear update sequences. We will mention how components can make it easier to debug. We will talk about the problem of objects applying meaning to data, causing coupling, and therefore with the dissolution of the object as the central entity, how the tyranny of the instance is mitigated.

In this section, we'll show how we can take an existing class and rewrite it in a component based fashion. We're going to tackle a fairly typical complex object, the Player class. Normally these classes get messy and out of hand quite quickly. We're going to assume it's a Player class designed for a generic 3rd person action game, and take a typically messy class as our starting point. We shall use listing 4.1 as a reference example of one such class.

```
 1   class Player {
 2   public:
 3     Player();
 4     ~Player();
 5     Vec GetPos(); // the root node position
 6     void SetPos( Vec ); // for spawning
 7     Vec GetSpeed(); // current velocity
 8     float GetHealth();
 9     bool IsDead();
10     int GetPadIndex(); // the player pad controlling me
11     float GetAngle(); // the direction the player is pointing
12     void SetAnimGoal( ... ); // push state to anim-tree
13     void Shoot( Vec target ); // fire the player's weapon
14     void TakeDamage( ... ); // take some health off, maybe animate
          for the damage reaction
15     void Speak( ... ); // cause the player to start audio/anim
```

---

[2]GPG:DG uses GO or Game-Objects, but we stick with the term entity because it has become the standard term.

```
16    void SetControllable( bool ); // no control in cut-scene
17    void SetVisible( bool ); // hide when loading / streaming
18    void SetModel( ... ); // init streaming the meshes etc
19    bool IsReadyForRender();
20    void Render(); // put this in the render queue
21    bool IsControllable(); // player can move about?
22    bool IsAiming(); // in normal move-mode, or aim-mode
23    bool IsClimbing();
24    bool InWater(); // if the root bone is underwater
25    bool IsFalling();
26    void SetBulletCount( int ); // reload is -1
27    void AddItem( ... ); // inventory items
28    void UseItem( ... );
29    bool HaveItem( ... );
30    void AddXP( int ); // not really XP, but used to indicate when
          we let the player power-up
31    int GetLevel(); // not really level, power-up count
32    int GetNumPowerups(); // how many we've used
33    float GetPlayerSpeed(); // how fast the player can go
34    float GetJumpHeight();
35    float GetStrength(); // for melee attacks and climb speed
36    float GetDodge(); // avoiding bullets
37    bool IsInBounds( Bound ); // in trigger zone?
38    void SetGodMode( bool ); // cheater
39  private:
40    Vec pos;
41    Vec up, forward, right;
42    Vec velocity;
43    Array<ItemType> inventory;
44    float health;
45    int controller;
46    AnimID idleAnim;
47    AnimID shootAnim;
48    AnimID reloadAnim;
49    AnimID movementAnim;
50    AnimID currentAnimGoal;
51    AnimID currentAnim;
52    int bulletCount;
53    float shotsPerSecond;
54    float timeSinceLastShot;
55    SoundHandle playingSoundHandle; // null most of the time
56    bool controllable;
57    bool visible;
58    AssetID playerModel;
59    LocomotionType currentLocomotiveModel;
60    int xp;
61    int usedPowerups;
62    int SPEED, JUMP, STRENGTH, DODGE;
63    bool cheating;
64  };
```

Listing 4.1: Monolithic Player class

This example class includes many of the types of things found in games, where the codebase has grown organically.

It's common for the Player class to have lots of helper functions to make writing game code easier.  Helper functions typically consider the Player as an instance in itself, from data in save through to rendering on screen.  It's not unusual for the Player class to touch nearly every aspect of a game, as the human player is the target of the code in the first place, the Player class is going to reference nearly everything too.

AI characters will have similarly gnarly looking classes if they are generalised rather than specialised.  Specialising AI was more commonplace when games needed to fit in smaller machines, but now, because the Player class has to interact with many of them over the course of the game, they tend to be unified into one type just like the player, if not the same as the player, to help simplify the code that allows them to interact.  As of writing, the way in which AI is differentiated is mostly by data, with behaviour trees taking the main stage for driving how AI thinks about its world.  Behaviour trees are another concept subject to various interpretations, so some forms are data-oriented design friendly, and others are not.

## 4.2   Away from the hierarchy

A recurring theme in articles and post-mortems from people moving from object-oriented hierarchies of gameplay classes to a component based approach is the transitional states of turning their classes into containers of smaller objects, an approach often called composition.  This transitional form takes an existing class and finds the boundaries between concepts internal to the class and attempts to refactor them out into new classes which can be owned or pointed to by the original class.  From our monolithic player class, we can see there are lots of things that are not directly related, but that does not mean they are not linked together.

Object-oriented hierarchies are *is-a* relationships, and

components and composition oriented designs are traditionally thought of as *has-a* relationships. Moving from one to the other can be thought of as delegating responsibility or moving away from being locked into what you are, but having a looser role and keeping the specialisation until further down the tree. Composition clears up most of the common cases of diamond inheritance issues, as capabilities of the classes are added by accretion as much as they are added by overriding.

The first move we need to make will be to take related pieces of our monolithic class and move them into their own classes, along the lines of composing, changing the class from owning all the data and the actions that modify the data into having instances which contain data and delegating actions down into those specialised structures where possible. We move the data out into separate structures so they can be more easily combined into new classes later. We will initially only separate by categories we perceive as being the boundaries between systems. For example, we separate rendering from controller input, from gameplay details such as inventory, and we split out animation from all.

Taking a look at the results of splitting the player class up, such as in listing 4.2, it's possible to make some initial assessments of how this may turn out. We can see how a first pass of building a class out of smaller classes can help organise the data into distinct, purpose oriented collections, but we can also see the reason why a class ends up being a tangled mess. When you think about the needs of each of the pieces, what their data requirements are, the coupling can become evident. The rendering functions need access to the player's position as well as the model, and the gameplay functions such as *Shoot(Vec target)* need access to the inventory as well as setting animations and dealing damage. Taking damage will need access to the animations and health. Things are already seeming more difficult to handle than expected, but what's really happening here is that it's becoming clear that code needs to cut across different

pieces of data. With just this first pass, we can start to see
that functionality and data don't belong together.

```
struct PlayerPhysical {
  Vec pos;
  Vec up, forward, right;
  Vec velocity;
};
struct PlayerGameplay {
  float health;
  int xp;
  int usedPowerups;
  int SPEED, JUMP, STRENGTH, DODGE;
  bool cheating;
  float shotsPerSecond;
  float timeSinceLastShot;
};
struct EntityAnim {
  AnimID idleAnim;
  AnimID shootAnim;
  AnimID reloadAnim;
  AnimID movementAnim;
  AnimID currentAnimGoal;
  AnimID currentAnim;
  SoundHandle playingSoundHandle; // null most of the time
};
struct PlayerControl {
  int controller;
  bool controllable;
};
struct EntityRender {
  bool visible;
  AssetID playerModel;
};
struct EntityInWorld {
  LocomotionType currentLocomotiveModel;
};
struct Inventory {
  Array<ItemType> inventory;
  int bulletCount;
};

class Player {
public:
  Player();
  ~Player();
  // ...
  // ... the member functions
  // ...
private:
  PlayerPhysical phsyical;
  PlayerGameplay gameplay;
  EntityAnim anim;
  PlayerControl control;
  EntityRender render;
  EntityInWorld inWorld;
  Inventory inventory;
};
```

Listing 4.2: Composite Player class

In this first step, we made the player class a container for the components. Currently, the player has the components, and the player class has to be instantiated to make a player exist. To allow for the cleanest separation into components in the most reusable way, it's worth attempting to move components into being managed by managers, and not handled or updated by their entities. In doing this, there will also be a benefit of cache locality when we're iterating over multiple entities doing related tasks when we move them away from their owners.

This is where it gets a bit philosophical. Each system has an idea of the data it needs in order to function, and even though they will overlap, they will not share all data. Consider what it is that a serialisation system needs to know about a character. It is unlikely to care about the current state of the animation system, but it will care about inventory. The rendering system will care about position and animation, but won't care about the current amount of ammo. The UI rendering code won't even care about where the player is, but will care about inventory and their health and damage. This difference of interest is at the heart of why putting all the data in one class isn't a good long-term solution.

The functionality of a class, or an object, comes from how the internal state is interpreted, and how the changes to state over time are interpreted too. The relationship between facts is part of the problem domain and could be called meaning, but the facts are only raw data. This separation of fact from meaning is not possible with an object-oriented approach, which is why every time a fact acquires a new meaning, the meaning has to be implemented as part of the class containing the fact. Dissolving the class, extracting the facts and keeping them as separate components, has given us the chance to move away from classes that instill permanent meaning at the expense of occasionally having to look up facts via less direct methods. Rather than store all the possibly associated data by meaning, we choose to only add meaning when necessary. We add meaning when it is part of the immediate problem we are trying to solve.

## 4.3   Towards managers

After splitting your classes up into components, you might find your classes look more awkward now they are accessing variables hidden away in new structures. But it's not your classes that should be looking up variables, but instead transforms on the classes. A common operation such as rendering requires the position and the model information, but it also requires access to the renderer. Such object boundary crossing access is seen as a compromise during game development, but here it can be seen as the method by which we move away from a class-centric approach to a data-oriented approach. We will aim at transforming our data into render requests which affect the graphics pipeline without referring to data unimportant to the renderer.

Referring to listing 4.3, we move to no longer having a player update, but instead an update for each component that makes up the player. This way, everyone entity's physics is updated before it is rendered, or could be updated while the rendering is happening on another thread. All entity's controls (whether they be player or AI) can be updated before they are animated. Having the managers control when the code is executed is a large part of the leap towards fully parallelisable code. This is where performance can be gained with more confidence that it's not negatively impacting other areas. Analysing which components need updating every frame, and which can be updated less frequently leads to optimisations that unlock components from each other.

In many component systems that allow scripting languages to define the actions taken by components or their

```
class Renderable {
  void RenderUpdate() {
    auto pos = gPositionArray[index];
    gRenderer.AddModel( playerModel, pos );
  }
};
class RenderManager {
  void Update() {
    gRenderer.BeginFrame();
    for( auto &renderable : renderArray ) {
      renderable.RenderUpdate();
    }
    gRenderer.SubmitFrame();
  }
};
class PhysicsManager {
  void Update() {
    for( auto &physicsRequest : physicsRequestArray ) {
      physicalArray[physicsRequest.index].UpdateValues(
          physicsRequest.updateData );
    }
    // Run physics simulation
    for( auto &physical : physicalArray ) {
      positionArray[physical.index].pos = physical.pos;
    }
  }
};
class Controller {
  void Update() {
    Pad pad = GetPad( controller );
    if( pad.IsPressed( SHOOT ) ) {
      if( inventoryArray[index].bulletCount > 0 )
        animRequest.Add( SHOOT_ONCE );
    }
  }
};
class PlayerInventory {
  void Update() {
    if( inv.bulletCount == 0 ) {
      if( animArray.contains( inv.index ) {
        anim = animArray[ index ];
        anim.currentAnim = RELOAD;
        inventoryArray[index].bulletCount = 6;
        anim.playingSoundHandle = PlaySound( GUNFIRE );
      }
    }
  }
};
class PlayerControl {
  void Update() {
    for( auto &control : controlArray ) {
      control.Update();
    }
    for( auto &inv : inventoryArray )  {
      inv.Update();
    }
  }
}
```

Listing 4.3: Manager ticked components

entities, performance can fall foul of the same inefficiencies present in an object-oriented program design. Notably, the dependency inversion practice of calling *Tick* or *Update* functions will often have to be sandboxed in some way which will lead to error checking and other safety measures wrapping the internal call. There is a good example of this being an issue with the older versions of Unity, where their component based approach allowed every instance to have its own script which would have its own call from the core of Unity on every frame. The main cost appeared to be transitioning in and out of the scripting language, crossing the boundary between the C++ at the core, and the script that described the behaviour of the component. In his article *10,000 Update() calls*[11], Valentin Simonov provided information on why the move to managers makes so much sense, giving details on what is costing the most when utilising dependency inversion to drive your general code update strategies. The main cost was in moving between the different areas of code, but even without having to straddle the language barrier, managers make sense as they ensure updates to components happen in sync.

What happens when we let more than just the player use these arrays? Normally we'd have some separate logic for handling player fire until we refactored the weapons to be generic weapons with NPCs using the same code for weapons probably by having a new weapon class that can be pointed to by the player or an NPC, but instead what we have here is a way to split off the weapon firing code in such a way as to allow the player and the NPC to share firing code without inventing a new class to hold the firing. In fact, what we've done is split the firing up into the different tasks it really contains.

Tasks are good for parallel processing, and with component based objects, we open up the opportunity to move most of our previously class oriented processes out, and into more generic tasks that can be dished out to whatever CPU or co-processor can handle them.

```
struct Orientation { Vec pos, up, forward, right; };
SparseArray<Orientation> orientationArray;
SparseArray<Vec> velocityArray;
SparseArray<float> healthArray;
SparseArray<int> xpArray, usedPowerupsArray, controllerID,
    bulletCount;
struct Attributes { int SPEED, JUMP, STRENGTH, DODGE; };
SparseArray<Attributes> attributeArray;
SparseArray<bool> godmodeArray, controllable, isVisible;
SparseArray<AnimID> currentAnim, animGoal;
SparseArray<SoundHandle> playingSound;
SparseArray<AssetID> modelArray;
SparseArray<LocomotionType> locoModelArray;
SparseArray<Array<ItemType> > inventoryArray;

int NewPlayer( int padID, Vec startPoint ) {
  int ID = newID();
  controllerID[ ID ] padID;
  GetAsset( "PlayerModel", ID ); // adds a request to put the
      player model into modelArray[ID]
  orientationArray[ ID ] = Orientation(startPoint);
  velocityArray[ ID ] = VecZero();
  return ID;
}
```

Listing 4.4: Sparse arrays for components

## 4.4 There is no entity

What happens when we completely remove the Player class?
If an entity can be represented by its collection of components, does it need any further identity than those self same
components? Like the values in the rows of a table, the components describe a single instance, but also like the rows in
a table, the table is also a set. In the universe of possibilities
of component combinations, the components which make up
the entity are not facts about the entity, but are the entity,
and are the only identity the entity needs. As an entity *is*
its current configuration of components, then there is the
possibility of removing the core Player class completely. Removing this class can mean we no longer think of the player
as being the centre of the game, but because the class no
longer exists, it means the code is no longer tied to a specific
singular entity. Listing 4.4 shows a rough example of how
you might develop this kind of setup.

Moving away from compile-time defined classes means many other classes can be invented without adding much code. Allowing scripts to generate new classes of entity by composition or prototyping increases their power dramatically, and cleanly increase the apparent complexity of the game without adding more actual complexity. Finally, all the different entities in the game will now run the same code at the same time, which simplifies and centralises your processing code, leading to more opportunity to share optimisations, and fewer places for bugs to hide.

# Chapter 5

# Hierarchical Level of Detail and Implicit-state

Consoles and graphics cards are not generally bottlenecked at the polygon rendering stage in the pipeline. Usually, they are bandwidth bound. If there is a lot of alpha blending, it's often fill-rate issues. For the most part, graphics chips spend a lot of their time reading textures, and texture bandwidth often becomes the bottleneck. Because of this, the old way of doing level of detail with multiple meshes with decreasing numbers of polygons is never going to be as good as a technique which takes into account the actual data required of the level of detail used in each renderable. The vast majority of stalls when rendering come from driver side processing, or from processing too much for what you want to actually render. Hierarchical level of detail can fix the problem of high primitive count which causes more driver calls than necessary.

The basic approach for art is to make optimisations by grouping and merging many low level of detail meshes into one single low level of detail mesh. This reduces the time spent in the setup of render calls which is beneficial in situations where driver calls are costly. In a typical very large scale environment, a hierarchical level of detail approach to game content can reduce the workload on a game engine by an order of magnitude as the number of entities in the scene considered for processing and rendering drops significantly.

Even though the number of polygons rendered may be exactly the same, or maybe even higher, the fact that the engine usually is only handling roughly the same number of entities at once on average increases stability and allows for more accurately targeted optimisations of both art and code.


## 5.1   Existence from Null to Infinity

If we consider that entities can be implicit based on their attributes, we can utilise the technique of hierarchical level of detail to offer up some optimisations for our code. In traditional level of detail techniques, as we move further away from the object or entity of interest, we lose details and fidelity. We might reduce polygon count, or texture sizes, or even the number of bones in a skeleton that drives the skinned mesh. Game logic can also degrade. Moving away from an entity, it might switch to a much coarser grain time step. It's not unheard of for behaviours of AI to migrate from a 50hz update to a 1hz update. In a hierarchical level of detail implementation, as the entity becomes closer, or more apparent to the player, it might be that only at that point does it even begin to exist.

Consider a shooter game where you are defending a base from incoming attacks. You are manning an anti-air turret, and the attackers come in squadrons of aircraft, you can see them all coming at once, over ten thousand aircraft in all, and up to a hundred at once in each squadron. You have to shoot them down or be inundated with gunfire and bombs, taking out both you and the base you are defending.

Running full AI, with swarming for motion and avoidance for your slower moving ordnance might be too much if it was run on all ten thousand ships every tick, but you don't need to. The basic assumption made by most AI programmers is that unless they are within attacking range, then they don't need to be running AI. This is true and offers an immediate speedup compared to the naïve approach. Hierarchical LOD provides another way to think about this, by changing the number of entities based on how they are perceived by the player. For want of a better term, *collective lodding* is a name that describes what is happening behind the scenes a little better. Sometimes there is no hierarchy, and yet, there can still be a change in the manner in which the elements are referenced between the levels of detail. The term collective lodding is inspired by the concept of a collective term. A murder of crows is a computational element, but each crow is a lower level of detail sub-element of the collective.

In the collective lodding version of the base defender game, there are a few wave entities which project squadron blips on the radar. The squadrons don't exist as their own entities until they get close enough. Once a wave's squadron is within range, the wave will decrease its squadron count and pop out a new squadron entity. The newly created squadron entity shows blips on the radar for each of its component aircraft. The aircraft don't exist yet, but they are implicit in the squadron in the same way the squadron was implicit in the wave. The wave continues to pop Squadrons as they come into range, and once its internal count has dropped to zero, it can delete itself as it now represents no entities. As a squadron comes into even closer range, it pops out its aircraft into their own entities and eventually deletes itself. As the aircraft get closer, traditional level of detail techniques kick in and their renderables are allowed to switch to higher resolution and their AI is allowed to run at a higher intelligence setting.

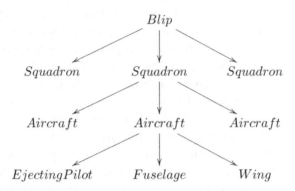

When the aircraft are shot at, they switch to a taken damage type. They are full health enemy aircraft unless they take damage. If an AI reacts to damage with fear, they may eject, adding another entity to the world. If the wing of the plane is shot off, then that also becomes a new entity in the world. Once a plane has crashed, it can delete its entity and replace it with a smoking wreck entity that will be much simpler to process than an aerodynamic simulation, faked or not.

If things get out of hand and the player can't keep the aircraft at bay and their numbers increase in size so much that any normal level of detail system can't kick in to mitigate it, collective lodding can still help by returning aircraft to squadrons and flying them around the base attacking as a group, rather than as individual aircraft. In the board game *Warhammer Fantasy Battle*, there were often so many troops firing arrows at each other, that players would often think of attacks by squads as being collections of attacks, and not actually roll for each individual soldier, rat, orc or whatever it was, but instead counted up how many troops they had, and rolled that many dice to see how many attacks got through. This is what is meant by attacking as a squadron. The aircraft no longer attack, instead, the likelihood an attack will succeed is calculated, dice are rolled, and that many attacks get through. The level of detail heuristic can be tuned so the nearest and front-most squadron are always the highest level of detail, effectively making them roll individually, and the ones behind the player maintain a very simplistic representation.

This is game development smoke and mirrors as a basic game engine element. In the past we have reduced the number of concurrent attacking AI[1], reduced the number of cars on screen by staggering the lineup over the whole race track[2], and we've literally combined people together into one person instead of having loads of people on screen at once[3]. This kind of reduction of processing is commonplace. Now consider using it everywhere appropriate, not just when a player is not looking.

## 5.2 Mementos

Reducing detail introduces an old problem, though. Changing level of detail in game logic systems, AI and such, brings with it the loss of high detail history. In this case, we need a way to store what is needed to maintain a highly cohesive player experience. If a high detail squadron in front of the player goes out of sight and another squadron takes their place, we still want any damage done to the first group to reappear when they come into sight again. Imagine if you had shot out the glass on all the aircraft and when they came round again, it was all back the way it was when they first arrived. A cosmetic effect, but one that is jarring and makes it harder to suspend disbelief.

When a high detail entity drops to a lower level of de-

---

[1] I believe this was Half-Life
[2] Ridge Racer was known for this
[3] Populous did this

tail, it should store a memento, a small, well-compressed nugget of data that contains all the necessary information in order to rebuild the higher detail entity from the lower detail one. When the squadron drops out of sight, it stores a memento containing compressed information about the amount of damage, where it was damaged, and rough positions of all the aircraft in the squadron. When the squadron comes into view once more, it can read this data and generate the high detail entities back in the state they were before. Lossy compression is fine for most things, it doesn't matter precisely which windows, or how they were cracked, maybe just that about 2/3 of the windows were broken.

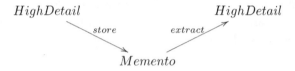

Another example is in a city-based free-roaming game. If AIs are allowed to enter vehicles and get out of them, then there is a good possibility you can reduce processing time by removing the AIs from the world when they enter a vehicle. If they are a passenger, then they only need enough information to rebuild them and nothing else. If they are the driver, then you might want to create a new driver type based on some attributes of the pedestrian before making the memento for when they exit the vehicle.

If a vehicle reaches a certain distance away from the player, then you can delete it. To keep performance high, you can change the priorities of vehicles that have mementos so they try to lose sight of the player thus allowing for earlier removal from the game. Optimisations like this are hard to coordinate in object-oriented systems as internal inspection of types isn't encouraged. Some games get around it by designing in ways to reset memento data as a gameplay element. The game *Zelda: Breath of the Wild* resets monsters during a Blood Moon, and by doing so, you as a player, are not surprised when you return to camps to find all the monsters are just as you left them.

## 5.3  JIT mementos

If a vehicle that has been created as part of the ambient population is suddenly required to take on a more important role, such as the car being involved in a firefight, it needs to gain detail. This detail must come from somewhere and must be convincing. It is important to generate new entities which don't seem overly generic or unlikely, given what the player knows about the game so far. Generating that data can be thought of as providing a memento to read from just in time. Just in time mementos, or JIT mementos, offers a way to create fake mementos that can provide continuity by utilising pseudo-random generators or hash functions to create suitable information on demand without relying on storing data anywhere. Instead, they rely only on information provided implicitly by the entity in need of it.

Instead of generating new characters from a global random number generator, it is possible to seed the generator with details about the thing that needs generation. For example, you want to generate a driver and some passengers, as you're about to get close enough to a car to need to render the people inside it. Just creating random characters from a set of lookup tables is good, but if you drive past them far enough for them to get out of rendering range, and then return, the people in the car might not look the same anymore as they had to be regenerated. Instead, generate the driver and passengers using some other unique attribute, such as the license plate, as a seed. This way, while you have not affected the result of generating the memento, you have no memory overhead to store it, and no object lifetime to worry about either, as it can always be reproduced from nothing again.

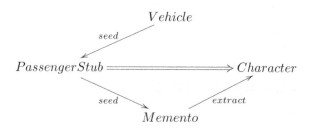

This technique is used all the time in landscape generators, where the landscape is seeded from the x,y location in
the map, so why not use it when generating the weather for
day 107 of the game? When generating Perlin noise, many
algorithms call upon a noise function, but to have a reproducible landscape, the noise function must be a repeatable
function, so it can create the same results over and over
again. If you're generating a landscape, it's preferred for the
noise function to be coherent, that is, for small variances in
the input function, only small changes should be observed
in the output. We don't need such qualities when generating
JIT mementos, and a hash function which varies wildly with
even the smallest change in the input will suffice.

An example of using this to create a JIT memento might
be to generate a house for a given landscape. First, take
any normal random number generator and seed it with the
location of the building. Given the landscape the house is on,
select from a building template and start generating random
numbers to answer questions about the house the same way
loading a file off disk answers questions about the object.
How large is the house? Is it small, medium, large? Generate
a random number and select one answer. How many rooms
does it have based on the size? 2 or 3 for small, or (int)(7
+ rand * 10) for large. The point is, once you have seeded
the random number generator, you're going to get the same
results back every time you run through the same process.
Every time you visit the house at {223.17,-100.5}, you're
going to see the same 4 (or more) walls, and it will have the
same paint job, broken windows, or perfect idyllic little frog

pond in the back garden.

JIT mementos can be the basis of a highly textured environment with memento style sheets or style guides which can direct a feel bias for any mementos generated in those virtual spaces. Imagine a city style guide that specifies rules for occupants of cars. The style guide might claim that businessmen might share, but are much less likely to, that families have children in the back seats with an older adult driving. It might declare that young adults tend to drive around in pairs. Style guides help add believability to any generated data. Add in local changes such as having types of car linked to types of drivers. Have convertibles driven by well-dressed types or kids, low riders driven almost exclusively by their stereotypical owner, and imports and modded cars driven by young adults. In a space game, dirty hairy pilots of cargo ships, well turned out officers commanding yachts, rough and ready mercenaries in everything from a single seater to a dreadnought. Then, once you have the flavour in place, allow for a little surprise to bring it to life fully.

JIT mementos are a good way to keep the variety up, and style guides bias that so it comes without the impression that everyone is different so everyone is the same. When these biases are played out without being strictly adhered to, you can build a more textured environment. If your environment is heavily populated with completely different people all the time, there is nothing to hold onto, no patterns to recognise. When there are no patterns, the mind tends to see noise or consider it to be a samey soup. Even the most varied virtual worlds look bland when there is too much content all in the same place. Walk along the street and see if you can spot any identical paving slabs. You probably can, but also see the little bits of damage, decay, dirt, mistakes, and blemishes. To make an environment believable, you have to make it look like someone took a lot of effort trying to make it all conform.

## 5.4   Alternative axes

As with all things, take away an assumption and you can find other uses for a tool. Whenever you read about, or work with a level of detail system, you will be aware that the constraint on what level of detail is shown has always been some distance function in space. It's now time to take the assumption, discard it, and analyse what is really happening.

First, we find that if we take away the assumption of distance, we can infer the conditional as some kind of linear measure. This value normally comes from a function which takes the camera position and finds the relative distance to the entity under consideration. What we may also realise when discarding the distance assumption is a more fundamental understanding of what we are trying to do. We are using a single runtime variable to control the presentation state of the entities of our game. We use runtime variables to control the state of many parts of our game already, but in this case, there is a passive presentation response to the variable, or axis being monitored. The presentation is usually some graphical, or logical level of detail, but it could be something as important to the entity as its own existence.

### 5.4.1   The true measure

Distance is the measure we normally use to identify what level of detail something should be at, but it's not the metric we really need, it's just very closely related. In fact, it's inversely related. The true metric of level of detail should be how much of our perception an entity is taking up. If an entity is very large, and far away, it takes up as much of our perception as something small and nearby. All this time we have talked about hierarchical level of detail the elephant in the room has been the language used. We had waves on our radar. They took up as much perception attention as a single squadron, and a single squadron took up as much perceptual space as a single aircraft when it was in firing range.

Understand this concept: level of detail should be defined by how the player perceives a thing, at the range it is at. If you internalise this, you will be on your way to making good decisions about where the boundaries are between your levels of detail.

## 5.4.2  Beyond space

Let's now consider what other variables we can calculate that present an opportunity to remove details from the game's representation. We should consider anything which presents an opportunity to no longer process data unnecessarily. If some element of a game is not the player's current concern, or will fade from memory soon enough, we can dissolve it away. If we consider the probability of the player caring about a thing as a metric, then we begin to think about recollection and attention as measurable quantities we can use to drive how we end up representing it.

An entity that you know has the player's attention, but is hidden, maintains a large stake on the player's perception. That stake allows the entity to maintain a higher priority on level of detail than it would otherwise deserve. For example, a character the player is chasing in an assassination game, may be spotted only once at the beginning of the mission, but will have to remain at a high consistency of attribute throughout the mission, as they are the object the player cares about the most, coming second only to primitive needs such as survival. Even if the character slips into the crowd, and is not seen again until much later, they must look just like they did when you first caught sight of them.

Ask the question, how long until a player forgets about something that might otherwise be important? This information will help reduce memory usage as much as distance.

If you have ever played *Grand Theft Auto IV*, you might have noticed that the cars can disappear just by not looking at them. As you turn around a few times you might notice the cars seem to be different each time you face their way. This is a stunning use of temporal level of detail. Cars which have been bumped into or driven and parked by the player remain where they were, because, in essence, the player put them there. Because the player has interacted with them, they are likely to remember they are there. However, ambient vehicles, whether they are police cruisers or civilian vehicles, are less important and don't normally get to keep any special status so can vanish when the player looks away.

At the opposite end of the scale, some games remember everything you have done. Kill enemies in the first few minutes of your game, loot their corpses, and chuck items around, then come back a hundred hours later and the items are still wherever you left them. Games like this store vast amounts of tiny details, and these details need careful storage otherwise they would cause continual and crushing performance degradation. Using spatially mapped mementos is one approach that can attempt to rationalise this kind of level of attention to player game interaction.

In addition to time-since-seen, some elements may base their level of detail on how far a player has progressed in the game, or how many of something a player has, or how many times they have done it. For example, a typical bartering animation might be cut shorter and shorter as the game uses the axis of *how many recent barters* to draw back the length of any non-interactive sections which could be caused by the event. This can be done simply, and the player will be thankful. Consider allowing multi-item transactions only after a certain number of single transactions have happened. In effect, you could set up gameplay elements, reactions to situations, triggers for tutorials, reminders, or extensions to gameplay options all through these abstracted level of detail style axes. Handling the idea of player expertise through axes of level of detail of gameplay mechanic depth or complexity.

This way of manipulating the present state of the game is safer from transition errors. These are errors that happen because going from one state to another may have set something to true when transitioning one direction, but might not set it back to false when transitioning the other way. You can think of the states as being implicit on the axis. When state is modified, it's prone to being modified incorrectly, or not modified at the right time. If state is tied to other variables, that is, if state is a function of other state, then it's less prone to inconsistency.

An example of where transition errors occur is in menu systems where all transitions should be reversible, sometimes you may find that going down two levels of menu, but back only one level, takes you back to where you started. For example, entering the options menu, then entering an adjust volume slider, but backing out of the slider might take you out of the options menu altogether. These bugs are common in UI code as there are large numbers of different layers of interaction. Player input is often captured in obscure ways compared to gameplay input response. A common problem with menus is one of ownership of the input for a particular frame. For example, if a player hits both the forward and backward button at the same time, a state machine UI might choose to enter whichever transition response comes first. Another might manage to accept the forward event, only to have the next menu accept the back event, but worst of all might be the unlikely, but seen in the wild, menu transitioning to two different menus at the same time. Sometimes the menu may transition due to external forces, and if there is player input captured in a different thread of execution, the game state can become disjoint and unresponsive. Consider a network game's lobby, where if everyone is ready to play, but the host of the game disconnects while you are entering into the options screen prior to game launch, in a traditional state-machine like approach to menus, where should the player return to once they exit the options screen?

The lobby would normally have dropped you back to a server search screen, but in this case, the lobby has gone away to be replaced with nothing. This is where having simple axes instead of state machines can prove to be simpler to the point of being less buggy and more responsive.

## 5.5    Collective lodding - or how to reduce your instance count.

It's an ugly term, and I hope one day someone comes up with a better one, but it's a technique that didn't need a name until people stopped doing it. Over the time it has taken to write this book, games have started to have too many instances. We're not talking about games that have hundreds of enemy spacecraft, battling each other in a desperate fight for superiority, firing off missile after missile, generating visual effects which spawn multiple GPU particles. We're talking about simple seeming games. We're talking about your average gardening simulator, where for some reason, every leaf on your plants is modeled as an instance, and every insect going around pollinating is an instance, and every plot of land in which your plants can grow is an instance, and every seed you sew is an instance, and each have their own lifetimes, components, animations, and their own internal state adding to the ever-growing complexity of the system as a whole.

I have a fictional farming game, where I harvest wheat. I have a field which is 100 by 100 tiles, each with wheat growing. In some games, those wheat tiles would be instances, and the wheat on the tiles would be instances too. There's little reason for this, as we can reduce the field down to some very small data. What do we actually need to know about the field and the wheat? Do we need to know the position of the wheat? We don't, because it's in a tiled grid. Do we need to know if the tile has wheat or not? Yes, but it doesn't need an object instance to tell us that. Do we need an object to render the wheat? It needs to blow in the wind, so don't we need to have it keep track of where it is to blow around and maintain momentum? No, because in almost all cases, cheating at this kind of thing is cheap and believable. Grass rendering works fine without an instance per blade of grass. The right data format for a field full of wheat could be as simple as 10,000 unsigned chars, with zero being no wheat, and values from 1 to 100 being how grown it is. The wheat doesn't have positions. The positions have wheat.

If you have a stack of blocks in Minecraft, you don't have 64 instances in your inventory slot, you just have a type, and a multiple. You have a stack. If you have a stack of plates in a restaurant sim, you don't have 10 plate instances, you have a stack of plates object with an int saying how many plates there currently are.

The underlying principle of this is making sure you have slots in the world, whether hand placed, or generated in a pattern, and keeping track of what's in them, rather than placing things in the world directly. Refer to things by how a stranger would name them. When you ask someone what is in a room, they won't say a sofa, a bookshelf, an armchair, another armchair, a coffee table, a TV stand, more book-shelves. No, they will say furniture. Look at your game from the outside. Use how the players describe what is on screen. Look at how they describe their inventory. Look at how they describe the game, understand their mental model, match that, and you will find a strong correlation to what is taking up the players perception space.

When normalising your data, look at how your rows are aligned to some kind of container. If you have any form of grid, from 1D to 4D, it's worth looking at how you can utilise it. Don't ignore other tesselations, such as triangle grids, or hexagon grids. Hexagon grids, in particular, get a bad name, but they can be represented by a square grid with different traversal functions. Don't give up just because the literal grid is irregular either, in some grid-based games, the centres of the cells are perturbed to give a more natural look, but the game code can be strict grid-based, leading to better solution space, and more likely easier for the player to reason about what they can and can't do.

# Chapter 6

# Searching

When looking for specific data, it's very important to remember why you're doing it. If the search is not necessary, then that's your biggest possible saving. Finding if a row exists in a table will be slow if approached naïvely. You can manually add searching helpers such as binary trees, hash tables, or just keep your table sorted by using ordered insertion whenever you add to the table. If you're looking to do the latter, this could slow things down, as ordered inserts aren't normally concurrent, and adding extra helpers is normally a manual task. In this chapter, we find ways to combat all these problems.

## 6.1  Indexes

Database management systems have long held the concept of an index. Traditionally, they were automatically added when a DBMS noticed a particular query had been run a large number of times. We can use this idea and implement a just-in-time indexing system in our games to provide the same kinds of performance improvement.

113

In SQL, every time you want to find out if an element exists, or even just generate a subset like when you need to find all the entities in a certain range, you will have to build it as a query. The query exists as an entity of a kind, and helps build intuition into the DBMS.

The query that creates the row or table generation can be thought of as an object which can hang around in case it's used again, and can transform itself depending on how it's used over time. Starting out as a simple linear search query (if the data is not already sorted), the process can find out that it's being used quite often through internal telemetry, and be able to discover that it generally returns a simply tunable set of results, such as the first N items in a sorted list. After some predefined threshold number of operations, lifetime, or other metric, it would be valuable for the query object to hook itself into the tables it references. Hooking into the insertion, modification, and deletion would allow the query to update its answers, rather than run the full query again each time it's asked.

This kind of smart object is what object-oriented programming can bring to data-oriented design. It can be a significant saving in some cases, but it can also be safe, due to its optionality.

If we build generalised backends to handle building queries into these tables, they can provide multiple benefits. Not only can we expect garbage collection of indexes which aren't in use, but they can also make the programs in some way self-documenting and self-profiling. If we study the logs of what tables had pushed for building indexes for their queries, then we can see data hotspots and where there is room for improvement. It may even be possible to have the code self-document what optimisation steps should be taken.

```
1   struct FullAnimKey {
2     float time;
3     Vec3 translation;
4     Vec3 scale;
5     Vec4 rotation; // sijk quaternion
6   };
7   struct FullAnim {
8     int numKeys;
9     FullAnimKey *keys;
10    FullAnimKey GetKeyAtTimeBinary( float t ) {
11      int l = 0, h = numKeys-1;
12      int m = (l+h) / 2;
13      while( l < h ) {
14        if( t < keys[m].time ) {
15          h = m-1;
16        } else {
17          l = m;
18        }
19        m = (l+h+1) / 2;
20      }
21      return keys[m];
22    }
23  };
```

Listing 6.1: Binary search through objects

## 6.2 Data-oriented Lookup

The first step in any data-oriented approach to searching is to understand the difference between the search criteria, and the data dependencies of the search criteria. Object-oriented solutions to searching often ask the object whether or not it satisfies some criteria. Because the object is asked a question, there can be a lot of code required, memory indirectly accessed, and cache lines filled but hardly utilised. Even outside of object-oriented code-bases, there's still a lot of poor utilisation of memory bandwidth. In listing 6.1, there is an example of simple binary search for a key in a naïve implementation of an animation container. This kind of data access pattern is common in animation libraries, but also in many hand-rolled structures which look up entries that are trivially sorted along an axis.

We can improve on this very quickly by understanding the dependence on the producer and the consumer of the process.  Listing 6.2, is a quick rewrite that saves us a lot of memory requests by moving out to a partial structure-of-arrays approach.  The data layout stems from recognising what data is needed to satisfy the requirements of the program.

First, we consider what we have to work with as inputs, and then what we need to provide as outputs.  The only input we have is a time value in the form of a float, and the only value we need to return in this instance is an animation key.  The animation key we need to return is dependent on data internal to our system, and we are allowing ourselves the opportunity to rearrange the data any way we like.  As we know the input will be compared to the key times, but not any of the rest of the key data, we can extract the key times to a separate array.  We don't need to access just one part of the animation key when we find the one we want to return, but instead, we want to return the whole key.  Given that, it makes sense to keep the animation key data as an array of structures so we access fewer cache lines when returning the final value.

It is faster on most hardware, but why is it faster?  The first impression most people get is that we've moved the keys from nearby the returned data, ensuring we have another fetch before we have the chance to return.  Sometimes it pays to think a bit further than what looks right at first glance.  Let's look at the data layout of the AnimKeys.

| t | tx | ty | tz | sx | sy | sz | rs | cacheline |
|---|----|----|----|----|----|----|----|-----------|
| ri | rj | rk | t | tx | ty | tz | sx | |
| sy | sz | rs | ri | rj | rk | t | tx | cacheline |
| ty | tz | sx | sy | sz | rs | ri | rj | |
| rk | t | tx | ty | tz | sx | sy | sz | cacheline |
| rs | ri | rj | rk | t | . | . | . | |

Primarily, the processing we want to be doing is all about finding the index of the key by hunting for through values in a list of times.  In the extracted times code, we're no longer looking for a whole struct by one of its members in an array

```
1   struct DataOnlyAnimKey {
2     Vec3 translation;
3     Vec3 scale;
4     Vec4 rotation; // sijk quaternion
5   };
6   struct DataOnlyAnim {
7     int numKeys;
8     float *keyTime;
9     DataOnlyAnimKey *keys;
10    DataOnlyAnimKey GetKeyAtTimeBinary( float t ) {
11      int l = 0, h = numKeys-1;
12      int m = (l+h) / 2;
13      while( l < h ) {
14        if( t < keyTime[m] ) {
15          h = m-1;
16        } else {
17          l = m;
18        }
19        m = (l+h+1) / 2;
20      }
21      return keys[m];
22    }
23  };
```

Listing 6.2: Binary search through values

of structs. This is faster because the cache will be filled with mostly pertinent data during the hunt phase. In the original layout, we one or two key times per cache line. In the updated code, we see 16 key times per cache line.

| t0 | t1 | t2 | t3 | t4 | t5 | t6 | t7 | cacheline |
| t8 | t9 | t10 | t11 | t12 | t13 | t14 | t15 | |

There are ways to organise the data better still, but any more optimisation requires a complexity or space time trade off. A basic binary search will home in on the correct data quite quickly, but each of the first steps will cause a new cache line to be read in. If you know how big your cache line is, then you can check all the values that have been loaded for free while you wait for the next cache line to load in. Once you have got near the destination, most of the data you need is in the cache and all you're doing from then on is making sure you have found the right key. In a cache line aware engine, all this can be done behind the scenes with a well-optimised search algorithm usable all over the game

code. It is worth mentioning again, every time you break out
into larger data structures, you deny your proven code the
chance to be reused.

A binary search is one of the best search algorithms for
using the smallest number of *instructions* to find a key value.
But if you want the fastest algorithm, you must look at what
takes time, and often, it's not the instructions.  Loading a
whole cache line of information and doing as much as you
can with that would be a lot more helpful than using the
smallest number of instructions. It is worth considering that
two different data layouts for an algorithm could have more
impact than the algorithm used.

As a comparison to the previous animation key finding
code, a third solution was developed which attempted to
utilise the remaining cache line space in the structure. The
structure that contained the number of keys, and the two
pointers to the times and the key data, had quite a bit of
space left on the cache line. One of the biggest costs on the
PS3 and Xbox360 was poor cache line utilisation, or CLU.
In modern CPUs, it's not quite as bad, partially because the
cache lines are smaller, but it's still worth thinking about
what you get to read for free with each request.   In this
particular case, there was enough cache line left to store
another 11 floating point values, which are used as a place
to store something akin to skip-list.

| times | | keys | | n | s0 | s1 | s2 | cacheline |
|---|---|---|---|---|---|---|---|---|
| s3 | s4 | s5 | s6 | s7 | s8 | s9 | s10 | |

Using the fact that these keys would be loaded into memory, we give ourselves the opportunity to interrogate some
data for free. In listing 6.3 you can see it uses a linear search
instead of a binary search, and yet it still manages to make
the original binary search look slow by comparison, and we
must assume, as with most things on modern machines, it
is because the path the code is taking is using the resources
better, rather than being better in a theoretical way, or using
fewer instructions.

```
struct ClumpedAnim {
  float *keyTime;
  DataOnlyAnimKey *keys;
  int numKeys;
  static const int numPrefetchedKeyTimes = (64-sizeof(int)-sizeof
      (float*)-sizeof(DataOnlyAnimKey*))/sizeof(float);
  static const int keysPerLump = 64/sizeof(float);
  float firstStage[numPrefetchedKeyTimes];
  DataOnlyAnimKey GetKeyAtTimeLinear( float t ) {
    for( int start = 0; start < numPrefetchedKeyTimes; ++start )
      {
      if( firstStage[start] > t ) {
        int l = start*keysPerLump;
        int h = l + keysPerLump;
        h = h > numKeys ? numKeys : h;
        return GetKeyAtTimeLinear( t, l );
      }
    }
    return GetKeyAtTimeLinear( t, numPrefetchedKeyTimes*
        keysPerLump );
  }
  DataOnlyAnimKey GetKeyAtTimeLinear( float t, int startIndex ) {
    int i = startIndex;
    while( i < numKeys ) {
      if( keyTime[i] > t ) {
        --i;
        break;
      }
      ++i;
    }
    if( i < 0 )
      return keys[0];
    return keys[i];
  }
};
```

Listing 6.3: Better cache line utilisation

```
i5-4430 @ 3.00GHz
Average 13.71ms [Full anim key - linear search]
Average 11.13ms [Full anim key - binary search]
Average  8.23ms [Data only key - linear search]
Average  7.79ms [Data only key - binary search]
Average  1.63ms [Pre-indexed - binary search]
Average  1.45ms [Pre-indexed - linear search]
```

If the reason for your search is simpler, such as checking for existence, then there are even faster alternatives. Bloom filters offer a constant time lookup. Even though it produces some false positives, it can be tweaked to generate a reasonable answer hit rate for very large sets. In particular, if you are checking for which table a row exists in, then bloom filters work very well, by providing data about which tables to look in, usually only returning the correct table, but sometimes more than one. The engineers at Google have used bloom filters to help mitigate the costs of something of a write-ahead approach with their BigTable technology[12], and use bloom filters to quickly find out if data requests should lookup their values in recent change tables, or should go straight to the backing store.

In relational databases, indexes are added to tables at runtime when there are multiple queries that could benefit from their presence. For our data-oriented approach, there will always be some way to speed up a search but only by looking at the data. If the data is not already sorted, then an index is a simple way to find the specific item we need. If the data is already sorted, but needs even faster access, then a search tree optimised for the cache line size would help.

Most data isn't this simple to optimise. But importantly, when there is a lot of data, it usually is simple to learn patterns from it. A lot of the time, we have to work with spatial data, but because we use objects, it's hard to strap on an efficient spatial reference container after the fact. It's virtually impossible to add one at runtime to an externally defined class of objects.

Adding spatial partitioning when your data is in a simple data format like rows allows us to generate spatial containers or lookup systems that will be easy to maintain and optimise for each particular situation. Because of the inherent reusability in data-oriented transforms, we can write some very highly optimised routines for the high-level programmers.

## 6.3 Finding lowest or highest is a sorting problem

In some circumstances, you don't even really need to search. If the reason for searching is to find something within a range, such as finding the closest food, or shelter, or cover, then the problem isn't really one of searching, but one of sorting. In the first few runs of a query, the search might literally do a real search to find the results, but if it's run often enough, there is no reason not to promote the query to a runtime-updating sorted-subset of some other tables' data. If you need the nearest three elements, then you keep a sorted list of the nearest three elements, and when an element has an update, insertion or deletion, you can update the sorted three with that information. For insertions or modifications which bring elements that are not in the set closer, you can check whether the element is closer and pop the lowest before adding the new element to the sorted best. If there is a deletion or a modification that makes one in the sorted set a contender for elimination, a quick check of the rest of the elements to find a new best set might be necessary. If you keep a larger than necessary set of best values, however, then you might find this never happens.

The trick is to find, at runtime, the best value to use that covers the solution requirement. The only way to do that is to check the data at runtime. For this, either keep logs or run the tests with dynamic resizing based on feedback from

```
 1   Array<int> bigArray;
 2   Array<int> bestValue;
 3   const int LIMIT = 3;
 4
 5   void AddValue( int newValue ) {
 6     bigArray.push( newValue );
 7     bestValue.sortedinsert( newValue );
 8     if( bestValue.size() > LIMIT )
 9       bestValue.erase(bestValue.begin());
10   }
11   void RemoveValue( int deletedValue ) {
12     bigArray.remove( deletedValue );
13     bestValue.remove( deletedValue );
14   }
15   int GetBestValue() {
16     if( bestValue.size() ) {
17       return bestValue.top();
18     } else {
19       int best = bigArray.findbest();
20       bestvalue.push( best );
21       return best;
22     }
23   }
```

Listing 6.4: keeping more than you need

the table's query optimiser.

## 6.4   Finding random is a hash/tree issue

For some tables, the values change very often.  For a tree representation to be high performance, it's best not to have a high number of modifications as each one could trigger the need for a rebalance. Of course, if you do all your modifications in one stage of processing, then rebalance, and then all your reads in another, then you're probably going to be okay still using a tree.

The C++ standard template library implementation of map for your compiler might not work well even when committing all modifications in one go, but a more cache line aware implementation of a tree, such as a B-tree, may help you. A B-tree has much wider nodes, and therefore is much shallower. It also has a much lower chance of making multiple changes at once under insert and delete operations, as each node has a much higher capacity. Typically, you will see some form of balancing going on in a red-black tree every other insert or delete, but in most B-tree implementations, you will have tree rotations occur relative to the width of the node, and nodes can be very wide. For example, it's not unusual to have nodes with 8 child nodes.

If you have many different queries on some data, you can end up with multiple different indexes. How frequently the entries are changed should influence how you store your index data. Keeping a tree around for each query could become expensive, but would be cheaper than a hash table in many implementations. Hash tables become cheaper where there are many modifications interspersed with lookups, trees are cheaper where the data is mostly static, or at least hangs around in one form for a while over multiple reads.

When the data becomes constant, a perfect hash can trump a tree. Perfect hash tables use pre-calculated hash functions to generate an index and don't require any space other than what is used to store the constants and the array of pointers or offsets into the original table. If you have the time, then you might find a perfect hash that returns the actual indexes. It's not often you have that long though.

For example, what if we need to find the position of someone given their name? The players won't normally be sorted by name, so we need a name to player lookup. This data is mostly constant during the game so would be better to find a way to directly access it. A single lookup will almost always trump following a pointer chain, so a hash to find an array entry is likely to be the best fit. Consider a normal hash table, where each slot contains either the element you're looking for, or a different element, and a way of calculating the next slot you should check. If you know you want to do one and only one lookup, you can make each of your hash buck-

ets as large as a cache line. That way you can benefit from
free memory lookups.

# Chapter 7

# Sorting

For some subsystems, sorting is a highly important function. Sorting the primitive render calls so they render from front to back for opaque objects can have a massive impact on GPU performance, so it's worth doing. Sorting the primitive render calls so they render from back to front for alpha blended objects is usually a necessity. Sorting sound channels by their amplitude over their sample position is a good indicator of priority.

Whatever you need to sort for, make sure you need to sort first, as usually, sorting is a highly memory intense business.

## 7.1  Do you need to?

There are some algorithms which seem to require sorted data, but don't, and some which require sorted data but don't seem to. Be sure you know whether you need to before you make any false moves.

A common use of sorting in games is in the render pass

where some engine programmers recommend having all your render calls sorted by a high bit count key generated from a combination of depth, mesh, material, shader, and other flags such as whether the call is alpha blended. This then allows the renderer to adjust the sort at runtime to get the most out of the bandwidth available. In the case of the rendering list sort, you could run the whole list through a general sorting algorithm, but in reality, there's no reason to sort the alpha blended objects with the opaque objects, so in many cases you can take a first step of putting the list into two separate buckets, and save some work overall. Also, choose your sorting algorithm wisely. With opaque objects, the most important part is usually sorting by textures then by depth, but that can change with how much your fill rate is being trashed by overwriting the same pixel multiple times. If your overdraw doesn't matter too much but your texture uploads do, then you probably want to radix sort your calls. With alpha blended calls, you just have to sort by depth, so choose an algorithm which handles your case best. Be aware of how accurately you need your data to be sorted. Some sorts are stable, others unstable. Unstable sorts are usually a little quicker. For analogue ranges, a quick sort or a merge sort usually offer slow but guaranteed accurate sorting. For discrete ranges of large $n$, a radix sort is very hard to beat. If you know your range of values, then a counting sort is a very fast two pass sort, for example, sorting by material, shader, or other input buffer index.

When sorting, it's also very important to be aware of algorithms that can sort a range only partially. If you only need the lowest or highest $n$ items of an $m$ long array, you can use a different type of algorithm to find the $n^{th}$ item, then sort all the items greater or less than the returned pivot. In some *selection algorithms* you will end with some guarantees about the data. Notably, *quickselect* will result in the $n^{th}$ item by sorting criteria residing in the $n^{th}$ position. Once complete, all items either side remain unsorted in their sub-ranges, but are guaranteed to be less than or more than the pivot, depending on the side of the pivot they fall.

```
template <class It, class T>
It unstable_remove( It begin, It end, const T& value )
{
  begin = find(begin, end, value);
  if (begin != end) {
    --end;
    *begin = move( *end );
  }
  return end;
}
```

Listing 7.1: A basic implementation of unstable_remove

If you have a general range of items which need to be sorted in two different ways, you can either sort with a specialised comparison function in a one-hit sort, or you can sort hierarchically. This can be beneficial when the order of items is less important for a subset of the whole range. The render queue is still a good example. If you split your sort into different sub-sorts, it makes it possible to profile each part of the sort, which can lead to beneficial discoveries.

You don't need to write your own algorithms to do this either. Most of the ideas presented here can be implemented using the STL, using the functions in algorithms. You can use std::partial_sort to find and sort the first $n$ elements, you can use std::nth_element to find the $n^{th}$ value as if the container was sorted. Using std::partition and std::stable_partition allow you to split a range by a criteria, effectively sorting a range into two sub-ranges.

It's important to be aware of the contracts of these algorithms, as something as simple as the erase/remove process can be very expensive if you use it without being aware that remove will shuffle all your data down, as it is required to maintain order. If there was one algorithm you should add to your collection, it would be your own version of remove which does not guarantee maintaining order. Listing 7.1 shows one such implementation.

## 7.2 Maintain by insertion sort or parallel merge sort

Depending on what you need the list sorted for, you could sort while modifying. If the sort is for some AI function that cares about priority, then you may as well insertion sort as the base heuristic commonly has completely orthogonal inputs. If the inputs are related, then a post insertion table wide sort might be in order, but there's little call for a full-scale sort.

If you really do need a full sort, then use an algorithm which likes being parallel. Merge sort and quick sort are somewhat serial in that they end or start with a single thread doing all the work, but there are variants which work well with multiple processing threads, and for small datasets there are special sorting network techniques which can be faster than better algorithms just because they fit the hardware so well[1].

## 7.3 Sorting for your platform

Always remember that in data-oriented development you must look to the data for information before deciding which way you're going to write the code. What does the data look like? For rendering, there is a large amount of data with different axes for sorting. If your renderer is sorting by mesh and material, to reduce vertex and texture uploads, then the data will show that there are a number of render calls which share texture data, and a number of render calls which share vertex data. Finding out which way to sort first could be figured out by calculating the time it takes to upload a texture, how long it takes to upload a mesh, how many ex-

---

[1]Tony Albrecht proves this point in his article on sorting networks
http://seven-degrees-of-freedom.blogspot.co.uk/2010/07/question-of-sorts.html

tra uploads are required for each, then calculating the total scene time, but mostly, profiling is the only way to be sure. If you want to be able to profile and get feedback quickly or allow for runtime changes in case your game has such varying asset profiles that there is no one solution to fit all, having some flexibility of sorting criteria is extremely useful and sometimes necessary. Fortunately, it can be made just as quick as any inflexible sorting technique, bar a small setup cost.

Radix sort is the fastest serial sort. If you can do it, radix sort is very fast because it generates a list of starting points for data of different values in a first pass, then operates using that data in a second pass. This allows the sorter to drop their contents into containers based on a translation table, a table that returns an offset for a given data value. If you build a list from a known small value space, then radix sort can operate very fast to give a coarse first pass. The reason radix sort is serial, is that it has to modify the table it is reading from in order to update the offsets for the next element that will be put in the same bucket. If you ran multiple threads giving them part of the work each, then you would find they were non-linearly increasing in throughput as they would be contending to write and read from the same memory, and you don't want to have to use atomic updates in your sorting algorithm.

It is possible to make this last stage of the process parallel by having each sorter ignore any values it reads which are outside its working set, meaning each worker reads through the entire set of values gathering for their bucket, but there is still a small chance of non-linear performance due to having to write to nearby memory on different threads. During the time the worker collects the elements for its bucket, it could be generating the counts for the next radix in the sequence, only requiring a summing before use in the next pass of the data, mitigating the cost of iterating over the whole set with every worker.

If your data is not simple enough to radix sort, you might be better off using a merge sort or a quicksort, but there are other sorts that work very well if you know the length of your sortable buffer at compile time, such as sorting networks. Through merge-sort is not itself a concurrent algorithm, the many early merges can be run in parallel, only the final merge is serial, and with a quick pre-parse of the to-be-merged data, you can finalise with two threads rather than one by starting from both ends (you need to make sure the mergers don't run out of data). Though quick sort is not a concurrent algorithm each of the substages can be run in parallel. These algorithms are inherently serial, but can be turned into partially parallelisable algorithms with $\mathcal{O}(\log n)$ latency.

When your n is small enough, a traditionally good technique is to write an in-place bubble sort. The algorithm is so simple, it is hard to write wrong, and because of the small number of swaps required, the time taken to set up a better sort could be better spent elsewhere. Another argument for rewriting such trivial code is that inline implementations can be small enough for the whole of the data and the algorithm to fit in cache[2]. As the negative impact of the inefficiency of the bubble sort is negligible over such a small $n$, it is hardly ever frowned upon to do this. In some cases, the fact that there are fewer instructions can be more important than the operational efficiency, as instruction eviction could cost more than the time saved by the better algorithm. As always, measure so you can be certain.

If you've been developing data-oriented, you'll have a transform which takes a table of $n$ and produces the sorted version of it. The algorithm doesn't have to be great to be better than bubble sort, but notice it doesn't cost any development time to use a better algorithm as the data is in the right shape already. Data-oriented development naturally

---

[2]It might be wise to have some inline sort function templates in your own utility header so you can utilise the benefits of miniaturisation, but don't drop in a bloated std::sort

leads us to reuse of good algorithms.

When looking for the right algorithm, it's worth knowing about more than you are presented during any coursework, and look into the more esoteric forms. For sorting, sometimes you want an algorithm that always sorts in the same amount of time, and when you do, you can't use any of the standard quick sorts, radix sorts, bubble or other. Merge sort tends to have good performance, but to get truly stable times when sorting, you may need to resort to sorting networks.

Sorting networks work by implementing the sort in a static manner. They have input data and run swap if necessary functions on pairs of values of the input data before outputting the final. The simplest sorting network is two inputs.

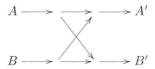

If the values entering are in order, the sorting crossover does nothing. If the values are out of order, then the sorting crossover causes the values to swap. This can be implemented as branch-free writes:

```
a' <= MAX(a,b)
b' <= MIN(a,b)
```

This is fast on any hardware. The MAX and MIN functions will need different implementations for each platform and data type, but in general, branch-free code executes a little faster than code that includes branches. In most current compilers, the MIN and MAX functions will be promoted to intrinsics if they can be, but you might need to finesse the data so the value is part of the key, so it is sorted along with the keys.

Introducing more elements:

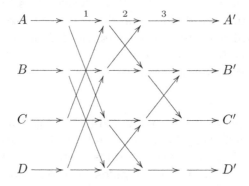

What you may notice here is that the critical path is not long (just three stages in total), the first stage is two concurrent sortings of A/C, and B/D pairs. The second stage, sorting A/B, and C/D pairs. The final cleanup sorts the B/C pair. As these are all branch-free functions, the performance is regular over all data permutations. With such a regular performance profile, we can use the sort in ways where the variability of sorting time length gets in the way, such as just-in-time sorting for subsections of rendering. If we had radix sorted our renderables, we can network sort any final required ordering as we can guarantee a consistent timing.

```
a' <= MAX(a,c)
b' <= MIN(b,d)
c' <= MAX(a,c)
d' <= MIN(b,d)
a'' <= MAX(a',b')
b'' <= MIN(a',b')
c'' <= MAX(c',d')
d'' <= MIN(c',d')
b''' <= MIN(b'',c'')
c''' <= MAX(b'',c'')
```

Sorting networks are somewhat like predication, the branch-free way of handling conditional calculations. Because sorting networks use a min/max function, rather than a conditional swap, they gain the same benefits when it comes to the actual sorting of individual elements. Given that sorting networks can be faster than radix sort for certain implementations, it goes without saying that for some types of calculation, predication, even long chains of it, will be faster than code that branches to save processing time. Just such an example exists in the *Pitfalls of Object Oriented Programming*[14] presentation, concluding that lazy evaluation costs more than the job it tried to avoid. I have no hard evidence for it yet, but I believe a lot of AI code could benefit the same, in that it would be wise to gather information even when you are not sure you need it, as gathering it might be quicker than deciding not to. For example, seeing if someone is in your field of vision, and is close enough, might be small enough that it can be done for all AI rather than just the ones requiring it, or those that require it occasionally.

# Chapter 8

# Optimisations and Implementations

When optimising software, you have to know what is causing the software to run slower than you need it to run. We find in most cases, data movement is what really costs us the most. Data movement is where most of the energy goes when processing data. Calculating solutions to functions, or running an algorithm on the data uses less energy. It is the fulfillment of the request for data in the first place that appears to be the largest cost. As this is most definitely true about our current architectures, we find implicit or calculable information is often much more useful than cached values or explicit state data.

If we start our game development by organising our data into arrays, we open ourselves up to many opportunities for optimisation. Starting with such a problem agnostic layout, we can pick and choose from tools we've created for other tasks, at worst elevating the solution to a template or a strategy, before applying it to both the old and new use cases.

In *Out of the Tar Pit*[4], it's considered poor form to add

135

state and complexity for the sake of performance until late
in the development of the solution. By using arrays to solve
the problem, and side-effect free transforms on those tables,
performance improvements can be made across systems in
general. The improvements can be applied at many sites in
the program with little fear of incompatibility, and a convic-
tion that we're not adding state, but augmenting the language in which we work.

The bane of many projects, and the cause of their late-
ness, has been the insistence on not doing optimisation pre-
maturely. The reason optimisation at late stages is so difficult is that many pieces of software are built up with instances of objects everywhere, even when not needed. Many
issues with object-oriented design are caused by the idea
that an instance is the unit of processing. Object-oriented
development practices tend to assume the instance is the
unit on which code will work, and techniques and standards
of practice treat collections of objects as collections of individuals.

When the basic assumption is that an object is a unique
and special thing with its own purpose, then the instructions
to carry out what it needs to do, will necessarily be selected
in some way dependent on the object. Accessing instructions
via the vtable pointer is the usual method by which operations are selected. The greater threat is when five, ten, or
a hundred individual instances, which could have been represented as a group, a swarm, or merely an increment on a
value, are processed as a sequence of individuals. There are
many cases where an object exists just because it seemed
to match the real world concept it was trying to represent at
the scale of the developer implementing it, rather than because it needed to function as a unique individual element
of which the user would be aware. It's easy to get caught up
implementing features from the perspective of what they are,
rather than how they are perceived.

# 8.1 When should we optimise?

When should optimisation be done? When is it truly premature? The answer lies in data of a different sort. Premature optimisation is when you optimise something without knowing whether it will make a difference. If you attempt to optimise something because in your mind it will *"speed things up a bit"*, then it can be considered premature, as it's not apparent there is anything to optimise.

Let's be clear here, without the data to show that a game is running slow, or running out of memory, then all optimisations are premature. If an application has not been profiled, but feels slow, sluggish, or erratic, then anything you do cannot be objectively defined as improving it, and any improvements you attempt to do cannot be anything but premature optimisations. The only way to stop premature optimisation is to start with real data. If your application seems slow, and has been profiled, and what is considered unacceptable is a clearly defined statement based on data, then anything you do to improve the solution will not be premature, because it has been measured, and can be evaluated in terms of failure, success, or progress.

Given that we think we will need to optimise at some point, and we know optimising without profiling is not actually optimising, the next question becomes clear. When should you start profiling? When should you start work on your profiling framework? How much game content is enough to warrant testing performance? How much of the game's mechanics should be in before you start testing them for performance spikes?

Consider a different question. Is the performance of your final product optional? Would you be able to release the game if you knew it had sections which ran at 5fps on certain hardware? If you answer that it's probably okay for your game to run at around 30fps, then that's a metric, even if it's quite imprecise. How do you know your game already isn't running at 5fps on one of your target audience's hardware configurations? If you believe there are lower limits to frame-rate, and upper limits to your memory usage, if there is an expected maximum time for a level to load before it's just assumed to be stuck, or a strong belief the game should at least not kill the battery on a phone when it's running, then you have, in at least some respect, agreed that performance is not optional.

If performance is not optional, and it requires real work to optimise, then start asking yourself a different set of questions. How long can you delay profiling? How much art or other content can you afford to redo? How many features are you willing to work on without knowing if they can be included in the final game? How long can you work without feedback on whether any of what you have done, can be included in the final product?

## 8.2   Feedback

Not knowing you are writing poor performance code doesn't just hurt your application. By not having feedback on their work, developers cannot get better, and myths and techniques which do not work are reinforced and perpetuated. Daniel Kahneman, in his book *Thinking, Fast and Slow*[13], provides some evidence that you can learn well from immediate reactions, but cannot easily pick up skills when the feedback is longer in arriving. In one part, he puts it in terms of psychotherapists being able to acquire strong intuitive skills in patient interaction, as they are able to observe the patient's immediate reactions, but they are less likely to be able to build strong intuitions for identifying the appropriate treatment for a patient, as the feedback is not always available, not always complete, and often delayed. Choosing to work without feedback would make no sense, but there is little option for many game developers, as third party engines offer very little in the way of feedback mechanisms for those learning or starting out on their projects. They do not provide mechanisms to apply budgets to separate aspects of their engines, other than the coarse grain of CPU, GPU, Physics, render, etc. They provide lots of tools to help fix performance when it has been identified as an issue, but can often provide feedback which is incomplete, or inaccurate to the final form of the product, as built-in profiling tools are not always available in fully optimised publishing ready builds.

You must get feedback on what is going on, as otherwise there is a risk the optimisations you will need to do will consume any polish time you have. Make sure your feedback is complete and immediate where possible. Adding metrics on the status of the performance of your game will help with this. Instant feedback on success or failure of optimisations helps mitigate the sunk cost fallacy that can intrude on rational discourse about a direction taken. If a developer has a belief in a way of doing things, but it's not helping, then it's better to know sooner rather than later. Even the most entrenched in their ways are more approachable with raw data, as curiosity is a good tonic for a developer with a wounded ego. If you haven't invested a lot of time and effort into an approach, then the feedback is even easier to integrate, as you're going to be more willing to throw the work away and figure out how to do it differently.

You also need to get the feedback about the right thing. If you find you've been optimising your game for a silky smooth frame rate and you think you have an average frame rate of 60fps, and yet your customers and testers keep coming back with comments about nasty frame spikes and dropout, then it could be that you're not profiling the right thing, or not profiling the right way. Sometimes it can be that you have to profile a game while it is being played. Sometimes it can be as simple as remembering to profile frame times on a per frame basis, not just an average.

Profiling doesn't have to be about frame rate. A frame

isn't a slow thing, something in that frame was slow.  An old-fashioned, but powerful way to develop software, is to provide budgets to systems and departments.  We're not talking about financial budgets here, but instead time, memory, bandwidth, disk space, or other limits which affect the final product directly.  If you give your frame a budget of 16ms, and you don't go over, you have a 60fps game, no ifs, no buts.  If you decide you want to maintain good level load times, and set yourself a budget of 4 seconds to load level data, then as long as you don't go over, no one is going to complain about your load times.

Beyond games, if you have a web-based retail site, you might want to be aware of latency, as it has an effect on your users.  It was revealed in a presentation in 2008 by Greg Linden that for every additional 100ms of latency, Amazon would experience a loss of 1% in sales.  It was also revealed that Google had statistics showing a 20% drop in site traffic was experienced when they added just half a second of latency to page generation.  Most scarily of all was a comment from TABB group in 2008, where they mention company wrecking levels of costs.

> TABB Group estimates that if a broker's electronic trading platform is 5 milliseconds behind the competition, it could lose at least 1% of its flow; that's $4 million in revenues per millisecond. Up to 10 milliseconds of latency could result in a 10% drop in revenues. From there it gets worse. If a broker is 100 milliseconds slower than the fastest broker, it may as well shut down its FIX engine and become a floor broker.

[1]

If latency, throughput, frame times, memory usage, or another resource is your limit, then budget for it.  What

---

[1]From *THE VALUE OF A MILLISECOND: FINDING THE OPTIMAL SPEED OF A TRADING INFRASTRUCTURE* by Viraf (Willy) Reporter

would cripple your business? Are you measuring it? How long can you go without checking that you're not already out of business?

## 8.2.1 Know your limits

Building budgets into how you work means, you can set realistic budgets for systems early and have them work at a certain level throughout development knowing they will not cause grief later in development. On a project without budgets, frame spikes may only become apparent near release dates as it is only then that all systems are coming together to create the final product. A system which was assumed to be quite cheap, could cause frame spikes in the final product, without any evidence being previously apparent. When you finally find out which system causes the spikes, it may be that it was caused by a change from a very long time ago, but as resources were plentiful in the early times of development on the project, the spikes caused by the system would have gone completely unnoticed, flying under the radar. If you give your systems budgets, violations can be recorded and raised as issues immediately. If you do this, then problems can be caught at the moment they are created, and the cause is usually within easy reach.

Build or get yourself a profiler that runs all the time. Ensure your profiler can report the overall state of the game when the frame time goes over budget. It's highly beneficial to make it respond to any single system going over budget. Sometimes you need the data from a number of frames around when a violation occurred to really figure out what is going on. If you have AI in your game, consider running continuous testing to capture performance issues as fast as your build machine churns out testable builds. In all cases, unless you're letting real testers run your profiler, you're never going to get real world profiling data. If real testers are going to be using your profiling system, it's worth considering how you gather data from it. If it's possible for you, see if you can get automatically generated profile data sent back to an analytics or metrics server, to capture issues without requiring user intervention.

# 8.3   A strategy for optimisation

You can't just open up an editor and start optimising. You need a strategy. In this section, we walk through just one such strategy. The steps have parallels in industries outside game development, where large companies such as Toyota optimise as part of their business model. Toyota has refined their techniques for ensuring maximum performance and growth, and the Toyota Production System has been the driving idea behind the Lean manufacturing method for the reduction of waste. There are other techniques available, but this subset of steps shares much with many of them.

## 8.3.1   Define the problem

Define your problem. Find out what it is you think is bad. Define it in terms of what is factual, and what is assumed to be a final good solution. This can be as simple as saying the problem is that the game is running at 25fps, and you need it to be at 30fps. Stick to clear, objective language.

It's important to not include any guesses in this step, so statements which include ideas on what or how to optimise should be prohibited. Consider writing it from the point of view of someone using the application, not from the perspective of the developer. This is sometimes called quality criteria, or customer requirements.

## 8.3.2 Measure

Measure what you need to measure. Unlike measuring randomly, targeted measuring is better for figuring out what is actually going on, as you are less likely to find a pattern in irrelevant data. P-hacking or data dredging can lead you to false convictions about causes of problems.

At this stage, you also need to get an idea of the quality of your measurements. Run your tests, but then run them again to make sure they're reproducible. If you can't reproduce the same results before you have made changes, then how are you going to be sure the changes you have made, have had any effect?

## 8.3.3 Analyse

The first step in most informal optimisation strategies: the guessing phase. This is when you come up with ideas about what could be the problem and suggest different ways to tackle the problem. In the informal optimisation process, you pick the idea which seems best, or at least the most fun to implement.

In this more formal strategy, we analyse what we have measured. Sometimes it's apparent from this step that the measurements didn't provide enough direction to come up with a good optimisation plan. If your analysis proves you don't have good data, the next step should be to rectify your ability to capture useful data. Don't tackle optimisation without understanding the cost associated with failing to understand the problem.

This is also the stage to make predictions. Estimate the expected impact of an improvement you plan to make. Don't just lightly guess, have a really good go at guessing with some number crunching. You won't be able to do it after the implementation, as you will have too much knowledge to make an honest guess. You will be suffering what some call the curse of knowledge. By doing this, you can learn about how good you are at estimating the impact of your optimisations, but also, you can get an idea of the relative impact of your change before you begin work.

### 8.3.4  Implement

The second step in most informal optimisation strategies; the implementation phase. This is when you make the changes you think will fix the problem.

If possible, do an experimental implementation of the optimisation to your solution. A program is a solution to a problem, it is a strategy to solve a data transform, and you should remember that when designing your experiment.

Before you consider the local version to be working, and indeed, worth working on, you must prove it's useful. Check the measurements you get from the localised experiment are in line with your expectations as measured from the integrated version.

If your optimisation is going to be perfect first time, then the experimental implementation will only be used as a proof that the process can be repeated and can be applicable in other circumstances. It will only really be useful as a teaching tool for others, in helping them understand the costs of the original process and the expected improvement under similar constraints.

If you are not sure the optimisation will work out first time, then the time saved by not doing a full implementation can be beneficial, as a localised experiment can be worked on faster. It can also be a good place to start when trying to build an example for third parties to provide support, as a smaller example of the problem will be easier to communicate through.

## 8.3.5 Confirm

This step is critical in more ways than expected. Some may think it an optional step, but it is essential for retaining the valuable information you will have generated while doing the optimisation.

Create a report of what you have done, and what you have found. The benefits of doing this are twofold. First, you have the benefit of sharing knowledge of a technique for optimisation, which clearly can help others hitting the same kind of issue. The second is that creating the report can identify any errors of measurement, or any steps which can be tested to ensure they were actually pertinent to the final changes committed.

In a report, others can point out any illogical leaps of reasoning, which can lead to even better understanding and can also help deny any false assumptions from building up in your understanding of how the machine really works. Writing a report can be a powerful experience that will give you valuable mental building blocks and the ability to better explain what happens under certain conditions.

## 8.3.6 Summary

Above all things, keep track. If you can, do your optimisation work in isolation of a working test bed. Make sure your timings are reproducible even if you have to get up to date with the rest of the project due to having to work on a bug or feature. Making sure you keep track of what you are doing with notes can help you understand what was in your head when you made earlier changes, and what you might not have thought about.

It is important to keep trying to improve your ability to see; to observe. You cannot make measurable progress if you cannot measure, and you cannot tell you have made an improvement without tools for identifying the improvement. Improve your tools for measuring when you can. Look for ways to look. Whenever you find that there was no way to know with the tools you had available, either find the tools you need or if you can't find them, attempt to make them yourself. If you cannot make them yourself, petition others, or commission someone else to create them. Don't give in to hopeful optimisations, because they will teach you bad habits and you will learn false facts from random chance proving you right.

## 8.4  Tables

To keep things simple, advice from multiple sources indicate that keeping your data as vectors has a lot of positive benefits. There are some reasons to use something other than the STL, but learn its quirks, and you can avoid a lot of the issues. Whether you use std::vector, or roll your own dynamically sized array, it is a good starting place for any future optimisations. Most of the processing you will do will be reading an array, transforming one array into another, or modifying a table in place. In all these cases, a simple array will suffice for most tasks.

Moving to arrays is good, moving to structure-of-arrays can be better. Not always. It's very much worth considering the access patterns for your data. If you can't consider the access patterns, and change is costly, choose based on some other criteria, such as readability.

Another reason to move away from arrays of objects, or arrays of structures, is to keep the memory accesses specific to their tasks. When thinking about how to structure your data, it's important to think about what data will be loaded and what data will be stored. CPUs are optimised for certain patterns of memory activity. Many CPUs have a cost associated with changing from read operations to write oper-

```
struct PosInfo
{
  vec3 pos;
  vec3 velocity;
  PosInfo():
    pos(1.0f, 2.0f, 3.0f),
    velocity(4.0f, 5.0f, 6.0f)
  {}
};

struct nodes
{
    std::vector<PosInfo> posInfos;
    std::vector<vec3> colors;
    std::vector<LifetimeInfo> lifetimeInfos;
} nodesystem;

// ...

for (size_t times = 0; times < trialCount; times++)
{
    std::vector<PosInfo>& posInfos = nodesystem.posInfos;
    for (size_t i = 0; i < node_count; ++i)
    {
      posInfos[i].pos += posInfos[i].velocity * deltaTime;
    }
}
```

Listing 8.1: Mixing hot reads with hot and cold writes

ations. To help the CPU not have to transition between read and write, it can be beneficial to arrange writing to memory in a very predictable and serial manner. An example of hot cold separation that doesn't take into account the importance of writing can be seen in the example code in listing 8.1 that attempts to update values which are used both for read and write, but are close neighbours of data which is only used for reading.

The code in listing 8.2 shows a significant performance improvement.

For the benefit of your cache, structs of arrays can be more cache-friendly if the data is not strongly related both for reading and writing. It's important to remember this is only true when the data is not always accessed as a unit, as one advocate of the data-oriented design movement assumed

```
1    struct nodes
2    {
3        std::vector<vec3> positions;
4        std::vector<vec3> velocities;
5        std::vector<vec3> colors;
6        std::vector<LifetimeInfo> lifetimeInfos;
7    };
8    // ...
9    nodes nodesystem;
10   // ...
11   for (size_t times = 0; times < trialCount; times++)
12   {
13     for (size_t i = 0; i < node_count; ++i)
14     {
15       nodesystem.positions[i] += nodesystem.velocities[i] *
             deltaTime;
16     }
17   }
```

Listing 8.2: Ensuring each stream is continuous

that structures of arrays were intrinsically cache-friendly, then put the x,y, and z coordinates in separate arrays of floats. It is possible to benefit from having each element in its own array when you utilise SIMD operations on larger lists. However, if you need to access the x,y, or z of an element in an array, then you more than likely need to access the other two axes as well. This means that for every element you will be loading three cache lines of float data, not one. If the operation involves a lot of other values, then this may overfill the cache. This is why it is important to think about where the data is coming from, how it is related, and how it will be used. Data-oriented design is not just a set of simple rules to convert from one style to another. Learn to see the connections between data. In this case, we see that in some circumstances, it's better to keep your vector as three or four floats if it's not commonly used as a value in an operation that will be optimised with SIMD instructions.

There are other reasons why you might prefer to not store data in trivial SoA format, such as if the data is commonly subject to insertions and deletions. Keeping free lists around to stop deletions from mutating the arrays can help alleviate the pressure, but being unable to guarantee every element

```
ProcessJoin( Func functionToCall ) {
  TableIterator A = t1Table.begin();
  TableIterator B = t2Table.begin();
  TableIterator C = t3Table.begin();
  while( !A.finished && !B.finished && !C.finished ) {
    if( A == B && B == C ) {
      functionToCall( A, B, C );
      ++A; ++B; ++C;
    } else {
      if( A < B || A < C ) ++A;
      if( B < A || B < C ) ++B;
      if( C < A || C < B ) ++C;
    }
  }
}
```

Listing 8.3: Zipping together multiple tables by merging

requires processing moves away from simple homogeneous transformations which are often the point of such data layout changes.

If you use dynamic arrays, and you need to delete elements from them, and these tables refer to each other through some IDs, then you may need a way to splice the tables together in order to process them as you may want to keep them sorted to assist with zipping operations. If the tables are sorted by the same value, then it can be written out as a simple merge operation, such as in listing 8.3.

This works as long as the == operator knows about the table types and can find the specific column to check against, and as long as the tables are sorted based on this same column. But what about the case where the tables are zipped together without being the sorted by the same columns? For example, if you have a lot of entities which refer to a modelID, and you have a lot of mesh-texture combinations which refer to the same modelID, then you will likely need to zip together the matching rows for the orientation of the entity, the modelID in the entity render data, and the mesh and texture combinations in the models. The simplest way to program a solution to this is to loop through each table in turn looking for matches such as in Listing 8.4. This so-

```
ProcessJoin( Func functionToCall ) {
  for( auto A : orientationTable ) {
    for( auto B : entityRenderableTable ) {
      if( A == B ) {
        for( auto C : meshAndTextureTable ) {
          if( A == C ) {
            functionToCall( A, B, C );
          }
        }
      }
    }
  }
}
```

Listing 8.4: Join by looping through all tables

lution, though simple to write, is incredibly inefficient, and should be avoided where possible. But as with all things, there are exceptions. In some situations, very small tables might be more efficient this way, as they will remain resident, and sorting them could cost more time.

Another thing you have to learn about when working with data which is joined on different columns is the use of join strategies. In databases, a join strategy is used to reduce the total number of operations when querying across multiple tables. When joining tables on a column (or key made up of multiple columns), you have a number of choices about how you approach the problem. In our trivial coded attempt, you can see we simply iterate over the whole table for each table involved in the join, which ends up being O($nmo$) or $\mathcal{O}(n^3)$ for roughly same size tables. This is no good for large tables, but for small ones it's fine. You have to know your data to decide whether your tables are big[2] or not. If your tables are too big to use such a trivial join, then you will need an alternative strategy.

You can join by iteration, or you can join by lookup[3], or you can even join once and keep a join cache around. Keep-

---

[2]dependent on the target hardware, how many rows and columns, and whether you want the process to run without trashing too much cache

[3]often a lookup join is called a join by hash, but as we know our data, we can use better row search algorithms than a hash when they are available

ing the join cache around makes it appear as if you can operate on the tables as if they are sorted in multiple ways at the same time.

It's perfectly feasible to add auxiliary data which will allow for traversal of a table in a different order. We add join caches in the same way databases allow for any number of indexes into a table. Each index is created and kept up to date as the table is modified. In our case, we implement each index the way we need to. Maybe some tables are written to in bursts, and an insertion sort would be slow, it might be better to sort on first read, or trash the whole index on modify. In other cases, the sorting might be better done on write, as the writes are infrequent, or always interleaved with many reads.

## 8.5 Transforms

Taking the concept of schemas a step further, a static schema definition can allow for a different approach to iterators. Instead of iterating over a container, giving access to an element, a schema iterator can become an accessor for a set of tables, meaning the merging work can be done during iteration, generating a context upon which the transform operates. This would benefit large, complex merges which do little with the data, as there would be less memory usage creating temporary tables. It would not benefit complex transforms as it would reduce the likelihood that the next set of data is in cache ready for the next cycle.

Another aspect of transforms is the separation of what from how. That is, separating the gathering or loading of data we will transform from the code which ultimately performs the operations on the data. In some languages, introducing map and reduce is part of the basic syllabus, in C++, not so much. This is probably because lists aren't part of the base language, and without that, it's hard to introduce powerful tools which require them. These tools, map and reduce, can be the basis of a purely transform and flow driven program. Turning a large set of data into a single result sounds eminently serial, however, as long as one of the steps, the reduce step, is associative, then you can reduce in parallel for a significant portion of the reduction.

A simple reduce, one made to create a final total from a mapping which produces values of zero or one for all matching elements, can be processed as a less and less parallel tree of reductions. In the first step, all reductions produce the total of all odd-even pairs of elements and produce a new list which goes through the same process. This list reduction continues until there is only one item left remaining. Of course, this particular reduction is of very little use, as each reduction is so trivial, you'd be better off assigning an $n^{th}$ of the workload to each of the $n$ cores and doing one final summing. A more complex, but equally useful reduction would be the concatenation of a chain of matrices. Matrices are associative even if they are not commutative, and as such, the chain can be reduced in parallel the same way building the total worked. By maintaining the order during reduction you can apply parallel processing to many things which would normally seem serial, so long as they are associative in the reduce step. Not only matrix concatenation, but also products of floating point values such as colour modulation by multiple causes such as light, diffuse, or gameplay related tinting. Building text strings can be associative, as can be building lists.

## 8.6   Spatial sets for collisions

In collision detection, there is often a broad-phase step which can massively reduce the number of potential collisions we check against. When ray casting, it's often useful to find the potential intersection via an octree, BSP, or other spatial query accelerator. When running pathfinding, sometimes it's useful to look up local nodes to help choose a starting node for your journey.

All spatial data-stores accelerate queries by letting them do less. They are based on some spatial criteria and return a reduced set which is shorter and thus less expensive to transform into new data.

Existing libraries which support spatial partitioning have to try to work with arbitrary structures, but because all our data is already organised by table, writing adaptors for any possible table layout is made simpler. Writing generic algorithms becomes easier without any of the side effects normally associated with writing code that is used in multiple places. Using the table-based approach, because of its intention agnosticism (that is, the spatial system has no idea it's being used on data which doesn't technically belong in space), we can use spatial partitioning algorithms in unexpected places, such as assigning audio channels by not only their distance from the listener, but also their volume and importance. Making a 5 dimensional spatial partitioning system, or even an $n$ dimensional one, would be an investment. It would only have to be written once and have unit tests written once, before it could be used and trusted to do some very strange things. Spatially partitioning by the quest progress for tasks to do seems a little overkill, but getting the set of all nearby interesting entities by their location, threat, and reward, seems like something an AI might consider useful.

## 8.7   Lazy evaluation for the masses

When optimising object-oriented code, it's quite common to find local caches of completed calculations hidden in mutable member variables. One trick found in most updating hierarchies is the dirty bit, the flag that says whether the child or parent members of a tree have decided this object needs updating. When traversing the hierarchy, this dirty bit causes branching based on data which has only just loaded, usually meaning there is no chance to guess the outcome and thus in most cases, causes memory to be read in preparation, when it's not required.

If your calculation is expensive, then you might not want to go the route that render engines now use. In render engines, it's often cheaper to do every scene matrix concatenation every frame than it is only doing the ones necessary and figuring out if they are.

For example, in the *Pitfalls of Object-Oriented Programming* [14] presentation by Tony Albrecht, in the early slides he declares that checking a dirty flag is less useful than not checking it, as when it does fail (the case where the object is not dirty) the calculation that would have taken 12 cycles is dwarfed by the cost of a branch misprediction (23-24 cycles). Things always move on, and in the later talk *Pitfalls revisited*[15], he notes that the previous improvement gained through manual devirtualization no longer provides any benefit. Whether it was the improvements in the compiler or the change in hardware, reality will always trump experience.

If your calculation is expensive, you don't want to bog down the game with a large number of checks to see if the value needs updating. This is the point at which existence-based-processing comes into its own again as existence in the dirty table implies it needs updating, and as a dirty element is updated it can be pushing new dirty elements onto the end of the table, even prefetching if it can improve bandwidth.

# 8.8 Necessity, or not getting what you didn't ask for

When you normalise your data you reduce the chance of another multifaceted problem of object-oriented development. C++'s implementation of objects forces unrelated data to share cache lines.

Objects collect their data by the class, but many objects, by design, contain more than one role's worth of data. This is because object-oriented development doesn't naturally allow for objects to be recomposed based on their role in a transaction, and also because C++ needed to provide a method by which you could have object-oriented programming while keeping the system level memory allocations overloadable in a simple way. Most classes contain more than just the bare minimum, either because of inheritance or because of the many contexts in which an object can play a part. Unless you have very carefully laid out a class, many operations which require only a small amount of information from the class will load a lot of unnecessary data into the cache in order to do so. Only using a very small amount of the loaded data is one of the most common sins of the object-oriented programmer.

Every virtual call loads in the cache line that contains the virtual-table pointer of the instance. If the function doesn't use any of the class's early data, then that will be cache line utilisation in the region of only 4%. That's a memory throughput waste, and cannot be recovered without rethinking how you dispatch your functions. Adding a final keyword to your class can help when your class calls into its own virtual functions, but cannot help when they are called via a base type.

In practice, only after the function has loaded, can the CPU load the data it wants to work on, which can be scattered across the memory allocated for the class too. It won't know what data it needs until it has decoded the instructions from the function pointed to by the virtual table entry.

## 8.9 Varying length sets

Throughout the techniques so far, there's been an implied table structure to the data. Each row is a struct, or each table is a row of columns of data, depending on the need of the transforms. When working with stream processing, for example, with shaders, we would normally use fixed size buffers. Most work done with stream processing has this same limitation, we tend to have a fixed number of elements for both sides.

For filtering where the input is known to be a superset of the output, there can be a strong case for an annealing structure. Outputting to multiple separate vectors, and concatenating them in a final reduce. Each transform thread has its own output vector, the reduce step would first generate a total and a start position for each reduce entry and then processes the list of reduces onto the final contiguous memory. A parallel prefix sum would work well here, but simple linear passes would suffice.

If the filtering was a stage in a radix sort, counting sort, or something which uses a similar histogram for generating offsets, then a parallel prefix sum would reduce the latency to generate the offsets. A prefix sum is the running total of a list of values. The radix sort output histogram is a great example because the bucket counts indicate the starting points through the sum of all histogram buckets that come prior. $o_n = \sum_{i=0}^{n-1} b_i$. This is easy to generate in serial form, but in parallel, we have to consider the minimum required operations to produce the final result. In this case, we can remember that the longest chain will be the value of the last offset, which is a sum of all the elements. This is normally optimised by summing in a binary tree fashion. Dividing and conquering: first summing all odd numbered slots with all even numbered slots, then doing the same, but for only the outputs of the previous stage.

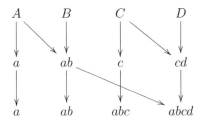

Then once you have the last element, backfill all the other elements you didn't finish on your way to making the last element. When you come to write this in code, you will find these backfilled values can be done in parallel while making the longest chain. They have no dependency on the final value so can be given over to another process, or managed by some clever use of SIMD.

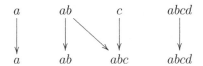

Parallel prefix sums provide a way to reduce latency, but are not a general solution which is better than doing a linear prefix sum. A linear prefix sum uses far fewer machine resources to do the same thing, so if you can handle the latency, then simplify your code and do the sum linearly.

Also, for cases where the entity count can rise and fall, you need a way of adding and deleting without causing any hiccups. For this, if you intend to transform your data in place, you need to handle the case where one thread can be reading and using the data you're deleting. To do this in a system where objects' existence was based on their memory being allocated, it would be very hard to delete objects that were being referenced by other transforms. You could use smart pointers, but in a multi-threaded environment, smart pointers cost a mutex to be thread safe for every reference and dereference. This is a high cost to pay, so how do we avoid it? There are at least two ways.

Don't have a mutex. One way to avoid the mutex is to use a smart pointer type which is bound to a single thread. In some game engines, there are smart pointer types that instead of keeping a mutex, store an identifier for the thread they belong to. This is so they can assert every access is made by the same thread. For performance considerations, this data doesn't need to be present in release builds, as the checks are done to protect against misuse at runtime caused by decisions made at compile time. For example, if you know the data should not be used outside of the audio subsystem, and the audio subsystem is running on a single thread of its own, lock it down and tie the memory allocation to the audio thread. Any time the audio system memory is accessed outside of the audio thread, it's either because the audio system is exposing memory to the outside systems or it's doing more work than it should in any callback functions. In either case, the assert will catch the bad behaviour, and fixes can be made to the code to counter the general issue, not the specific case.

Don't delete. If you are deleting in a system that is constantly changing, then you would normally use pools anyway. By explicitly not deleting, by doing something else instead, you change the way all code accesses data. You change what the data represents. If you need an entity to exist, such as a CarDriverAI, then it can stack up on your table of CarDriverAIs while it's in use, but the moment it's not in use, it won't get deleted, but instead marked as not used. This is not the same as deleting, because you're saying the entity is still valid, won't crash your transform, but it can be skipped as if it were not there until you get around to overwriting it with the latest request for a CarDriverAI. Keeping dead entities around can be as cheap as keeping pools for your components, as long as there are only a few dead entities in your tables.

## 8.10   Joins as intersections

Sometimes, normalisation can mean you need to join tables together to create the right situation for a query. Unlike RDBMS queries, we can organise our queries much more carefully and use the algorithm from merge sort to help us zip together two tables. As an alternative, we don't have to output to a table, it could be a pass-through transform which takes more than one table and generates a new stream into another transform. For example, per entityRenderable, join with entityPosition by entityID, to transform with AddRenderCall( Renderable, Position ).

## 8.11   Data-driven techniques

Apart from finite state machines, there are some other common forms of data-driven coding practices. Some are not very obvious, such as callbacks. Some are very obvious, such as scripting. In both these cases, data causing the flow of code to change will cause the same kind of cache and pipeline problems as seen in virtual calls and finite state machines.

Callbacks can be made safer by using triggers from event subscription tables. Rather than have a callback which fires off when a job is done, have an event table for done jobs so callbacks can be called once the whole run is finished. For example, if a scoring system has a callback from "badGuyDies", then in an object-oriented message watcher you would have the scorer increment its internal score whenever it received the message that a badGuyDies. Instead, run each of the callbacks in the callback table once the whole set of badGuys has been checked for death. If you do that and execute every time all the badGuys have had their tick, then you can add points once for all badGuys killed. That means one read for the internal state, and one write. Much better than multiple reads and writes accumulating a final score.

For scripting, if you have scripts which run over multiple entities, consider how the graphics kernels operate with branches, sometimes using predication and doing both sides of a branch before selecting a solution. This would allow you to reduce the number of branches caused merely by interpreting the script on demand. If you go one step further an actually build SIMD into the scripting core, then you might find you can use scripts for a very large number of entities compared to traditional per entity serial scripting. If your SIMD operations operate over the whole collection of entities, then you will pay almost no price for script interpretation[4].

### 8.11.1  SIMD

SIMD operations can be very beneficial as long as you have a decent chunk of work to do, such as making an operation that handles updating positions of particles (see listing 8.5). This example of SIMDifying some code is straightforward, and in tests ran about four times faster than both the array of structs code and the naïve struct of arrays code.

In many optimising compilers, simple vectorisation is carried out by default, but only as far as the compiler can figure things out. It's not often very easy to figure these things out.

SIMD operations on machines which support SSE, allow you to get more data into the CPU in one go. Many people started out by putting their 3D vectors into SIMD units, but that doesn't allow full utilisation of the SIMD pipeline. The

---

[4]Take a look at the section headed *The Massively Vectorized Virtual Machine* on the BitSquid blog http://bitsquid.blogspot.co.uk/2012/10/a-data-oriented-data-driven-system-for.html

```
void SimpleUpdateParticles( particle_buffer *pb, float delta_time
    ) {
  float g = pb->gravity;
  float gd2 = g * delta_time * delta_time * 0.5f;
  float gd = g * delta_time;
  for( int i = 0; i < NUM_PARTICLES; ++i ) {
    pb->posx[i] += pb->vx[i] * delta_time;
    pb->posy[i] += pb->vy[i] * delta_time + gd2;
    pb->posz[i] += pb->vz[i] * delta_time;
    pb->vy[i] += gd;
  }
}

void SIMD_SSE_UpdateParticles( particle_buffer *pb, float
    delta_time ) {
  float g = pb->gravity;
  float f_gd = g * delta_time;
  float f_gd2 = pb->gravity * delta_time * delta_time * 0.5f;

  __m128 mmd = _mm_setr_ps( delta_time, delta_time, delta_time,
      delta_time );
  __m128 mmgd = _mm_load1_ps( &f_gd );
  __m128 mmgd2 = _mm_load1_ps( &f_gd2 );

  __m128 *px = (__m128*)pb->posx;
  __m128 *py = (__m128*)pb->posx;
  __m128 *pz = (__m128*)pb->posz;
  __m128 *vx = (__m128*)pb->vx;
  __m128 *vy = (__m128*)pb->vy;
  __m128 *vz = (__m128*)pb->vz;

  int iterationCount = NUM_PARTICLES / 4;
  for( int i = 0; i < iterationCount; ++i ) {
    __m128 dx = _mm_mul_ps(vx[i], mmd );
    __m128 dy = _mm_add_ps( _mm_mul_ps(vy[i], mmd ), mmgd2 );
    __m128 dz = _mm_mul_ps(vz[i], mmd );
    __m128 newx = _mm_add_ps(px[i], dx);
    __m128 newy = _mm_add_ps(py[i], dy);
    __m128 newz = _mm_add_ps(pz[i], dz);
    __m128 newvy = _mm_add_ps(vy[i], mmgd);
    _mm_store_ps((float*)(px+i), newx);
    _mm_store_ps((float*)(py+i), newy);
    _mm_store_ps((float*)(pz+i), newz);
    _mm_store_ps((float*)(vy+i), newvy);
  }
}
```

Listing 8.5: Simple particle update with SIMD

example loads in four different particles at the same time, and updates them all at the same time too. This very simple technique also means you don't have to do anything clever with the data layout, as you can just use a naïve struct of arrays to prepare for SIMDification once you find it has become a bottleneck.

## 8.12 Structs of arrays

In addition to all the other benefits of keeping your runtime data in a database style format, there is the opportunity to take advantage of structures of arrays rather than arrays of structures. SoA has been coined as a term to describe an access pattern for object data. It is okay to keep hot and cold data side by side in an SoA object as data is pulled into the cache by necessity rather than by accidental physical location.

If your animation timekey/value class resembles this:

```
struct Keyframe
{
  float time, x,y,z;
};
struct Stream
{
  Keyframe *keyframes;
  int numKeys;
};
```

Listing 8.6: animation timekey/value class

then when you iterate over a large collection of them, all the data has to be pulled into the cache at once. If we assume that a cache line is 64 bytes, and the size of floats is 4 bytes, the Keyframe struct is 16 bytes. This means that every time you look up a key time, you accidentally pull in four keys and all the associated keyframe data. If you are doing a binary search of a 128 key stream, it could mean you end up loading 64 bytes of data and only using 4 bytes of it in up to 5 of the steps. If you change the data layout so the searching takes place in one array, and the data is stored separately, then you get structures that look like this:

```
struct KeyData
{
  float x,y,z;
  // consider padding out to 16 bytes long
};
struct stream
{
  float *times;
  KeyData *values;
  numKeys;
};
```

Listing 8.7: struct of arrays

Doing this means that for a 128 key stream, the key times only take up 8 cache lines in total, and a binary search is going to pull in at most three of them, and the data lookup is guaranteed to only require one, or two at most if your data straddles two cache lines due to choosing memory space efficiency over performance.

Database technology was here first. In DBMS terms, it's called column-oriented databases and they provide better throughput for data processing over traditional row-oriented relational databases simply because irrelevant data is not loaded when doing column aggregations or filtering. There are other features that make column-store databases more efficient, such as allowing them to collect many keys under one value instead of having a key value 1:1 mapping, but database advances are always being made, and it's worth hunting down current literature to see what else might be worth migrating to your codebase.

# Chapter 9

# Helping the compiler

Compilers are rather good at optimising code, but there are ways in which we code that make things harder. There are tricks we use that break assumptions the compiler can make. In this section, we will look at some of the things we do that we should try not to, and we look at how to introduce some habits that will make it easier for the compiler to do what we mean, not what we say.

## 9.1   Reducing order dependence

If the compiler is unable to deduce that the order of operations is not important to you, then it won't be able to do work ahead of schedule. When composing the translated code into intermediate representation form, there's a quality some compilers use called static single assignment form, or SSA. The idea is that you never modify variables once they are initially assigned, and instead create new ones when a modification becomes required. Although you cannot actually use this in loops, as any operations which carry through would require the assigned value to change, you can get close to it, and in doing so, you can help the compiler understand what you mean when you are modifying and assigning values. Skimming the available features and tutorials in languages such as Haskell, Erlang, and Single-Assignment C can give you the necessary hints to write your code in a single assignment manner.

Writing code like this means you will see where the compiler has to branch more easily, but also, you can make your writes more explicit, which means that where a compiler might have had to break away from writing to memory, you can force it to write in all cases, making your processing more homogeneous, and therefore more likely to stream better.

## 9.2   Reducing memory dependency

Linked lists are expensive due to dependencies, but dependencies of a different sort. Memory being slow, you want to be able to load it in time for your operations, but when the address you need to load is itself still being loaded, you can't cheat anymore. Pointer driven tree algorithms are slow, not because of the memory lookups, but because the memory lookups are chained together.

If you want to make your map or set implementation run faster, move to a wide node algorithm such as a B-tree, or B*-tree. Hopefully, at some point soon, the STL will allow you to chose the method by which `std::map` and `std::set` are implemented.

When you have an entity component system using the compositional style, and you have a pointer based composition, then the two layers of pointers to get to the component is slowing you down. If you have pointers inside those components, you're just compounding the problem.

Attempt where possible to reduce the number of hops to

get to the data you need. Each hop that depends on previous data is potentially a stall waiting for main memory.

## 9.3 Write buffer awareness

When writing, the same issues need to be considered as when reading. Try to keep things contiguous where possible. Try to keep modified values separated from read-only values, and also from write-only values.

In short, write contiguously, in large amounts at a time, and use all the bytes, not a small part of them. We need to try to do this, as not only does it help with activation and deactivation of different memory pages, but also opens up opportunities for the compiler to optimise.

When you have a cache, sometimes it's important to find ways to bypass it. If you know that you won't be using the data you're loading more than once or at least not soon enough to benefit from caching, then it can be useful to find ways to avoid polluting the cache. When you write your transforms in simple ways, it can help the compiler promote your operations from ones which pollute the cache, to instructions that bypass the cache completely. These streaming operations benefit the caches by not evicting randomly accessed memory.

In the article *What every programmer should know about memory*[18], Ulrich Drepper talks about many aspects of memory which are interesting to get the most out of your computer hardware. In the article, he used the term non-temporality to describe the kinds of operations we call streaming. These non-temporal memory operations help because they bypass the cache completely, which naïvely would seem to be a poor choice, but as the name suggests, streaming data is not likely to be recalled into registers any time soon, so having it available in the cache is pointless, and merely evicts potentially useful data. Streaming operations, therefore, allow you some control over what you consider important to be in cache, and what is almost certainly not.

## 9.4 Aliasing

Aliasing is when it's possible for pointers to reference the same memory, and therefore require reloading between reads if the other pointer has been written to. A simple example could be where the value we're looking for is specified by reference, rather than by value, so if any functions that could potentially affect the memory being referred to by that lookup reference, then the reference must be re-read before doing a comparison. The very fact it is a pointer, rather than a value, is what causes the issue.

A reason to work with data in an immutable way comes in the form of preparations for optimisation. C++, as a language, provides a lot of ways for the programmer to shoot themselves in the foot, and one of the best is that pointers to memory can cause unexpected side effects when used without caution. Consider this piece of code:

```
char buffer[ 100 ];
buffer[0] = 'X';
memcpy( buffer+1, buffer, 98 );
buffer[ 99 ] = '\0';
```

Listing 9.1: byte copying

This is perfectly correct code if you just want to get a string filled with 99 'X's. However, because this is possible, memcpy has to copy one byte at a time. To speed up copying, you normally load in a lot of memory locations at once, then save them out once they are all in the cache. If your input data can be modified by writes to your output buffer, then you have to tread very carefully. Now consider this:

```
1  int q=10;
2  int p[10];
3  for( int i = 0; i < q;  ++i )
4    p[i] = i;
```

Listing 9.2: trivially parallelisable code

The compiler can figure out that q is unaffected, and can happily unroll this loop or replace the check against q with a register value. However, looking at this code instead:

```
1  void foo( int* p, const int &q )
2  {
3    for( int i = 0; i < q; ++i)
4      p[i] = i;
5  }
6
7  int q=10;
8  int p[10];
9  foo( p, q );
```

Listing 9.3: potentially aliased int

The compiler cannot tell that q is unaffected by operations on p, so it has to store p and reload q every time it checks the end of the loop. This is called aliasing, where the address of two variables that are in use are not known to be different, so to ensure functionally correct code, the variables have to be handled as if they might be at the same address.

# 9.5 Return value optimisation

If you want to return multiple values, the normal way is to return via reference arguments, or by filling out an object passed by reference. In many cases, return by value can be very cheap as many compilers can turn it into a non-copy operation.

When a function attempts to return a structure by constructing the value in place during the return, it is allowed to move the construction straight into the value that will receive it, without doing a copy at all.

Utilising `std::pair` or other small temporary `structs` can help by making more of your code run on value types, which are not only inherently easier to reason about, but also easier to optimise by a compiler.

## 9.6   Cache line utilisation

It is a truth universally acknowledged that a single memory request will always read in at least one complete cache line. That complete cache line will contain multiple bytes of data. At the time of writing this book, the most common cache line size seems to have stabilized at 64 bytes. With this information, we can speculate about what data will be cheap to access purely by their location relative to other data.

In Searching (Chapter 6), we utilise this information to decide the location and quantity of data that is available for creating the rapid lookup table included in the example that uses a two-layer linear search that turns out to be faster than a binary search.

When you have an object you will be loading into memory, calculate the difference between a cache line and the size of the object. That difference is how much memory you have left to place data you can read for free. Use this space to answer the common questions you have about the class, and you will often see speedups as there will be no extra memory accesses.

For example, consider a codebase that partially migrated to components, and still has an entity class which points to optional rows in component arrays. In this case, we can cache the fact the entity has elements in those arrays in the latter part of the entity class as a bitset. This would mean the entity on entity interactions could save doing a lookup into the arrays if there was no matching row. It can also improve render performance as the renderer can immediately tell that there is no damage done, so will just show a full health icon or nothing at all.

In the example code in listing 16.11 in Chapter 16, an attempt is made to use more of an object's initial cache line to answer questions about the rest of the object, and you can see various levels of success in the results. In the case of fully caching the result, a massive improvement was gained. If the result cannot be quickly calculated and needs to be calculated on demand, caching that there was something to do was a factor of four improvement. Caching the result when you can, had differing levels of performance improvement, based on the likelihood of hitting a cached response. In all, using the extra data you have on your cache line is always an improvement over simple checking.

```
i5-4430 @ 3.00GHz
Average 11.31ms [Simple, check the map]
Average  9.62ms [Partially cached query (25%)]
Average  8.77ms [Partially cached presence (50%)]
Average  3.71ms [Simple, cache presence]
Average  1.51ms [Partially cached query (95%)]
Average  0.30ms [Fully cached query]
```

So, in summary, keep in mind, every time you load any memory at all, you are loading in a full cache line of bytes. Currently, with 64-byte cache lines, that's a 4x4 matrix of floats, 8 doubles, 16 ints, a 64 character ASCII string, or 512 bits.

## 9.7 False sharing

When a CPU core shares no resources with another, it can always operate at full speed independently, right? Well, sometimes no. Even if the CPU core is working on independent data, there are times it can get choked up on the cache.

On the opposite side of the same issue as writing linearly, when you are writing out data to the same cache line, it can interfere with threading. Due to the advancement of compilers, it seems this happens far less frequently than it should, and when attempting to reproduce the issue to give ideas on the effect it can have, only by turning off optimisations is it possible to witness the effect with trivial examples.

The idea is that multiple threads will want to read from and write to the same cache line, but not necessarily the same memory addresses in the cache line. It's relatively easy to avoid this by ensuring any rapidly updated variables are kept local to the thread, whether on the stack or in thread local storage. Other data, as long as it's not updated regularly, is highly unlikely to cause a collision.

There has been a lot of talk about this particular problem, but the real-world is different from the real-world problems supposed. Always check your problems are real after optimisation, as well as before, as even the high and mighty have fallen for this as a cause of massive grief.

So, how can you tell if this problem is real or not? If your multi-threaded code is not growing at a linear rate of processing as you add cores, then you might be suffering from false sharing, look at the where your threads are writing, and try to remove the writes from shared memory where possible until the last step. The common example given is of adding up some arrays and updating the sum value in some global shared location, such as in listing 9.4.

In the FalseSharing function, the sums are written to as a shared resource, and each thread will cause the cache to clean up and handle that line being dirty for each of the other cores before they can update their elements in the cache line. In the second function, LocalAccumulator, each thread sums up their series before writing out the result.

```
void FalseSharing() {
  int sum=0;
  int aligned_sum_store[NUM_THREADS] __attribute__((aligned(64)))
      ;
#pragma omp parallel num_threads(NUM_THREADS)
  {
    int me = omp_get_thread_num();
    aligned_sum_store[me] = 0;
    for (int i = me; i < ELEMENT_COUNT; i += NUM_THREADS ) {
      aligned_sum_store[me] += CalcValue( i );
    }
#pragma omp atomic
    sum += aligned_sum_store[me];
  }
}

void LocalAccumulator() {
  int sum=0;
#pragma omp parallel num_threads(NUM_THREADS)
  {
    int me = omp_get_thread_num();
    int local_accumulator = 0;
    for (int i = me; i < ELEMENT_COUNT; i += NUM_THREADS ) {
      local_accumulator += CalcValue( i );
    }
#pragma omp atomic
    sum += local_accumulator;
  }
}
```

Listing 9.4: False sharing

# 9.8   Speculative execution awareness

Speculative execution helps as it executes instructions and prepares data before we arrive at where we might need them, effectively allowing us to do work before we know we need it, but sometimes it could have a detrimental effect. For example, consider the codebase mentioned previously, that had partially migrated to components. The bit arrays of which optional tables it was currently resident could lead, through speculation, to loading in details about those arrays. With speculative execution, you will need to watch out for the code accidentally prefetching data because it was waiting to find out the result of a comparison. These speculative operations have been in the news with SPECTRE and MELTDOWN vulnerabilities.

These branch prediction caused reads can be reduced by pre-calculating predicates where possible, storing the result of doing a common query in your rows is a big win for most machines and a massive one for machines with poor memory latency or high CPU bandwidth to memory bandwidth ratios. Moving to techniques where branch mispredictions cause the smallest side-effects to the data is a generally good idea. Even caching only when you can, storing the result back in the initial section, can save bandwidth over time.

In the cache line utilisation section, the numbers showed that the possibility of getting data seemed to affect how fast the process went, much more than it would be expected, which leads to a belief that speculative loads of unnecessary data were potentially harming overall throughput.

Even if all you are able to cache is whether a query will return a result, it can be beneficial. Avoiding lookups into complex data structures by keeping data on whether or not there are entries matching that description can give speed boosts with very few detrimental side-effects.

# 9.9 Branch prediction

One of the main causes of stalling in CPUs comes down to not having any work to do, or having to unravel what they have already done because they predicted badly. If code is speculatively executed, and requests memory that is not needed, then the load has become a wasteful use of memory bandwidth. Any work done will be rejected and the correct work has to be started or continued. To get around this issue, there are ways to make code branch free, but another way is to understand the branch prediction mechanism of the CPU and help it out.

If you make prediction trivial, then the predictor will get it right most of the time. If you ensure the conditions are consistently true or false in large chunks, the predictor will make fewer mistakes. A trivial example such as in listing 9.5 will predict to either do or not do the accumulation, based on the incoming data. The work being done here can be optimised away by most compilers using a conditional move instruction if the CPU supports it. If you make the work done a little more realistic, then even with full optimisations turned on, you can see a very large difference[1] if you can sort the data so the branches are much more predictable. The other thing to remember is that if the compiler can help you, let it. The optimised trivial example is only trivial in comparison to other common workloads, but if your actual work is trivially optimised into a conditional execution, then sorting your data will be a waste of effort.

```
i5-4430 @ 3.00GHz
Average  4.40ms [Random branching]
Average  1.15ms [Sorted branching]
Average  0.80ms [Trivial Random branching]
Average  0.76ms [Trivial Sorted branching]
```

---

[1]On an i5-4430 the unsorted sum ran in 4.2ms vs the sorted sum running in 0.8ms. The trivial version, which was likely mostly compiled into CMOVs, ran in 0.4ms both sorted and unsorted

```
1   int SumBasedOnData() {
2     int sum=0;
3     for (int i = 0; i < ELEMENT_COUNT; i++) {
4       if( a[i] > 128 ) {
5         sum += b[i];
6       }
7     }
8     return sum;
9   }
```

Listing 9.5: Doing work based on data

Branching happens because of data, and remember the reason why branching is bad is not that jumps are expensive, but the work being done because of a misprediction will have to be undone. Because of this, it's valuable to remember that a vtable pointer is data too. When you don't batch update, you won't be getting the most out of your branch predictor, but even if you don't hit the branch predictor at all, you may still be committing to sequences of instructions based on data.

## 9.10 Don't get evicted

If you're working with others, as many are, then perhaps the simplest solution to a lot of issues with poor cache performance has to take into account other areas of the code. If you're working on a multi-core machine (you are, unless we went back in time), then there's a good chance that all processes are sharing and contending for the caches on the machine. Your code will be evicted from the cache, there is no doubt. So will your data. To reduce the chance or frequency of your code and data being evicted, keep both code and data small and process in bursts when you can.

It's very simple advice. Not only is small code less likely to be evicted, but if it's done in bursts it will have had a chance to get a reasonable amount of work before being overwritten. Some cache architectures don't have any way to tell if the

```
void Amplify( float *a, float mult, int count )
{
  for( int i = 0; i < count; ++i ) {
    a[i] *= mult;
  }
}
```

Listing 9.6: Trivial amplification function

elements in the cache have been used recently, so they rely on when they were added as a metric for what should be evicted first. In particular, some Intel CPUs can have their L1 and L2 cache lines evicted because of L3 needing to evict, but L3 doesn't have full access to LRU information. The Intel CPUs in question have some other magic that reduces the likelihood of this happening, but it does happen.

To that end, try to find ways to guarantee to the compiler that you are working with aligned data, in arrays that are multiples of 4 or 8, or 16, so the compiler doesn't need to add preambles and postamble code to handle unaligned, or irregularly sized arrays. It can be better to have 3 more dead elements in an array and handle it as an array of length $N*4$.

## 9.11  Auto vectorisation

Auto vectorisation will help your applications run faster just by enabling it and forming your code in such a way that it is possible for the compiler to make safe assumptions, and change the instructions from scalar to vector.

There are many trivial examples of things which can be cleanly vectorised. The first example is found in listing 9.6, which is simple enough to be vectorised by most compilers when optimisations are turned on. The issue is that there are few guarantees with the code, so even though it can be quite fast to process the data, this code will take up a lot more space than is necessary in the instruction cache.

```
typedef float f16 __attribute__((aligned(16)));

void Amplify( f16 *a, float mult, int count )
{
  count &= -4;
  for( int i = 0; i < count; ++i ) {
    a[i] *= mult;
  }
}
```

Listing 9.7: Amplification function with alignment hints

```
typedef float f16 __attribute__((aligned(16)));

void Amplify( f16 *a, float mult, int count )
{
  count &= -4;
  for( int i = 0; i < count; ++i ) {
    if( a[i] < 0 )
      break;
    a[i] *= mult;
  }
}
```

Listing 9.8: Breaking out, breaks vectorisation

If you can add some simple guarantees, such as by using aligned pointers, and by giving the compiler some guarantees about the number of elements, then you can cut the size of the emitted assembly, which on a per case basis won't help, but over a large codebase, it will increase the effectiveness of your instruction cache as the number of instructions to be decoded is slashed. Listing 9.7 isn't faster in isolated test beds, but the size of the final executable will be smaller, as the generated code is less than half the size. This is a problem with micro-benchmarks, they can't always show how systems work together or fight against each other. In real-world tests, fixing up the alignment of pointers can improve performance dramatically. In small test beds, memory throughput is normally the only bottleneck.

A thing to watch out for is making sure the loops are trivial and always run their course. If a loop has to break based on data, then it won't be able to commit to doing all elements

```
1    typedef float f16 __attribute__((aligned(16)));
2
3    void Amplify( f16 *a, float mult, int count )
4    {
5      count &= -4;
6      for( int i = 0; i < count; ++i ) {
7        f16 val = a[i] * mult;
8        if( val > 0 )
9          a[i] = val;
10       else
11         a[i] = 0;
12     }
13   }
```

Listing 9.9: Vectorising an if

of the processing, and that means it has to do each element
at a time. In listing 9.8 the introduction of a break based on
the data turns the function from a fast parallel SIMD operation auto-vectorisable loop, into a single stepping loop. Note
that branching in and of itself does not cause a breakdown in
vectorisation, but the fact the loop is exited based on data.
For example, in listing 9.9, the branch can be turned into
other operations. It's also the case that calling out to a function can often break the vectorisation, as side effects cannot
normally be guaranteed. If the function is a constexpr, then
there's a much better chance it can be consumed into the
body of the loop, and won't break vectorisation. On some
compilers, there are certain mathematical functions which
are available in a vectorised form, such as min, abs, sqrt,
tan, pow, etc. Find out what your compiler can vectorise. It
can often help to write your series of operations out longhand
to some extent, as trying to shorten the C++ code, can lead
to slight ambiguities with what the compiler is allowed to do.
One thing to watch out for in particular is making sure you
always write out. If you only write part of the output stream,
then it won't be able to write out whole SIMD data types, so
write out to your output variable, even if it means reading it
in, just to write it out again.

Aliasing can also affect auto vectorisation, as when pointers can overlap, there could be dependencies between differ-

```
void CombineNext( float *a, int count )
{
  for( int i = 0; i < count - 1; ++i ) {
    a[i] += a[i+1]
  }
}

void CombineFours( float *a, int count )
{
  for( int i = 0; i < count - 4; ++i ) {
    a[i] += a[i+4]
  }
}
```

Listing 9.10: Aliasing affecting vectorisation

ent members of the same SIMD register. Consider the listing
9.10, where the first version of the function increments each
member by its direct neighbour. This function is pointless
but serves us as an example. The function will create a pair-
wise sum all the way to the end float by float. As such, it
cannot be trivially vectorised. The second function, though
equally pointless, makes large enough steps that auto vectorisation can find a way to calculate multiple values per
step.

Different compilers will manage different amounts of vectorisation based on the way you write your code, but in general, the simpler you write your code, the more likely the
compiler will be able to optimise your source.

Over the next decade, compilers will get better and better.
Clang already attempts to unroll loops far more than GCC
does, and many new ways to detect and optimise simple code
will likely appear. At the time of writing, the online Compiler
Explorer provided by Matt Godbolt[2], provides a good way to
see how your code will be compiled into assembly, so you
can see what can and will be vectorised, optimised out, re-
arranged, or otherwise mutated into the machine-readable
form. Remember that the number of assembly instructions
is not a good metric for fast code, that SIMD operations are

---

[2]https://godbolt.org/

not inherently faster in all cases, and measuring the code running cannot be replaced by stroking your chin[3] while thinking about whether the instructions look cool, and you should be okay.

---

[3]or even *stroking a beard, or biting a pencil (while making a really serious face)*, as one reviewer pleaded

# Chapter 10

# Concurrency

Any book on game development practices for contemporary and future hardware must cover the issues of concurrency. There will come a time when we have more cores in our computers than we have pixels on screen[1], and when that happens, it would be best if we were already coding for it, in a style which allows for maximal throughput with the smallest latency. Thinking about how to solve problems for five, ten or even one hundred cores isn't going to keep you safe. You must think about how your algorithms would work when you have an infinite number of cores. The real question is, can you make your code and algorithms work for N cores?

Writing concurrent software is a hard task because most people think they understand threading and can't get their heads around all the different corner cases that are introduced when you share the same memory as another thread. Fixing these with mutexes and critical sections can become a minefield of badly written code that works only 99% of the time. For any real concurrent development we have to stop thinking about ownership, and start thinking about our code transforming data. Every time you get a deadlock or a race

---

[1]We were getting close, but 4K just moved the goalposts.

condition in threaded code, it's because there's some ownership issue. If you code from a data transform point of view,
then there are some simple ground rules which provide very
stable tools for developing truly concurrent software.

## 10.1  What it means to be thread-safe

Academics consistently focus on what is possible and correct, rather than what is practical and usable, which is why
we've been inundated with multi-threaded techniques which
work, but cause a lot of unnecessary pain when used in a
high-performance system such as a game. The idea that
something is thread-safe implies more than just its ability
to be used safely in a multi-threaded environment. There
are lots of thread-safe functions which aren't mentioned because they seem trivial, but it's a useful distinction to make
when you are tracking down what could be causing a strange
thread issue. There are functions without side-effects, such
as the intrinsics for sin, sqrt, which return a value given
a value. There is no way they can cause any other code
to change behaviour, and no other code can change its behaviour either[2]. In addition to these very simple functions,
there are the simple functions that change things in an idempotent fashion, such as memset.

Thread-safe implies it doesn't just access its own data,
but accesses some shared data without causing the system
to enter into an inconsistent state. Inconsistent state is a
natural side effect of multiple processes accessing and writing to shared memory. It is these side effects which are the
cause of many bugs in multi-threaded code, which is why
the developers of the Erlang language chose to limit the programmer to code which doesn't have side-effects. Any code
which relies on reading from a shared memory before writing back an adjusted value can cause inconsistent state as

---

[2]If you discount the possibility of other code changing the floating point
operation mode

```
1  int shared = 0;
2  void foo() {
3    int a = shared;
4    a += RunSomeCalculation();
5    shared = a;
6  }
```

Listing 10.1: Very leaky shared value

```
1  int shared = 0;
2  Mutex sharedMutex;
3  void foo() {
4    sharedMutex.acquire();
5    int a = shared;
6    a += RunSomeCalculation();
7    shared = a;
8    sharedMutex.release();
9  }
```

Listing 10.2: Safer shared value

there is no way to guarantee the writing will take place before anyone else reads it before they modify it. Listing 10.1 shows a really poor example.

Making this work in practice is hard and expensive. The standard technique used to ensure the state is consistent is to make the value update atomic. How this is achieved depends on the hardware and the compiler. Most hardware has an atomic instruction that can be used to create thread-safety through mutual exclusions. On most hardware, the atomic instruction is a compare and swap, or CAS. Building larger tools for thread-safety from this has been the mainstay of multi-threaded programmers and operating system developers for decades, but with the advent of multi-core consoles, programmers not well versed in the potential pitfalls of multi-threaded development are suffering because of the learning cliff involved in making all their code work perfectly over six or more hardware threads.

Using mutual exclusions, it's possible to rewrite the first example. The code in listing 10.2 works a bit better, and will have fewer cases of unexpected change. This function

```
// directly modifying
int RunSomeCalculation() {
    int val = 4 + ++shared;
}

// indirectly modifying
int foo2() {
    sharedMutex.acquire();
    // oops, the base thread is the same, so reentrant or recursive
        lock doesn't block.
    shared += 1;
    sharedMutex.release();
    return shared;
}
int RunSomeCalculation() {
    int val = foo2() + 9;
}
```

Listing 10.3: Examples of how the mutexes can be circumvented

will now always finish its task without some other thread damaging its data via this same call. Every time one of the hardware threads encounters this code, it stops all processing until the mutex is acquired. Once it's acquired, no other hardware thread can enter into these instructions until the current thread releases the mutex at the far end. That is the only guarantee though, as it could be that RunSomeCalculation changes shared either directly or indirectly, or something changes shared without invoking the mutexes. See the examples in listing 10.3.

Every time a thread-safe function enters a mutex section, the whole machine needs to stop to do just one thing, that is, it needs to make sure it's allowed into that section of code by some atomic operation. At the time of writing, a mutex takes around 4 times as long as reading from L2 cache[3]. Every time you use a mutex, you make the code thread-safe by making it serial. Every time you use a mutex, to some extent, you make your code run badly on infinite core machines. If you frequently hit mutexes and stall, you're making it even worse. If nothing else, remember that by definition, a mutex

---

[3]You can see the figures on latency in Latency Numbers Every Programmer Should Know [16]

is itself shared state.

Thread-safe, therefore, is another way of saying: not concurrent, but won't break anything. Concurrency is when multiple threads are doing their thing without any mutex calls, semaphores, or other locking techniques which help maintain consistency by serialising tasks. Concurrent means at the same time. A lot of the problems solved by academics using thread-safety to develop their multi-threaded applications needn't be mutex bound. There are many ways to skin a cat, and many ways to avoid a mutex. Mutexes are only necessary when more than one thread shares write privileges on a piece of memory. If you can redesign your algorithms so they only ever require one thread to be given write privilege, then you can work towards a fully concurrent system.

Ownership is key to developing most concurrent algorithms. Concurrency only happens when the code cannot be in a bad state, not because it checks before doing work, but because the design is such that no process can interfere with another in any way.

## 10.2 Inherently concurrent operations

When working with tables of data, many operations are inherently concurrent. Transforms which take one table and generate the next step, such as those of physics systems or AI state such as finite state machines, are inherently concurrent. You could provide a core per row/element and there would be no issues at all. Setting up the local bone transforms from a skeletal animation data stream, ticking timers, producing condition values for later use in condition tables. All these are completely concurrent tasks. Anything which could be implemented as a pixel or vertex shader is inherently concurrent, which is why parallel processing languages such as shader models, do not cheaply allow for random write to memory and don't allow accumulators across elements.

Seeing that these operations are inherently concurrent, we can start to see it's possible to restructure our game from an end result perspective. We can use the idea of a structured query to help us find our critical path back to the game state. Many table transforms can be split up into much smaller pieces, possibly thinking along the lines of map reduce, bringing some previously serial operations into the concurrent solution set.

Any $N$ to $N$ transform is perfectly concurrent. Any $N$ to $<= N$ is perfectly concurrent, but depending on how you handle output NULLs, you could end up wasting memory. A reduce stage is necessary, but that could be managed by a gathering task after the main task has finished, or at least, after the first results have started coming in.

Any uncoupled transforms can be run concurrently. Ticking all the finite state machines can happen at the same time as updating the physics model and the graphics culling system building the next frame's render list. As long as all your different game state transforms are independent from each other's current output, they can be dependent on each other's original state and still maintain concurrency.

For example, the physics system can update while the renderer and the AI rely on the positions and velocities of the current frame. The AI can update while the animation system can rely on the previous set of states.

Multi-stage transforms, such as physics engine broad-phase, detection, reaction and resolution, will traditionally be run in series while the transforms inside each stage run concurrently. Standard solutions to these stages require all data has finished processing from each previous stage, but if you can find some splitting planes for the elements during the first stage, you can then remove temporal cohesion from the processing because you can know what is necessary for the next step and hand out jobs from finished subsets of each stage's results.

Concurrent operation assumes that each core operating on the data is free to access the data without interference, but there is a way that seemingly unconnected processes can end up getting in each other's way. Most systems have multiple layers of cache, and this is where the accident can happen.

## 10.3   Queues as gateways, and "Now"

When you don't know how many items you are going to get out of a transform, such as when you filter a table to find only the X which are Y, you need run a reduce on the output to make the table non-sparse. Doing this can be log(N) latent, that is pairing up rows takes serial time based on log(N). But, if you are generating more data than your input data, then you need to handle it very differently. Mapping a table out onto a larger set can be managed by generating into gateways, which once the whole map operation is over, can provide input to the reduce stage. The gateways are queues which are only ever written to by the Mapping functions, and only ever read by the gathering tasks such as Reduce. There is always one gateway per Map runtime. That way, there can be no sharing across threads. A Map can write that it has put up more data, and can set the content of that data, but it cannot delete it or mark any written data as having been read. The gateway manages a read head, which can be compared with the write head to find out if there are any waiting elements. Given this, a gathering gateway or reduce gateway can be made by cycling through all known gateways and popping any data from the gateway read heads. This is a fully concurrent technique and would be just as at home in variable CPU timing solutions as it is in standard programming practices as it implies a consistent state through ownership of their respective parts. A write will stall until the read has allowed space in the queue.  A read will either return "no data" or stall until the write head shows there is something more to read.

When it comes to combining all the data into a final output, sometimes it's not worth recombining it into a different shape, in which case we can just have an array of arrays.

Transforming an array of arrays maintains most of the efficiency of contiguous arrays. Arrays of arrays is a linear representation of data which allows for efficient storage of arbitrary lists of data. If we use arrays of arrays for input to transforms, we need to iterate over each subarray as a separate loop. In tests performed where an iterator was aware of the array of arrays, the fact it accesses the root structure created noise for the memory access requests enough to reduce the performance of the operations. In summary, it was better to keep the transform code simple and call the loop code recursively.

Moving away from transforms, there is the issue of *now* that crops up whenever we talk about concurrency. Sometimes, when you are continually updating data in real time, not per frame, but actual real time, there is no safe time to get the data or process it. Truly concurrent data analysis has to handle reading data which has literally only just arrived or is in the process of being retired. Data-oriented development helps us find a solution to this by not having a concept of now but a concept only of the data. If you are writing a network game, and you have a lot of messages coming in about a player, and their killers and victims, then to get accurate information about their state you have to wait until they are already dead. With a data-oriented approach, you only try to generate the information that is needed when it's needed. This saves trying to analyse packets to build some predicted state when the player is definitely not interesting, and gives more up to date information as it doesn't have to wait until the object representing the data has been updated before any of the most recent data can be seen or acted on.

The idea of now is present only in systems that are serial. There are multiple program counters when you have multiple cores, and when you have thousands of cores, there are thousands of different nows. Humans think of things happening at a certain time, but sometimes you can take so long doing something that more data has arrived by the time you're finished reacting to it, and that data can negate the result.

Take for example the idea of a game which tries to get the lowest possible latency between player control pad and avatar reaction on-screen. In a lot of games, you have to put up with the code reading the pad state, then the pad state being used to adjust animations, then the animations adjusting the renderables, then the rendering system rastering and finally, the raster system swapping buffers. An example is shown in diagram 10.1.

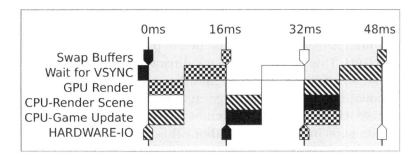

Figure 10.1: The effect of input can sometimes take three frames to be seen on screen

Many games have triple buffering and animation systems that don't update instantly. Some engines have extra buffering. Some engines submit a render frame based on current frame logic, shortening the pipeline.

In these cases, the player could potentially be left until the last minute before checking pad status and apply an emergency patch to the in-flight renderQueue. If you allowed a pad read to adjust the animation system's history rather than its current state, you could request that it update its historical commits to the render system, and potentially affect the next frame rather than the frame three buffer swaps from now. Alternatively, have some of the game run all potential player initiated events in parallel, then choose from the outcomes based on what really happened, then you can have the same response time but with less patching of data.

If all this sounds crazy and preposterous, then I have news for you. In the time since the first online version of this book and now, the development of VR headsets has brought about processes very similar to this. The first of the techniques developed by VR vendors works by creating a best guess at what will happen in the time between the start of rendering and the moment the visuals arrive on screen. This technique is used in almost all VR systems in some way, and is all about prediction, rather than low latency as such. After the rendering data is prepared, many vendors update the final camera matrices just before pushing commands to the GPU. This needs some slack during the visibility culling stage, so elements which might otherwise be culled in a traditional render pipeline are given a higher chance to appear, and so will make it into the render. Jerky head motion would create gaps in the render without this slack. Some vendors go another step further and commit to adjusting the copy to the screen to compensate for the change in head motion since the frame had finished being generated by the GPU. This transform is applied where we might normally do the swap buffers. Just before swapping, we render where the old head position would have rendered, in the frame of the new head position. This tiny last minute update reduces the latency down to a miniscule 3ms where it is being used. Finally, some vendors also update the final copying adjustment (sometimes called a reprojection) during the screen horizontal refresh, right along with the rolling shutter of the screen update. Doing this, or showing black frames between visible frames gives a much better persistence of vision effect than if they were to present an image and leave it there for the whole time available. All these kinds of last minute adjustment are the reason why watching the display of a VR headset can look odd unless you're actually wearing it, as the screen update is matching the head as its highest priority.

As technology moves forward, and we get wider bandwidth for processing, and more demand for lower latency, we will find other techniques to do more ahead of time. Just as CPUs waste time working on branches that were wrong, and cache lines load in more memory than we need, we are very likely to continue to do even more wasteful work in the future in the battle for lower latency and higher throughput.

# Chapter 11

# Finite State Machines

Turning data-driven processes into data-oriented solutions can seem difficult at times, as there are many ways in which algorithms designed by computer scientists can miss the reality of the hardware with which we now work. In many of the programming courses available, the attention is almost entirely on the algorithmic complexity and programs target abstract machines which don't have hardware backing their operations.

We also carry the burden of a language designed a long time ago, back when hardware was much simpler. You are programming with a language which has been extended, but is still rooted in C. Some choices made about the implementation of the language and supporting libraries were made with the hardware of the day as their main concern. Alexander Stepanov (designer of the C++ Standard Template Library) admits that hardware advances have had a big impact, and has said openly[1] that some decisions made when STL was first conceived, have negative consequences with today's hardware.

---

[1] In *Interviews: Alexander Stepanov and Daniel E. Rose Answer Your Questions* http://interviews.slashdot.org/story/15/01/19/159242/

Node-based data structures, which have low locality of reference, make much less sense. If I were
designing STL today, I would have a different set
of containers. For example, an in-memory B*-tree
is a far better choice than a red-black tree for implementing an associative container.

When you have little control over the data, such as in
scripting language support, you might need a completely
different approach, but with some techniques, there is a
way to migrate. In this chapter, we will take a well known,
highly data-driven programming technique and move to a
data-oriented approach. This is done to show how you can
analyse the required inputs and outputs and create a solution which is less wasteful than the original or traditional
form.

# What are they?

Finite state machines are a solid solution to many game logic
problems. They are one of the basic building blocks of a lot
of AI code and provide logical state frameworks for user interfaces. Notoriously convoluted finite state machines rule the
world of memory card operations and network lobbies, while
simple ones hold domain over point and click adventure puzzle logic. Finite state machines are highly data-driven in that
they react to what is sometimes called an alphabet of signals,
and change state based on both the signal received, and their
current state.

A finite state machine consists of a state, normally represented by an enum or an integer, sometimes a string, which
informs the system as a whole as to which events it is currently interested in. The events are sometimes referred to as
an alphabet. These can also be enums, integers, or strings.

The concept of an alphabet is more of a formal definition

of the translation than you will come across in much working code, and you will often see code that does its own checks, and then either continues on as normal or calls a state machine function to cause a state change. For now, think of the alphabet as the criteria upon which a transition should occur.

We have two sets of elements, and each relates to the other: the states, and the alphabet. You can think of how events are handled in a finite state machine as either having the alphabet elements linking states to each other or as states linking to new states by alphabet. The following example shows how a set of states (A, B, and C) transition to each other via an alphabet (d, e, and f).

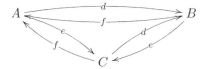

In some finite state machines, there are defined *end* states, which can simply be states that have no possible next state, as they don't respond to any event or alphabet entry.

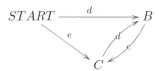

In some finite state machines, there are defined *start* states, which are just states that have no events leading to them.

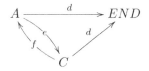

Finally, one state is selected as the starting point. This selected state does not have to be one of the *start* states, but once the first transition has occurred, no *start* states can be reached through the normal means of state transition.

It is common to implement simple artificial intelligence through a finite state machine. The state of the finite state machine represents a current plan of action for the entity, the events or alphabet can be driven by predefined sensors or queries about the world, and the choice of connections in the setup of the finite state machine make up the strategy of the AI. For example, a trivial AI to drive an NPC farmer could have states for being at home, heading to the fields, working the fields, and heading home. Sensors or queries to drive the alphabet could include things like what time of day it is, and the current position of the farmer.

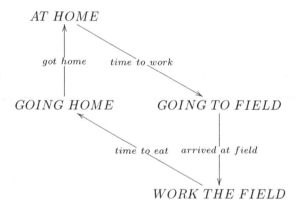

Starting at home, in the morning, when the time advances past the point where the farmer should be heading to the fields, that event can trigger the change of state to the heading-to-field state. The change of state could be used to create the path to the field, but the fact the farmer is in the heading-to-field state could be used to direct a passive movement and pathfinding system. Once the farmer has made it to the field, the state will change again, as the position of the farmer now matches the field, and the event of being at the field could be used to trigger the state change to working.

More complicated finite state machines are possible, including hierarchical finite state machines which include layers of action and reaction. As an example of a hierarchical finite state machine, consider a more complex entity, such as a guard of some sort. The guard has high-level states of *patrolling, investigating suspicious activity, chasing down a spotted intruder*. In the state of patrolling, the guard may have substates of *patrol, take a break, report in*. In the state of investigating, the guard may have substates of *move to suspicious location, look for evidence*. In the chasing state, the guard could have *following target in sight, going to last known location, guessing at where the target went, caught intruder and escort them where they need to go*. In each of the deeper states, the overall thought process of the AI is concentrated on that general plan, but the higher level state can be monitoring things such as how long it has been since the guard saw the intruder, whether there are any remaining areas to investigate, whether a sound was heard, or an intruder was seen. All these higher level triggers will be used to transition between the higher level states.

Finite state machines can be used for other logical progressions, such as resource streaming systems, user interfaces, and even maintaining the current state of the player character to change what they can and can't do. A player cannot shoot while they are reloading. A player cannot jump while they are in the air. Well, okay, they might be able to jump, but it would be a double jump, which is probably going to be handled differently anyway, so the statement still counts. Finite state machines can be used in a lot of different places and can replace a lot of conditional logic in our entity loops and updates.

It may be apparent at this stage, that finite state machines are useful, but are also inherently data-driven systems. Data-driven systems tend to be less organised around what is good for memory access, and finite state machines, with their state variables, do indeed request random memory for doing their alphabet checks based on their internal state and possibly on external state too. This leads to inefficiencies very similar to those present in virtual table lookup in C++.

When we think about finite state machines and data-oriented design, we might be thinking about using them to control a large number of entities simultaneously. Attempting to drive singular machines in a data-oriented approach can add a small benefit of making the system a little easier to debug, but this chapter is mostly about the benefits of migrating from an instance oriented data-driven approach to a way to utilise parallel execution, and the framework we will look at is one which is more easily tuned for throughput.

## 11.1   Tables as states

Finite state machines have another drawback which can be unclear when you begin to work with them, in that they represent a state of something. The problem is that the state is singular, not plural[2]. In some cases the problem is mitigated through hierarchical states, in other cases is it circumvented by introducing more states simultaneously, and in yet other cases, states are pushed onto a stack, so as to be able to return to them later. All these solutions provide techniques to get around the limitations of the core tenet of state being singular. If we could get around this limitation, then we may not need lots of clever techniques. The solution can be found in where the state is stored. The reason there is only one state at once is there is normally a single variable in which the state is held. When we free state from the confines of the container, in effect, having the state own the machine, not the machine owning the state, we expand the opportunities to create different numbers of simultaneous state as the out-

---

[2]Behaviour trees are a way around this problem as they can be implemented without a central state, but implicit state based on input alone

come of a transition. We can have states which lead to simultaneous states, or no state at all, or states which are aware of their child states, or states that know they need to return to another state, all within the same system, but defined by a data-driven process. Potentially new finite state machine techniques can be developed and implemented, without a call for new code to be written to handle the new technique.

If we wish to implement finite state machines without objects to contain them, and without state variables to instruct their flow, we can implement states as components of an entity. This could be seen as similar to the object-oriented approach to finite state machines. The object-oriented design pattern State prefers to have an object instance that represents the state of the machine, and allow the object instance to have its own state represented through member variables so it can keep track of information present when that state is current. These member variables lock the average object-oriented approach to a singular state, but moving the state from being a pointer in the instance, to the instancing being a pointer in the state isn't a great leap, and hence the comparison.

If you utilise the runtime dynamic polymorphism inherent in the data-oriented approach to component management, you can provide these characteristics based only on the existence of rows in tables. We do not need a state variable which would divert the flow according to internal state. We don't need an object to contain any state-dependent data for analysis of the alphabet.

At the fundamental level, a finite state machine requires a reaction to an alphabet. If we place the alphabet handling code in components that are mapped to states of a finite state machine, then we can either have these components destroy themselves and create new state components, or produce output tables of transitions which will be committed later. If each state is represented by an entry in a state table, and any entity in that state represented by a row existing in the state table, then we can run each state in turn, collecting any transitions in buffers, then committing these changes after everything has finished a single update step. If we wish to work in-place, then we need to do a little book-keeping, to ensure states don't bubble along the sequence of state updates (unless we actually want that) and we don't delete potentially needed states until all processing is complete.

In most games, finite state machines don't use an explicit alphabet to drive the state transitions, and we need to consider that too. When writing state behaviours, it's often the case that the behaviour itself will drive the state transition. This being the normal case of hand-rolled finite state machines, this is the version we profiled in the example code in listings 16.12, 16.13, and 16.14. Truly data-driven finite state machines and behaviour trees such as those used in commercial engines, the ones which drive scripts by behaviour, would seem like they could benefit from this technique too, but the hypothesis remains untested.

Finite state machines can be difficult to debug due to their data-driven nature. Data-driven code is normally harder to debug because the programmer cannot just look at the code to understand the program flow, but also has to follow the data that is being presented as well. Being able to move to an easier to debug framework should reduce development time. In the author's experience, being able to log all the transitions over time reduced some AI problems down to merely grepping through some logs before fixing an errant condition based only on an unexpected transition logged with its cause data.

Keeping the state as a table entry can also let the FSM do some more advanced work, such as managing level of detail or culling. If your renderables have a state of potentially visible, then you can run the culling checks on just these entities rather than those not even up for consideration this frame. Using collective lodding with FSMs allows for game flow logic such as allowing the triggering of a game state change to emit the state's linked entities, which could provide a good point for debugging any problems.

## 11.2 Implementing transitions

Canonical finite state machines normally have an input stream which modifies the internal state as fast as new signals arrive. This can lead to very fast state switching and is useful in some applications which don't have designated frames. In most game engines, finite state machines and other state transition systems normally work on a frame by frame basis, which can cause bugs and latency of its own, but for the sake of simplicity of explanation, it's the approach we're using here. Frame-based updates also maintain the parallelism we want. Table based finite state machines will only run one update based on all signals available at the time of the tick. There should be no fear that this is a limit of the system, as if there are more than one conditional responses matching the input state, then it is fine to continue to process any new states which have transpired, and it's still valid to go to more than one state at once as a result.

Consider the finite state machine in a point and click adventure, where the character has to find three objects. In most games, the logic would be defined as a single state waiting for all objects to be found. In a table driven finite state machine, you have a choice. Stick with the original approach, or there could be three different tables representing each of the objects, or three entries with data about which object it's waiting upon. While any table is populated, the game logic will not progress. You would make the decision about which technique to use based on whether there was normally only one agent, or if there were often more than a hundred, using judgement for the middle ground.

In a table driven finite state machine, the transition event approach can be implemented as inserts and deletes. If you

want to do in-place transitions, then the code that runs
on the elements of the tables would be set up to react to
the input signals, the alphabet, and would directly insert
and delete rows in other state tables. This means that in
both cases the finite state machine can react to multiple signals in a deterministic way because the state will not change
before it has finished processing all the possible condition
matches. There is no inherent temporal coupling in the transition queue design, and only some small changes are required to allow the direct approach to safely parallelise. Traditional finite state machines don't allow for multiple reactions at once as they transition from one state to another,
naturally reacting on the order of signals, which is perfect
for a finite state machine built for a lexer or parser, but possibly not for a generic gameplay state machine.

## 11.3   Condition tables as triggers

Sometimes a finite state machine transition has side effects.
Some purer alphabet driven finite state machines allow you
to add callbacks on transitions, so you can attach onEnter,
onExit, and onTransition effects. Because the state table
approach can have a natural rhythm of states to transition
requests to new states, it's simple to hook into any transition request table and add a little processing before the state
table row modifications are committed. Consider where normally you would have a transition for an AI going from asleep
to awake. When the manager of the table processes the entries to create the new awake state, it can also trigger any
*GetUp* animations or sound effects, but as a separate concern from the act of going from sleeping to waking. This idea
of decorating the transition is a powerful aspect brought into
object-oriented programming from the functional programming languages, but has always brought with it additional
hidden complexity. Adding it in as an aside during a commit
step in a transition from one state to another gives the deco-
rator an explicit location for processing and a natural place

to debug it.

You can use hooks for logging, telemetry, or game logic that is watching certain states. If you have a finite state machine for mapping input to player movement, it's important to have it react to a player state that adjusts the control method. For example, if the player has different controls when underwater, the onEnter of the inWater state table could change the player input mapping to allow for floating up or sinking down. It would also be a good idea to attach any oxygen-level gauge hooks here too. If there is meant to be a renderable for the oxygen-level, it should be created by the player entering the inWater state. It should also be hooked into the inWater onExit transition table, as it will probably want to reset or begin regenerating at that point.

Let's return to the guard. High-level states can have their own tables. When a guard has a state of patrolling, they will also have a state of doing the rounds, which, after that state feels like it's done enough, creates an entry on the taking a break state table, or creates a reporting in entry, which themselves, will push back and re-create a doing the rounds state when they are done. If a doing the rounds state notices something suspicious, it can push it up to the patrolling state as an event, and that state can handle the event. If the patrolling state thinks it's important it can change to investigating by deleting all subtable entries and adding a new suspicion state entry. If the patrolling state catches sight of the intruder, then that event can be sent up the same way. If the suspicious sighting seems unrelated to the noticed intruder, the suspicion state could be activated simultaneously or could be stacked on a pending state table, ready to return to once the chasing is over. When a high-level state changes, it needs to tell any substates that it is transitioning, and they can handle this either by stashing their state away into a memento or by merely deleting. For example, the suspicion state would want to remember what it had already investigated, so would stash away that information, but the chasing state would determine what to stash based on the outcome. If it had found the intruder, then it could dump all information about where the intruder has been and guesses of where they are, but if the state timed out, then the state could stash away, or even transfer potential suspicious locations to the suspicious state storage.

In addition to handling game AI, the same multi-state benefits apply to player input mapping. If the player is being asked to reload, and they want to change weapon instead, the reload state can be stashed away for that weapon, and if they switch back, the reload can be resumed. If you use a state variable, instead of an entry, then you may lose that information. Even down to simple common events such as jumping, the state of being on the ground would listen to the jump button differently from the state of being in the air, and double-jump could just be a state which is created from ground-jump. Ground-jump could be a state that times out on landing, or goes away on jump being pressed, as when the jump button is pressed it would be a second press of the jump button and would transition to double-jump.

One of the greatest benefits of being able to hook into states and transitions is being able to keep track of changes in game state for syncing. If you are trying to keep a network game synchronised, knowing exactly what happened and why can be the difference between a 5 minute and 5 day debugging session.

## 11.4  Double buffered finite state machines

You can implement finite state machines in a read-only mode, making the transitions only affect a future output buffer. If you have large states, with many pieces, then it can be beneficial to implement a copy on write state storage.

Normally, it's mentioned that global variables are bad,

and that the singleton pattern is just as bad, but it's not often mentioned how that also can be said of shared state via smart pointers. Large projects in the games industry overrun their schedule when using managed languages due to shared state, that state being the ownership of objects, that shared state causes memory leaks which are hard to track down. Why mention that here? To implement a low memory cost double buffered approach to your game, you only have one good choice, and that is to share data between frames or updates.

To share data between frames safely, you will need to guard against modifying state. One way to cleanly implement shared state is to allow for smart pointers to data that represent state, but immutably. Copying your game state from one frame to the next might seem like overkill, but if all you're doing is copying pointers to large state objects, then it's not so bad. State is then modified by creating a new state object from the old one, also constant, replacing the old state in the current frame. Doing this, it should be possible to create many more frames of historical data, which might be useful for your application or game as replay data, or undo states.

If you're going with double or more buffered, every state is considered, updated, then pushed out the other side, this means you will have very similar costs every single update.

As the input state is read-only, you can see exactly why and how an FSM got where it is. You can even build in the ability to re-run your application from an earlier point. You can then break into the code to see what happened, and what the inputs did to the machine.

As every machine state is copied to a final output buffer, this system costs a write for every machine, every update, regardless of whether there was a transition or not. If you can work with level of detail techniques, then the number of copies can be reduced to a more reasonable level.

As a final mitigation against unwanted copying, you can reduce the amount of state copied by creating different pace streams of state analysis. Adding entries to certain tables could be considered putting the machines to sleep, having them update and check to see if they need to return to full capacity in a less frequent cycle, but also, if you have different streams, some could be full copy read-only transforms, and others could be more traditional state migration in place.

# Chapter 12

# In Practice

Data-oriented development is not rooted in theory, but practice. Because of this, it's hard to describe the methodology without some practical examples. In this chapter, I will document some experiences with the data-oriented approach.

## 12.1  Data-manipulation

### 12.1.1  The Cube

In a strange game, at a startup with a rather famous founder, there was a call to handle a large amount of traffic from a large number of clients, potentially completely fragmented, and yet also completely synchronised. The plan was to develop a service capable of handling a large number of incoming packets of *update* data while also compiling it into compressed *output* data which could be sent to the client all with a minimal turnaround time.

The system was developed in C++11 on Linux and followed the basic tenets of data-oriented design from day one.

The data was loaded, but not given true context. Manipulations on the data were procedures that operated on the data given other data. This was a massive time saver when the servers needed a complete redesign. The speed of data processing was sufficient to allow us to run all the services in debug[1].

When the server went live, it wasn't the services that died, it was the login. Nginx is amazing, but under that amount of load on a single server, with so many of the requests requiring a lock on an SQL DB backend for Facebook integration, the machine reached its limit very quickly. For once, we think PHP itself wasn't to blame. We had to redesign all the services so they could work in three different situations so as to allow the server to become a distributed service. By not locking down data into contexts, it was relatively easy to change the way the data was processed, to reconfigure the single service that previously did all the data consumption, collation, and serving, into three different services which handled incoming data, merging the multiple instances, and serving the data on the instances. In part, this was due to a very procedural approach, but it was also down to data separation. The data, even between levels of detail, was not linked together or bound by an object context. The lack of binding allows for simpler recombination of procedures, simpler rewriting of procedures, and simpler repurposing of procedures from related services. This is something the object-oriented approach makes harder because you can be easily tempted to start adding base classes and inheriting to gain common functionality or algorithms. As soon as you do that, you start tying things together by what they mean rather than what they are, and then you lose the ability to reuse code.

---

[1] anyone remembering developing on a PS2 will likely attest to the minimal benefit you get from optimisations when your main bottleneck is the VU and GS. The same was true here, we had a simple bottleneck of the size of the data and the operations to run on it. Optimisations had minimal impact on processing speed, but they did impact our ability to debug the service when it did crash.

## 12.1.2 Rendering order

While working on the in-house engine at a small games company, we came up with an idea for how to reimplement the renderer that should have been much more efficient, not just saving CPU cycles, but also allowing for platform-specific optimisations at runtime by having the renderer analyse the current set of renderables and organise the whole list of jobs by what caused the least program changes, texture changes, constant changes and primitive render calls. The system seemed too good to be true, and though we tried to write the system, the company never finished it. After the company dissolved, when I did finish it, I didn't have access to a console[2], so I was only able to test out the performance on a PC. As expected the new system was faster, but only marginally. With hindsight, I now see that the engine was only marginally more efficient because the tests were being run on a system that would only see marginal improvements, but even the x86 architecture saw improvements, which can be explained away as slightly better control flow and generally better cache utilisation.

First, let me explain the old system.

All renderables came from a scene graph. There could be multiple scene graph renders per frame, which is how the 2D and 3D layers of the game were composited, and each of them could use any viewport, but most of them just used the fullscreen viewport as the engine hadn't been used for a split screen game, and thus the code was probably not working for viewports anyway. Each scene graph render to viewport would walk the scene[3] collecting transforms, materials, colour tints, and meshes, to render, at which point the node that contained the mesh would push a render element onto the queue for rendering into that viewport. This queue-

---

[2]The target platforms of the engine included the PlayStation2 and the Nintendo Wii along with Win32.

[3]sometimes multiple cameras belonged to the same scene and the scene graph would be walked multiple times

ing up of elements to render seemed simple and elegant at the time. It meant programmers could quickly build up a scene and render it, most of the time using helpers which loaded up the assets and generated the right nodes for setting textures, transforms, shader constants, and meshes. These rendering queues were then sorted before rendering. Sorted by material only for solid textures, and sorted back to front for alpha blended materials. This was the old days of fixed function pipelines and only minimal shader support on our target platforms. Once the rendering was done, all the calculated combinations were thrown away. This meant that for everything that was rendered, there was definitely a complete walk of the scene graph.

The new system, which was born before we were aware of data-oriented design, but was definitely born of looking at the data, was different in that it no longer required walking the scene graph. We wanted to maintain the same programmer friendly front edge API, so maintained the facade of a scene graph walk, but instead of walking the graph, we only added a new element to the rendering when the node was added, and only removed it when it was removed from the scene graph. This meant we had a lot of special code that looked for multiple elements registered in multiple viewport lists, but, other than that, a render merely looked up into the particular node it cared about, gathered the latest data, and processed it pulling when it required it rather than being pushed things it didn't even care about.

The new system benefited from being a simple list of pointers from which to fetch data (the concept of a dirty transform was removed, all transforms were considered to be dirty every frame), and the computation was simplified for sorting as all the elements that were solid were already sorted from the previous render, and all the alpha blended elements were sorted because they belonged to the set of alpha blended elements. This lack of options accounted for some saved time, but the biggest saving probably came from the way the data was being gathered per frame rather than being generated from an incoherent tree. A tree that, to traverse, required many pointer lookups into virtual tables as all the nodes were base classed to a base node type and all update and render calls were virtual causing many misses all the way through each of the tree walks.

In the end, the engine was completely abandoned as the company dissolved, but it was the first time we had taken an existing codebase and (though inadvertently) converted it to data-oriented.

## 12.1.3 Keeping track of damage

During the development of a AAA multiplayer code base there came a point where it became more and more important that we kept track of damage dealt to every player from every player. Sometimes this would be because we want to estimate more accurately how much health a player had. Sometimes this would be because we needed to know who saved who and thus who got a teammate saved bonus, or who got the assist. We kept a tight ship on the game, we tried to keep the awards precise as far as we could go, no overcompensating for potentially lost packets. There was no faking because we wanted a fair and competition grade experience where players could make all the difference through skill, not through luck.

To do this, we needed to have a system that kept track of all the bullets fired, but not fail when we missed some, or when they arrived out of order. What we needed was a system which could be interrogated at any point, but could receive data about things that had happened out of order, in effect re-writing the past. It needed to be able to heal itself in case of oddities, and last but not least, it needed to be really quick so we could query it many times per frame.

The solution was built as a simple list of things that happened and at what time. Initially, the data was organised as a list of structures with a sorted list of pointers to the data for quick queries about events over time, but after profiling the queries with and without the sorted list, it was clear the cost of maintaining a sorted list outweighed the benefits. Doing a one time sort on the data only when needed to satisfy a query was better. There were only two queries which benefited from the sorted data, and they were not called frequently. When they were called, they didn't need to be extremely fast as they were called as the result of player death. Death not only happened less often than once a frame, but also regularly resulted in there being less to update as the player cared a lot less about visibility checks and handling network traffic[4]. This simple design allowed for many different queries to run over the core data, and allowed for anyone to add another new query easily because there was no data-hiding getting in the way of any new kind of access. Object-oriented approaches to this kind of data handling often provide a gateway to the data but marshal it so the queries become heavyweight and consistently targeted for optimisation. With a very simple data structure and open access to the data in any form, any new query could be as easily optimised as an existing one.

## 12.2  Game entities

### 12.2.1  Converting an object-oriented player

While working on a little space game which ended up being a boat game in caverns[5] and it was the first time I intentionally changed a game from object-oriented to component-oriented. The ships all had their rendering positions, their health, speed, momentum, ammo recharge timers etc, and

---

[4]dead men don't care about bullets and don't really care that much about what other players are doing for a few frames

[5]due to concerns that a 2D space game might be misinterpreted as the next title by the company I was working for at the time

these were all part of a base ship class which was extended to be a player class, and inherited from a basic element which was extended to also include the loot drops and the dangerous ice blocks. All this is pretty standard practice, and from the number of codebases I have seen, it's pretty light on the scale of inheritance with which games normally end up. Still, I had this new tool in my bag, the component-oriented approach, and specifically existential processing. I wanted to try it out, see if it really did impact the profile of the game in any significant way. I started with the health values. I made a new component for health, and anyone who was at full health, or was dead, was not given an instance of the component. The player ship and the enemy ships all had no health values until they were shot and found wanting.

Transitioning to the component based health took a while. Translating any game from one programming paradigm to another is not a task to be taken lightly, even when your game code is small and you've only spent sixty hours developing the game so far. Once the game was back up though, the profile spoke loud and clear of the benefits. I had previously spent some time in health code every frame, this was because the ships had health regenerators which ran and updated the health every time they got an update poll. They needed to do an update because they were updated, not because they needed to, and they didn't have any way to opt out before the componentisation, as the update to health was part of the ship update. Now the health update only ran over the active health instances and removed itself once it reached max health rather than bounce off the max health.

This relatively small change allowed me to massively increase the number of small delicate ships in the game (ships which would beat the player ship by overrunning it rather than being able to withstand the player's fire and get close in to do some damage), and also lead to another optimisation: componentising the weapon recharge timer.

If the first change was a success, then the second was a

major success. Instead of keeping track of when a weapon
was ready to fire again, the time it would become available
was inserted into a sorted list of recharge times. Only the
head of the list was checked every global update, meaning
a large number of weapons could be recharging at once and
none of them caused any data access until they were very
nearly or actually ready.

This immediate success led me to believe the data-
oriented design movement was really important and needed
to be spread around, and probably caused my sudden dis-
trust of object-oriented programming. From that point
on, all I could see was cache-misses and pointless update
checks.

## 12.2.2   People don't really exist.

*A Mathematician, a Biologist and a Physicist are sitting
in a street cafe watching people going in and coming out
of the house on the other side of the street.*

*First, they see two people going into the house. Time
passes. After a while they notice three persons coming
out of the house.*

*The Physicist: "The measurement wasn't accurate.".*
*The Biologists conclusion: "They have reproduced".*
*The Mathematician: "If now exactly 1 person enters the
house then it will be empty again."*

The followers in an infamous god game were little objects when they were running around, and though the code
changed quite a bit from the initial lists of pointers to people
structures, and thus became unwieldy, there was one element that was a perfect example of hierarchical level of detail in the game logic. The followers, once they had started to
build a building, disappeared. They were no longer required
in any way, so they were reduced to a mere increment of
the number of people in a building. An object-oriented programmer disputed this being a good way to go, "but what if
the person has a special weapon, or is a special character?".
Logic prevailed. If there was a special weapon, I explained,
then there would have been a count of those in the house,

or the weapon would have become owned by the house, and
as for a special character, the same kind of exception could
be made, but in reality, which is where we firmly plant ourselves when developing in the data-oriented paradigm, these
potential changes had not yet been requested. By the end of
the development, they still hadn't.

Another example from the god game prototype was the
use of duck-typing. Instead of adding a base class for people
and houses, just to see if they were meant to be under control
of the local player, we used a function template to extract a
boolean value. Duck typing doesn't require anything more
than certain member functions or variables being available.
They don't have to be in the same place, or come bundled
into a base class: they just have to be present.

When teaching data-oriented design, I find the biggest
hurdle is convincing programmers that data-oriented design
is possible for some areas of development. It's very easy
to accidentally assume you need to bundle things into objects, especially after years of training and teaching object-
oriented development. It won't come naturally and you will
keep catching yourself building things as objects first then
making them more relational afterwards. It will take time to
fully remove the muscle memory of putting related things in
the same class, but worry not, I'm sure all data-oriented developers go through this transition where they know they're
not coding data-oriented, but they don't quite know how to
do it yet.

### 12.2.3  Lazy evaluation molasses

The idea of lazy evaluation makes so much sense, and yet
it's precisely that kind of sense that makes little sense for a
computer. I remember there was a dirty bit check before an
update in some of the global update code on an open world
$3^{rd}$ person shooter, something I would have done a hundred
times over before I started to get a better feel for what the

computer was doing, and found one of the best lines-of-code to time-saved ratio fixes I ever found in a triple A game. The dirty bit check was just before the code that actually did the work of updating the instance. This meant the CPU had to preload the *fixup* code while it was checking the dirty bit, and because the fixup code was virtual functions based, it meant the code was loading the virtual table value and the function was preloaded all the while the dirty bit was about to say it wasn't necessary to do any of it. To make matters worse, the code was inside an if, implying to most compilers that it would be the more likely taken branch[6]. The fix was simple. Build up a local array of objects to actually do an update of, then do them all at once. Because the code to do the update wasn't preloaded, the whole update took a lot less time. You can have your lazy evaluation, but don't preload the work to do by accident if you don't have to.

## 12.2.4   Component-oriented design

While at a small games company, I found an article about Dungeon Seige proclaiming the benefit of components when developing a game. The GOs or Game Objects which were used were components that could be stitched together to create new compound objects.

Taking that as inspiration, I looked at all our different scene-graph nodes, gameplay helper classes and functions we commonly used and tried to distil them into their elements. I started by just making components such as *PlayerCharacter* and *AICharacter*, adding a *Prop* element before realising where I was going wrong. The object-oriented mindset had told me to look at the compounds, not the elements, so I went back to the drawing board and started dissecting the objects again. Component-oriented development works out best when you completely explode all your compounds,

---

[6]profile guided optimisation might have saved a lot of time here, but the best solution is to give the profiler and optimiser a better chance by leaving them less to do

then recombine when you find the combinations are consistent, or when combining makes more sense to computation.

After I was done fully dissecting our basic game classes I had a long list of separate, elements which by themselves did very little[7]. At this point, I added the bootstrap code to generate the scene. Some components required other components at runtime, so I added a *requires* trait to the components, much like #include, except to make this work for teardown, I also added a count so components went away much like reference counted smart pointers folded away. The initial demo was a simple animated character running around a 3D environment, colliding with props via the collision Handler.

In the beginning, I had a container entity which maintained a list of components. Once I had a first working version, I stepped back and thought about the system. I started to see that the core entity wasn't really necessary. As long as any update components were updated, then the game would tick on. As long as the entity's components could find their requirement components, then the game would work. I shifted to having an implicit entity based on the UID I generate on entity creation. This meant all entities were really only the components that were linked to that ID, as the ID didn't index into an array of entity objects, or point to an allocated entity, it was merely an ID off which to hang all the components.

Adding features to a class at runtime was now possible. I could inject an additional property into the existing entities because I had centred the entities around a key, and not any kind of central class. The next step from here was to add components via a scripting language so it would be possible to develop new gameplay code while running the game. Unfortunately, this never happened, but some MMO engine developers have done precisely this.

---

[7]Position, Velocity, PlayerInputMapper, VelocityFromInput, MeshRender, SkinnedMeshRender, MatrixPalette, AnimPlayer, AnimFromInput, and CollisionHandler, to name a few.

The success of this demo convinced me that components would play a major role in our continuing game development, but alas, we only used the engine for one more product and the time to bring the new component-based system up to speed for the size of the last project was estimated to be counterproductive. Mick West released an article about how when he was at Neversoft, he did manage to convert the Tony Hawks code-base to components[8] which means it's not impossible to migrate, it's just not easy. If we were to start component-oriented... well that's a different story, normally told by Scott Bilas.

---

[8]http://cowboyprogramming.com/2007/01/05/evolve-your-heirachy/

# Chapter 13

# Maintenance and reuse

When object-oriented design was first promoted, it was said to be easier to modify and extend existing code bases than the more traditional procedural approach. Though it is not true in practice, it is often cited by object-oriented developers when reading about other programming paradigms. Regardless of their level of expertise, an object-oriented programmer will very likely cite the extensible, encapsulating nature of object-oriented development as a boon when it comes to working on larger projects.

Highly experienced but more objective developers have admitted or even written about how object-oriented C++ is not highly suited to big projects with lots of dependencies, but can be used as long as you follow strict guidelines such as those found in the *Large-scale C++* book[2]. For those who cannot immediately see the benefit of the data-oriented development paradigm with respect to maintenance and evolutionary development, this chapter covers why it is easier than working with objects.

# 13.1   Cosmic hierarchies

Whatever you call them, be it Cosmic Base Class, Root of all Evil, Gotcha #97, or CObject, having a base class that everything derives from has pretty much been a universal failure point in large C++ projects. The language does not naturally support introspection or duck typing, so it has difficulty utilising CObjects effectively. If we have a database driven approach, the idea of a cosmic base class might make a subtle entrance right at the beginning by appearing as the entity to which all other components are adjectives about, thus not letting anything be anything other than an entity. Although component–based engines can often be found sporting an EntityID as their owner, not all require owners. Not all have only one owner. When you normalise databases, you find you have a collection of different entity types. In our level file example, we saw how the objects we started with turned into a MeshID, TextureID, RoomID, and a PickupID. We even saw the emergence through necessity of a DoorID. If we pile all these Ids into a central EntityID, the system should work fine, but it's not a necessary step. A lot of entity systems do take this approach, but as is the case with most movements, the first swing away from danger often swings too far. The balance is to be found in practical examples of data normalisation provided by the database industry.

# 13.2   Debugging

The prime causes of bugs are the unexpected side effects of a transform or an unexpected corner case where a conditional didn't return the correct value. In object-oriented programming, this can manifest in many ways, from an exception caused by de-referencing a null, to ignoring the interactions of the player because the game logic hadn't noticed it was meant to be interactive.

Holding the state of a system in your head, and *playing computer* to figure out what is going on, is where we get the idea that programmers absolutely need to be in the zone to get any real work done. The reality is probably far less thrilling. The reality is closer to the fear that programmers only need to be in the zone if the code is nearing deadly levels of complexity.

## 13.2.1 Lifetimes

One of the most common causes of the null dereference is when an object's lifetime is handled by a separate object to the one manipulating it. For example, if you are playing a game where the badguys can die, you have to be careful to update all the objects that are using them whenever the badguy gets deleted, otherwise, you can end up dereferencing invalid memory which can lead to dereferencing null pointers because the class has destructed. Data-oriented development tends towards this being impossible as the existence of an entity in an array implies its processability, and if you leave part of an entity around in a table, you haven't deleted the entity fully. This is a different kind of bug, but it's not a crash bug, and it's easier to find and kill as it's just making sure that when an entity is destroyed, all the tables it can be part of also destroy their elements too.

## 13.2.2 Avoiding pointers

When looking for data-oriented solutions to programming problems, we often find pointers aren't required, and often make the solution harder to scale. Using pointers where null values are possible implies each pointer doesn't only have the value of the object being pointed at, but also implies a boolean value for whether or not the instance exists. Removing this unnecessary extra feature can remove bugs, save time, and reduce complexity.

```
bool SingleReturn( int numDucks ) {
  bool valid = true;
  // must be 10 or fewer ducks.
  if( numDucks > 10 ) valid = false;
  // number of ducks should be even.
  valid = ( numDucks & 1 ) == 0;
  // can't have negative ducks.
  if( numDucks < 0 ) valid = false;
  return valid;
}
bool RecursiveCheck( Node * node  ) {
  bool valid = true;
  if( node ) {
    valid = node->Valid();
    valid &= RecursiveCheck( node->sibling );
    valid &= RecursiveCheck( node->child );
  }
  return valid;
}
```

Listing 13.1: Modifying state can shadow history

## 13.2.3  Bad State

Bugs have a lot to do with not being in the right state. Debugging, therefore, becomes a case of finding out how the game got into its current, broken state.

Whenever you assign a value to a variable, you are destroying history. Take the example in listing 13.1. The ideal of having only one return statement in a function can cause this kind of error with greater frequency than expected. Having more than one return point has its own problems. What's important is once you have got to the end of the function, it's hard to figure out what it was that caused it to fail validation. You can't even breakpoint the bail points. The recursive example is even more dangerous, as there's a whole tree of objects and it will recurse through all of them before returning, regardless of value, and again, is impossible to breakpoint.

When you encapsulate your state, you hide internal changes. This quickly leads to adding lots of debugging logs. Instead of hiding, data-oriented suggests keeping data in simple forms. Potentially, leaving it around longer than required can lead to highly simplified transform inspection. If you have a transform that appears to work, but for one odd case it doesn't, the simplicity of adding an assert and not deleting the input data can reduce the amount of guess-work and toil required to generate the reproduction required to understand the bug and make a clean fix. If you keep most of your transforms as one-way, that is to say, they take from one source, and produce or update another, then even if you run the code multiple times it will still produce the same results as it would have the first time. The transform is idempotent. This useful property allows you to find a bug symptom, then rewind and trace through the causes without having to attempt to rebuild the initial state.

One way of keeping your code idempotent is to write your transforms in a single assignment style. If you operate with multiple transforms but all leading to predicated join points, you can guarantee yourself some timings, and you can look back at what caused the final state to turn out like it did without even rewinding. If your conditions are condition tables, just leave the inputs around until validity checks have been completed then you have the ability to go into any live system and check how it arrived at that state. This alone should reduce any investigation time to a minimum.

## 13.3  Reusability

A feature commonly cited by the object-oriented developers which seems to be missing from data-oriented development is reusability. The idea that you won't be able to take already written libraries of code and use them again, or on multiple projects, because the design is partially within the implementation. To be sure, once you start optimising your code to the particular features of a software project, you do end up with code which cannot be reused. While developing data-oriented projects, the assumed inability to reuse source code would be significant, but it is also highly unlikely. The truth is found when considering the true meaning of reusability.

Reusability is not fundamentally concerned with reusing source files or libraries. Reusability is the ability to maintain an investment in information, or the invention of more vocabulary with which to communicate intention, such as with the STL, or with other libraries of structural code. In the primary example of reuse as sequences of actions, this is a wealth of knowledge for the entity that owns the development IP and is very nearly what patents are built on. In the latter, the vocabulary is often stumbled upon, rather than truly invented.

Copyright law has made it hard to see what resources have value in reuse, as it maintains the source as the object of its discussion rather than the intellectual property represented by the source. The reason for this is that ideas cannot be copyrighted, so by maintaining this stance, the copyrighter keeps hold of this tenuous link to a right to withhold information. Reusability comes from being aware of the information contained within the medium it is stored. In our case, it is normally stored as source code, but the information is not the source code. With object-oriented development, the source can be adapted (adapter pattern) to any project we wish to venture. However, the source is not the information. The information is the order and existence of tasks that can and will be performed on the data. Viewing the information this way leads to an understanding that any reusability a programming technique can provide comes down to its mutability of inputs and outputs. Its willingness to adapt a set of temporally coupled tasks into a new usage framework is how you can find out how well it functions reusably.

In object-oriented development, you apply the information inherent in the code by adapting a class that does the job, or wrapper it, or use an agent. In data-oriented development, you copy the functions and schema and transform into and out of the input and output data structures around the time you apply the information contained in the data-oriented transform.

Even though, at first sight, data-oriented code doesn't appear as reusable on the outside, the fact is, it maintains the same amount of information in a simpler form, so it's more reusable as it doesn't carry the baggage of related data or functions like object-oriented programming, and doesn't require complex transforms to generate the input and extract from the output like procedural programming tends to generate due to the normalising.

Duck typing, not normally available in object-oriented programming due to a stricter set of rules on how to interface between data, can be implemented with templates to great effect, turning code which might not be obviously reusable into a simple strategy, or a sequence of transforms which can be applied to data or structures of any type, as long as they maintain a naming convention.

The object-oriented C++ idea of reusability is a mixture of information and architecture. Developing from a data-oriented transform centric viewpoint, architecture just seems like a lot of fluff code. The only good architecture that's worth saving is the actualisation of data-flow and transform. There are situations where an object-oriented module can be used again, but they are few and far between because of the inherent difficulty interfacing object-oriented projects with each other.

The most reusable object-oriented code appears as interfaces to agents into a much more complex system. The best example of an object-oriented approach that made everything easier to handle, that was highly reusable, and was fully encapsulated was the FILE type from stdio.h which is used as an agent into whatever the platform and OS would need to open, access, write, and read to and from a file on the system.

## 13.4   Reusable functions

Apart from the freedom of extension when it comes to keeping all your data in simple linear arrangements, there is also an implicit tendency to turn out accidentally reusable solutions to problems. This is caused by the data being formatted much more rigidly, and therefore when it fits, can almost be seen as a type of duck-typing. If the data can fit a transform, a transform should be able to act on it. Some would argue, just because the types match, it doesn't mean the function will create the expected outcome, but in addition to this being avoidable by not reusing code you don't understand, in some cases, all you need is to know the signature to understand the transform. As an extreme example, it's possible to understand a fair number of Haskell functions purely based on their arguments. Finally, because the code becomes much more penetrable, it takes less time to look at what a transform is doing before committing to reusing it in your own code.

Because the data is built in the same way each time, handled with transforms and always being held in the same types of container, there is a very good chance there are multiple design agnostic optimisations which can be applied to many parts of the code. General purpose sorting, counting, searches and spatial awareness systems can be attached to new data without calling for OOP adapters or implementing interfaces so *Strategies* can run over them. This is why it's possible to have generalised query optimisations in databases, and if you start to develop your code this way, you can carry your optimisations with you across more projects.

# 13.5 Unit testing

Unit testing can be very helpful when developing games, but because of the object-oriented paradigm making programmers think about code as representations of objects, and not as data transforms, it's hard to see what can be tested. Linking together unrelated concepts into the same object and requiring complex setup state before a test can be carried out, has given unit testing a stunted start in games as object-oriented programming caused simple tests to be hard to write. Making tests is further complicated by the addition of the non-obvious nature of how objects are transformed when they represent entities in a game world. It can be very hard to write unit tests unless you've been working with them for a while, and the main point of unit tests is that someone who doesn't fully grok the system can make changes without falling foul of making things worse.

Unit testing is mostly useful during refactorings, taking a game or engine from one code and data layout into another one, ready for future changes. Usually, this is done because the data is in the wrong shape, which in itself is harder to do if you normalise your data as you're more likely to have left the data in an unconfigured form. There will obviously be times when even normalised data is not sufficient, such as when the design of the game changes sufficient to render the original data-analysis incorrect, or at the very least, ineffective or inefficient.

Unit testing is simple with data-oriented technique because you are already concentrating on the transform. Generating tables of test data would be part of your development, so leaving some in as unit tests would be simple, if not part of the process of developing the game. Using unit tests to help guide the code could be considered to be partial following the test-driven development technique, a proven good way to generate efficient and clear code.

Remember, when you're doing data-oriented development

your game is entirely driven by stateful data and stateless transforms.  It is very simple to produce unit tests for your transforms.  You don't even need a framework, just an input and output table and then a comparison function to check the transform produced the right data.

## 13.6  Refactoring

During refactoring, it's always important to know you've not broken anything by changing the code.  Allowing for such simple unit testing gets you halfway there.  Another advantage of data-oriented development is that, at every turn, it peels away the unnecessary elements.  You might find refactoring is more a case of switching out the order of transforms than changing how things are represented.  Refactoring normally involves some new data representation, but as long as you build your structures with normalisation in mind, there's going to be little need of that.  When it is needed, tools for converting from one schema to another could be written once and used many times.

It might come to pass, as you work with normalised data, that you realise the reason you were refactoring so much in the first place, was that you had embedded meaning in the code by putting the data in objects with names, and methods that did things to the objects, rather than transformed the data.

# Chapter 14

# What's wrong?

What's wrong with object-oriented design? Where's the harm in it?

Over the years, game developers have fallen into a style of C++ that is so unappealing to hardware that the managed languages don't seem all that much slower in comparison. The pattern of usage of C++ in game development was so appallingly mismatched to the hardware of the PlayStation 3 and Xbox 360 generation, it is no wonder an interpreted language is only in the region of 50% slower under normal use and sometimes faster[1] in their specialist areas. What is this strange language that has embedded itself into the minds of C++ game developers? What is it that makes the fashionable way of coding games one of the worst ways of making use of the machines we're targeting? Where, in essence, is the harm in game-development style object-oriented C++?

Some of this comes from the initial interpretation of what object-oriented means, as game developers tended to believe that object-oriented meant you had to map instances of ev-

---

[1]http://keithlea.com/javabench/ tells the tale of the server JVM being faster than C++. There are some arguments against the results, but there are others backing it up. Read, make up your own mind.

erything you cared about into the code as instances of objects. This form of object-oriented development could be interpreted as instance-oriented development, and it puts the singular unique entity ahead of the program as a whole. When put this way, it is easier to see some of the problems that can arise. Performance of an individual is very hard to decry as poor, as object methods are hard to time accurately, and unlikely to be timed at all. When your development practices promote individual elements above the program as a whole, you will also pay the mental capacity penalty, as you have to consider all operations from the point of view of the actors, with their hidden state, not from a point of view of value semantics.

Another issue is it appears that performance has not been ignored by the language designers, but potentially instead it has been tested for quality in isolation. This could be because the real world uses of C++ are quite different from the expectation of the library providers, or it could be the library providers are working to internal metrics instead of making sure they understand their customer. It's the opinion of the author, when developing a library, or a set of templates for use in C++, it shouldn't just be possible to tune performance out of the code you are using, it should come as default. If you make it possible to tune performance, you trade features for understanding and performance. This is a poor trade for game developers, but has been accepted, as the benefit of a common language is a very tempting offer.

## 14.1   The harm

*Claim: Virtuals don't cost much, but if you call them a lot it can add up.*
*aka - death by a thousand paper cuts*

The overhead of a virtual call is negligible under simple inspection. Compared to what you do inside a virtual call, the extra dereference required seems petty and very likely not to have any noticeable side effects other than the cost of a dereference and the extra space taken up by the virtual table pointer. The extra dereference before getting the pointer to the function we want to call on this particular instance seems to be a trivial addition, but let's have a closer look at what is going on.

A class that has derived from a base class with virtual methods has a certain structure to it. Adding any virtual methods to a class instantly adds a virtual table to the executable, and a virtual table pointer as the implicit first data member of the class. There is very little way around this. It's allowed in the language specification for the data layout of classes to be up to the compiler to the point where they can implement such things as virtual methods by adding hidden members and generating new arrays of function pointers behind the scenes. It is possible to do this differently, but it appears most compilers implement virtual tables to store virtual method function pointers. It's important to remember virtual calls are not an operating system level concept, and they don't exist as far as the CPU is concerned, they are just an implementation detail of C++.

When we call a virtual method on a class we have to know what code to run. Normally we need to know which entry in the virtual table to access, and to do that we read the first data member in order to access the right virtual table for calling. This requires loading from the address of the class into a register and adding an offset to the loaded value. Every non-trivial virtual method call is a lookup into a table, so in the compiled code, all virtual calls are really function pointer array dereferences, which is where the offset comes in. It's the offset into the array of function pointers. Once the address of the real function pointer is generated, only then can instruction decoding begin. There are ways to not call into the virtual table, notably with C++11, there has been some progress with the `final` keyword that can help as classes that cannot be overridden can now know that if they call

```
 1  #include <stdio.h>
 2
 3  class B {
 4    public:
 5    B() {}
 6    virtual ~B() {}
 7    virtual void Call() { printf( "Base\n" ); }
 8    void LocalCall() {
 9      Call();
10    }
11  };
12
13  class D final : public B {
14    public:
15    D() {}
16    ~D() {}
17    virtual void Call() { printf( "Derived\n" ); }
18    void LocalCall() {
19      Call();
20    }
21  };
22
23  B *pb;
24  D *pd;
25
26  int main() {
27    D *d = new D;
28    pb = pd = d;
29
30    pb->LocalCall();
31    // prints "Derived" via virtual call
32    pd->LocalCall();
33    // prints "Derived" via direct call
34  }
```

Listing 14.1: A simple derived class

into themselves, then they can call functions directly. This doesn't help for polymorphic calls, or call sites that access the methods from the interface without knowing the concrete type (see listing 14.1), but it can occasionally help with some idioms such as private implementation (pImpl), and the curiously recurring template pattern.

For multiple inheritance it is slightly more convoluted, but basically, it's still virtual tables, but now each function will define which class of vtable it will be referencing.

So let's count up the actual operations involved in this method call: first we have a load, then an add, then another load, then a branch. To almost all programmers this doesn't seem like a heavy cost to pay for runtime polymorphism. Four operations per call so you can throw all your game entities into one array and loop through them updating, rendering, gathering collision state, spawning off sound effects. This seems to be a good trade-off, but it was only a good trade-off when these particular instructions were cheap.

Two out of the four instructions are loads, which don't seem like they should cost much, but unless you hit a nearby cache, a load takes a long time and instructions take time to decode. The add is very cheap[2], to modify the register value to address the correct function pointer, but the branch is not always cheap as it doesn't know where it's going until the second load completes. This could cause an instruction cache miss. All in all, it's common to see a chunk of time wasted due to a single virtual call in any significantly large scale game. In that chunk of time, the floating point unit alone could have finished naïvely calculating lots of dot products, or a decent pile of square roots. In the best case, the virtual table pointer will already be in memory, the object type the same as last time, so the function pointer address will be the same, and therefore the function pointer will be in cache too, and in that circumstance it's likely the branch won't stall as the instructions are probably still in the cache too. But this best case is not always the common case for all types of data.

Consider the alternative, where your function ends, and you are returning some value, then calling into another function. The order of instructions is fairly well known, and to the CPU looks very similar to a straight line. There are no deviations from getting instructions based on just following the program counter along each function in turn. It's possible to guess quite far ahead the address of any new functions that will be called, as none of them are dependent on data. Even with lots of function calls, the fact they are deducible at compile time makes them easy to prefetch, and pretranslate.

---

[2]Adding to a register before accessing memory is free on most platforms

The implementation of C++ doesn't like how we iterate over objects. The standard way of iterating over a set of heterogeneous objects is to literally do that, grab an iterator and call the virtual function on each object in turn. In normal game code, this will involve loading the virtual table pointer for each and every object. This causes a wait while loading the cache line, and cannot easily be avoided. Once the virtual table pointer is loaded, it can be used, with the constant offset (the index of the virtual method), to find the function pointer to call, however, due to the size of virtual functions commonly found in game development, the table won't be in the cache. Naturally, this will cause another wait for load, and once this load has finished, we can only hope the object is actually the same type as the previous element, otherwise, we will have to wait some more for the instructions to load.

Even without loads, not knowing which function will be called until the data is loaded means you rely on a cache line of information before you can be confident you are decoding the right instructions.

The reason virtual functions in games are large is that game developers have had it drilled into them that virtual functions are okay, as long as you don't use them in tight loops, which invariably leads to them being used for more architectural considerations such as hierarchies of object types, or classes of solution helpers in tree-like problem-solving systems (such as pathfinding, or behaviour trees).

Let's go over this again: many developers now believe the best way to use virtuals is to put large workloads into the body of the virtual methods, so as to mitigate the overhead of the virtual call mechanism. [3] However, doing this, you can virtually guarantee not only will a large portion of the instruction and data cache be evicted by each call to update(), but most branch predictor slots may become dirty too, and fail to offer any benefit when the next update() runs. As-

---

[3]There are parallels with task systems, where you want to mitigate the cost of setup and tear down of tasks.

suming virtual calls don't add up because they are called on high-level code is fine until they become the general programming style, leading to developers failing to think about how they affect the application, ultimately leading to millions of virtual calls per second. All those inefficient calls are going to add up and impact the hardware, but they hardly ever appear on any profiles. The issue isn't that it's not there, it's that it's spread thinly over the whole of the processing of the machine. They always appear somewhere in the code being called.

Carlos Bueno's book *Mature Optimization Handbook*[17], talks about how it's very easy to miss the real cause of slowness by blindly following the low hanging fruit approach. This is where the idea of creating a hypothesis can prove useful, as when it turns out to not reap the expected rewards, you can retrace and regroup faster. For Facebook, they traced what was causing evictions and optimised those functions, not for speed, but to remove as much as possible the chance that they evicted other data from the cache.

In C++, classes' virtual tables store function pointers by their class. The alternative is to have a virtual table for each function and switch function pointer on the type of the calling class. This works fine in practice and does save some of the overhead as the virtual table would be the same for all the calls in a single iteration of a group of objects. However, C++ was designed to allow for runtime linking to other libraries, libraries with new classes that may inherit from the existing codebase. The design had to allow a runtime linked class to add new virtual methods, and have them callable from the original running code. If C++ had gone with function oriented virtual tables, the language would have had to runtime patch the virtual tables whenever a new library was linked, whether at link-time for statically compiled additions, or at runtime for dynamically linked libraries. As it is, using a virtual table per class offers the same functionality but doesn't require any link-time or runtime modification to the virtual tables as the tables are oriented by the classes, which by the language design are immutable during link-time.

Combining the organisation of virtual tables and the order in which games tend to call methods, even when running through lists in a highly predictable manner, cache misses are commonplace. It's not just the implementation of classes that causes these cache misses, it's any time data is the deciding factor in which instructions are run. Games commonly implement scripting languages, and these languages are often interpreted and run on a virtual machine. However the virtual machine or JIT compiler is implemented, there is always an aspect of data controlling which instructions will be called next, and this causes branch misprediction. This is why, in general, interpreted languages are slower, they either run code based on loaded data in the case of bytecode interpreters or they compile code just in time, which though it creates faster code, causes issues of its own.

When a developer implements an object-oriented framework without using the built-in virtual functions, virtual tables and this pointers present in the C++ language, it doesn't reduce the chance of cache miss unless they use virtual tables by function rather than by class. But even when the developer has been especially careful, the very fact they are doing object-oriented programming with game developer access patterns, that of calling singular virtual functions on arrays of heterogeneous objects, they are still going to have some of the same instruction decode and cache misses as found with built-in virtuals. That is, the best they can hope for is one less data dependent CPU state change per virtual call. That still leaves the opportunity for two mispredictions.

So, with all this apparent inefficiency, what makes game developers stick with object-oriented coding practices? As game developers are frequently cited as a source of how the bleeding edge of computer software development is progressing, why have they not moved away wholesale from the problem and stopped using object-oriented development practices all together?

# 14.2 Mapping the problem

*Claim: Objects provide a better mapping from the real world description of the problem to the final code solution.*

Object-oriented design when programming in games starts with thinking about the game design in terms of entities. Each entity in the game design is given a class, such as ship, player, bullet, or score. Each object maintains its own state, communicates with other objects through methods, and provides encapsulation so when the implementation of a particular entity changes, the other objects that use it or provide it with utility do not need to change. Game developers like abstraction, because historically they have had to write games for not just one target platform, but usually at least two. In the past, it was between console manufacturers, but now game developers have to manage between Windows™ and console platforms, plus the mobile targets too. The abstractions in the past were mostly hardware access abstractions, and naturally some gameplay abstractions as well, but as the game development industry matured, we found common forms of abstractions for areas such as physics, AI, and even player control. Finding these common abstractions allowed for third party libraries, and many of these use object-oriented design as well. It's quite common for libraries to interact with the game through agents. These agent objects contain their own state data, whether hidden or publicly accessible, and provide functions by which they can be manipulated inside the constraints of the system that provided them.

The game design inspired objects (such as ship, player, level) keep hold of agents and use them to find out what's going on in their world. A player interacts with physics, input, animation, other entities, and doing this through an object-oriented API hides much of the details about what's actually required to do all these different tasks.

The entities in object-oriented design are containers for

data and a place to keep all the functions that manipulate that data. Don't confuse these entities with those of entity systems, as the entities in object-oriented design are immutable of class over their lifetime. An object-oriented entity does not change class during its lifetime in C++ because there is no process by which to reconstruct a class in place in the language. As can be expected, if you don't have the right tools for the job, a good workman works around it. Game developers don't change the type of their objects at runtime, instead, they create new and destroy old in the case of a game entity that needs this functionality. But as is often the case, because the feature is not present in the language, it is underutilised even when it would make sense.

For example, in a first-person shooter, an object will be declared to represent the animating player mesh, but when the player dies, a clone would be made to represent the dead body as a rag doll. The animating player object may be made invisible and moved to their next spawn point while the dead body object with its different set of virtual functions, and different data, remains where the player died so as to let the player watch their dead body. To achieve this sleight of hand, where the dead body object sits in as a replacement for the player once they are dead, copy constructors need to be defined. When the player is spawned back into the game, the player model will be made visible again, and if they wish to, the player can go and visit their dead clone. This works remarkably well, but it is a trick that would be unnecessary if the player could become a dead rag doll rather than spawn a clone of a different type. There is an inherent danger in this too, the cloning could have bugs, and cause other issues, and also if the player dies but somehow is allowed to resurrect, then they have to find a way to convert the rag doll back into the animating player, and that is no simple feat.

Another example is in AI. The finite state machines and behaviour trees that run most game AI maintain all the data necessary for all their potential states. If an AI has three states, { Idle, Making-a-stand, Fleeing-in-terror } then it has the data for all three states. If the Making-a-stand has a scared-points accumulator for accounting their fear, so they can fight, but only up until they are too scared to continue, and the Fleeing-in-terror has a timer so they will flee, but only for a certain time, then Idle will have these two unnecessary attributes as well. In this trivial example, the AI class has three data entries, { state, how-scared, flee-time }, and only one of these data entries is used by all three states. If the AI could change type when it transitioned from state to state, then it wouldn't even need the state member, as that functionality would be covered by the virtual table pointer. The AI would only allocate space for each of the state tracking members when in the appropriate state. The best we can do in C++ is to fake it by changing the virtual table pointer by hand, dangerous but possible, or setting up a copy constructor for each possible transition.

Apart from immutable type, object-oriented development also has a philosophical problem. Consider how humans perceive objects in real life. There is always a context to every observation. The humble table, when you look at it, you may see it to be a table with four legs, made of wood and modestly polished. If so, you will see it as being a brown colour, but you will also see the reflection of the light. You will see the grain, but when you think about what colour it is, you will think of it as being one colour. However, if you have the training of an artist, you will know what you see is not what is actually there. There is no solid colour, and if you are looking at the table, you cannot see its precise shape, but only infer it. If you are inferring it is brown by the average light colour entering your eye, then does it cease to be brown if you turn off the light? What about if there is too much light and all you can see is the reflection off the polished surface? If you close one eye and look at its rectangular form from one of the long sides, you will not see right angle corners, but instead, a trapezium. We automatically adjust for this and classify objects when we see them. We apply our prejudices to them and lock them down to make reasoning about them easier. This is why object-oriented development is so appealing to us. However, what we find easy to consume as humans, is not optimal for a computer. When we think about game entities being objects, we think about them as wholes. But a computer has no concept of objects, and only sees objects as being badly organised data and functions randomly called on it.

If you take another example from the table, consider the table to have legs about three feet long. That's someone's standard table. If the legs are only one foot long, it could be considered to be a coffee table. Short, but still usable as a place to throw the magazines and leave your cups. But when you get down to one inch long legs, it's no longer a table, but instead, just a large piece of wood with some stubs stuck on it. We can happily classify the same item but with different dimensions into three distinct classes of object. Table, coffee table, a lump of wood with some little bits of wood on it. But, at what point does the lump of wood become a coffee table? Is it somewhere between 4 and 8 inch long legs? This is the same problem as presented about sand, when does it transition from grains of sand to a pile of sand? How many grains are a pile, are a dune? The answer must be that there is no answer. The answer is also helpful in understanding how a computer thinks. It doesn't know the specific difference between our human classifications because to a certain degree even humans don't.

The class of an object is poorly defined by what it is, but better by what it does. This is why duck typing is a strong approach. We also realise, if a type is better defined by what it can do, then when we get to the root of what a polymorphic type is, we find it is only polymorphic in terms of what it can do. In C++, it's clear a class with virtual functions can be called as a runtime polymorphic instance, but it might not have been clear that if it didn't have those functions, it would not need to be classified in the first place. The reason multiple inheritance is useful stems from this. Multiple inheritance just means an object can behave, that is react, to certain impulses. It has declared that it can fulfil some contract of polymorphic function response. If polymorphism is just the ability for an object to fulfil a functionality contract, then we don't need virtual calls to handle that every time, as there are other ways to make code behave differently based on the object.

In most games engines, the object-oriented approach leads to a lot of objects in very deep hierarchies. A common ancestor chain for an entity might be: PlayerEntity → CharacterEntity → MovingEntity → PhysicalEntity → Entity → Serialisable → ReferenceCounted → Base.

These deep hierarchies virtually guarantee multiple indirect calls when calling virtual methods, but they also cause a lot of pain when it comes to cross-cutting code, that is code that affects or is affected by unrelated concerns, or concerns incongruous to the hierarchy. Consider a normal game with characters moving around a scene. In the scene you will have characters, the world, possibly some particle effects, lights, some static and some dynamic. In this scene, all these things need to be rendered, or used for rendering. The traditional approach is to use multiple inheritance or to make sure there is a `Renderable` base class somewhere in every entity's inheritance chain. But what about entities that make noises? Do you add an audio emitter class as well? What about entities that are serialised vs those that are explicitly managed by the level? What about those that are so common they need a different memory manager (such as the particles), or those that only optionally have to be rendered (like trash, flowers, or grass in the distance). This has been solved numerous times by putting all the most common functionality into the core base class for everything in the game, with special exceptions for special circumstances, such as when the level is animated, when a player character is in an intro or death screen, or is a boss character (who is special and deserves a little more code). These hacks are only necessary if you don't use multiple inheritance, but when you use multiple inheritance you then start to weave a web that could ultimately end up with virtual inheritance and the complexity of state that brings with it. The compromise almost always turns out to be some form of cosmic base class anti-pattern.

Object-oriented development is good at providing a human oriented representation of the problem in the source code, but bad at providing a machine representation of the solution. It is bad at providing a framework for creating an optimal solution, so the question remains: why are game developers still using object-oriented techniques to develop games? It's possible it's not about better design, but instead, making it easier to change the code. It's common knowledge that game developers are constantly changing code to match the natural evolution of the design of the game, right up until launch. Does object-oriented development provide a good way of making maintenance and modification simpler or safer?

## 14.3   Internalised state

*Claim: Encapsulation makes code more reusable. It's easier to modify the implementation without affecting the usage. Maintenance and refactoring become easy, quick, and safe.*

The idea behind encapsulation is to provide a contract to the person using the code rather than providing a raw implementation. In theory, well written object-oriented code that uses encapsulation is immune to damage caused by changing how an object manipulates its data. If all the code using the object complies with the contract and never directly uses any of the data members without going through accessor functions, then no matter what you change about how the class fulfils that contract, there won't be any new bugs introduced by any change. In theory, the object implementation can change in any way as long as the contract is not modified, but only extended. This is the open closed principle. A class should be open for extension, but closed for modification.

A contract is meant to provide some guarantees about how a complex system works. In practice, only unit testing can provide these guarantees.

Sometimes, programmers unwittingly rely on hidden features of objects' implementations. Sometimes the object they rely on has a bug that just so happens to fit their use case. If that bug is fixed, then the code using the object no longer works as expected. The use of the contract, though it was kept intact, has not helped the other piece of code to maintain working status across revisions. Instead, it provided false hope that the returned values would not change. It doesn't even have to be a bug. Temporal couplings inside objects or accidental or undocumented features that go away in later revisions can also damage the code using the contract without breaking it.

Consider an implementation that maintained an internal list in sorted order, and a use case that accidentally relied on it (an unforeseen bug in the user's use case, not an intentional dependency), but when the maintainer pushes out a *performance enhancing update*, the only thing the users are going to see is a pile of new bugs, and they will likely assume the performance update is suspect, not their own code.

A concrete example could be an item manager that kept a list of items sorted by name. If the function returns all the item types that match a filter, then the caller could iterate the returned list until it found the item it wanted. To speed things up, it could early-out if it found an item with a name later than the item it was looking for, or it could do a binary search of the returned list. In both those cases, if the internal representation changed to something that wasn't ordered by name, then the code would no longer work. If the internal representation was changed so it was ordered by hash, then the early-out and binary search would be completely broken.

In many linked list implementations, there is a decision

made about whether to store the length of the list or not. The choice to store a count member will make multi-threaded access slower, but the choice not to store it will make finding the length of the list an $\mathcal{O}(n)$operation. For situations where you only want to find out whether the list is empty, if the object contract only supplies a get_count() function, you cannot know for sure whether it would be cheaper to check if the count was greater than zero, or check if the begin() and end() are the same. This is another example of the contract being too little information.

Encapsulation only seems to provide a way to hide bugs and cause assumptions in programmers. There is an old saying about assumptions, and encapsulation doesn't let you confirm or deny them unless you have access to the source code. If you have, and you need to look at it to find out what went wrong, then all the encapsulation has done is add another layer to work around rather than add any useful functionality of its own.

## 14.4   Instance oriented development

*Claim: Making every object an instance makes it very easy to think about what an object's responsibilities are, what its lifetime looks like, and where it belongs in the world of objects.*

The first problem with instance thinking is that everything is centred around the idea of one item doing a thing, and that is a sure way to lead to poor performance.

The second, and more pervasive issue with instance thinking is it leads to thinking in the abstract about instances, and using full objects as building blocks for thought can lead to very inefficient algorithms. When you hide the internal representation of an item even from the programmer using it, you often introduce issues of translation from one way of thinking about an object to another, and back again.

Sometimes you may have an item that needs to change another object, but cannot reach it in the world it finds itself, so has to send a message to its container to help it achieve the goal of answering a question about another entity. Unfortunately, it's not uncommon for programs to lose sight of the data requirement along these routes, and send more than necessary in the query, or in the response, carrying around not only unnecessary permissions, but also unnecessary limitations due to related system state.

As an example of how things can go wrong, imagine a city building game where the population has happiness ratings. If each individual citizen has a happiness rating, then they will need to calculate that happiness rating. Let's assume the number of citizens isn't grossly overwhelming, with maybe a maximum of a thousand buildings and up to ten citizens per building. If we only calculate the happiness of the citizens when necessary, it will speed things up, and in at least one game where these numbers are similar, lazy evaluation of the citizen happiness was the way things were done. How the happiness is calculated can be an issue if it is worked out from the perspective of the individual, rather than the perspective of the city. If a citizen is happy when they are close to work, close to local amenities, far from industrial locations, and able to get to recreational areas easily, then a lot of the happiness rating comes from a kind of pathfinding. If the result of pathfinding is cached, then at least the citizens in the same building can benefit, but every building will have small differences in distances to each of the different types of building. Running pathfinding over that many instances is very expensive.

If instead, the city calculates happiness, it can build a map of distances from each of the types of building under consideration as a flood fill pass and create a general distance map of the whole city using a Floyd-Warshall algorithm to help citizens decide on how close their places of work are. Normally, substituting an $\mathcal{O}(n^3)$algorithm for an $\mathcal{O}(n^2)$could be seen as silly, but the pathfinding is being done for each citizen, so becomes $O(n^2m)$ and is not in fact algorithmically superior. Finally, this is the real world, and doing the pathing itself has other overheads, and running the Floyd-Warshall algorithm to generate a lookup before calculating happiness means the work to calculate happiness can be simpler (in data storage terms), and require fewer branches off into supporting code. The Floyd-Warshall algorithm can also have a partial update run upon it, using the existing map to indicate which items need to be updated. If running from the instance point of view, knowing a change to the topology or the type of buildings nearby would require doing some form of distance check per instance.

In conclusion, abstractions form the basis of solving difficult problems, but in games, we're often not solving difficult algorithmic problems at a gameplay level. To the contrary, we have a tendency to abstract too early, and object-oriented design often gives us an easy and recognisable way to commit to abstractions without rendering the costs apparent until much later, when we have become too dependent upon them to clear them away without impacting other code.

## 14.5   Hierarchical design vs change

*Claim: Inheritance allows reuse of code by extension. Adding new features is simple.*

Inheritance was seen as a major reason to use classes in C++ by game programmers. The obvious benefit was being able to inherit from multiple interfaces to gain attributes or agency in system objects such as physics, animation, and rendering. In the early days of C++ adoption, the hierarchies were shallow, not usually going much more than three layers deep, but later it became commonplace to find more than nine levels of ancestors in central classes such as that of the player, their vehicles, or the AI players. For example, in Unreal Tournament, the minigun ammo object had this:

Miniammo → TournamentAmmo → Ammo → Pickup → Inventory → Actor → Object

Game developers use inheritance to provide a robust way to implement polymorphism in games, where many game entities can be updated, rendered, or queried en-mass, without any hand coded checking of type. They also appreciate the reduced copy-pasting, because inheriting from a class also adds functionality to a class. This early form of mix-ins was seen to reduce errors in coding as there were often times where bugs only existed because a programmer had fixed a bug in one place, but not all of them. Gradually, multiple inheritance faded into interfaces only, the practice of only inheriting from one real class, and any others had to be pure virtual interface classes as per the Java definition.

Although it seems like inheriting from class to extend its functionality is safe, there are many circumstances where classes don't quite behave as expected when methods are overridden. To extend a class, it is often necessary to read the source, not just of the class you're inheriting, but also the classes it inherits too. If a base class creates a pure virtual method, then it forces the child class to implement that method. If this was for a good reason, then that should be enforced, but you cannot enforce that every inheriting class implements this method, only the first instantiable class inheriting it. This can lead to obscure bugs where a new class sometimes acts or is treated like the class it is inheriting from.

A feature missing from C++ also is the idea of being non-virtual. You cannot declare a function as not being virtual. That is, you can define that a function is an override, but you cannot declare that it is not an override. This can cause issues when common words are used, and a new virtual method is brought into existence. If it overlaps extant functions with the same signature, then you likely have a bug.

Another pitfall of inheritance in C++ comes in the form of runtime versus compile time linking. A good example is

```
class A {
  virtual void foo( int bar = 5 ) { cout << bar; }
};
class B : public A {
  void foo( int bar = 7 ) { cout << bar * 2; }
};
int main( int argc, char *argv[] ) {
  A *a = new B;
  a->foo();
  return 0;
}
```

Listing 14.2: Runtime, compile-time, or link-time?

default arguments on method calls and badly understood overriding rules. What would you expect the output of the program in listing 14.2 to be?

Would you be surprised to find out it reported a value of 10? Some code relies on the compiled state, some on run-time. Adding new functionality to a class by extending it can quickly become a dangerous game as classes from two layers down can cause coupling side effects, throw exceptions (or worse, not throw an exception and quietly fail), circumvent your changes, or possibly just make it impossible to implement your feature as they might already be taking up the namespace or have some other incompatibility with your plans, such as requiring a certain alignment or need to be in a certain bank of ram.

Inheritance does provide a clean way of implementing runtime polymorphism, but it's not the only way as we saw earlier. Adding a new feature by inheritance requires revisiting the base class, providing a default implementation, or a pure virtual, then providing implementations for all the classes that need to handle the new feature. This requires modification to the base class, and possible touching all of the child classes if the pure virtual route is taken. So even though the compiler can help you find all the places where the code needs to change, it has not made it significantly easier to change the code.

Using a type member instead of a virtual table pointer can give you the same runtime code linking, could be better for cache misses, and could be easier to add new features and reason about because it has less baggage when it comes to implementing those new features, provides a very simple way to mix and match capabilities compared to inheritance, and keeps the polymorphic code in one place. For example, in the fake virtual function go-forward, the class Car will step on the gas. In the class Person, it will set the direction vector. In the class UFO, it will also just set the direction vector. This sounds like a job for a switch statement fall through. In the fake virtual function re-fuel, the class Car and UFO will start a re-fuel timer and remain stationary while their fuelling-up animations play, whereas the Person class could just reduce their stamina-potion count and be instantly re-fuelled. Again, a switch statement with fall through provides all the runtime polymorphism you need, but you don't need to multiple inherit in order to provide different functionality on a per class per function level. Being able to pick what each method does in a class is not something inheritance is good at, but it is something desirable, and non inheritance based polymorphism does allow it.

The original reason for using inheritance was that you would not need to revisit the base class, or change any of the existing code in order to extend and add functionality to the codebase, however, it is highly likely you will at least need to view the base class implementation, and with changing specifications in games, it's also quite common to need changes at the base class level. Inheritance also inhibits certain types of analysis by locking people into thinking of objects as having IS-A relationships with the other object types in the game. A lot of flexibility is lost when a programmer is locked out of conceptualising objects as being combinations of features. Reducing multiple inheritance to interfaces, though helping to reduce the code complexity, has drawn a veil over the one good way of building up classes as compound objects. Although not a good solution in itself as it still abuses the cache, a switch on type seems to offer similar functionality to virtual tables without some of the associated baggage. So why put things in classes?

## 14.6  Divisions of labour

*Claim: Modular architecture for reduced coupling and better testing*

The object-oriented paradigm is seen as another tool in the kit when it comes to ensuring quality of code. Strictly adhering to the open closed principle, always using accessors, methods, and inheritance to use or extend objects, programmers write significantly more modular code than they do if programming from a purely procedural perspective. This modularity separates each object's code into units. These units are collections of all the data and methods that act upon the data. It has been written about many times that testing objects is simpler because each object can be tested in isolation.

However, we know it to be untrue, due to data being linked together by purpose, and purposes being linked together by data in a long chain of accidental relationships.

Object-oriented design suffers from the problem of errors in communication. Objects are not systems, and systems need to be tested, and systems comprise of not only objects, but their inherent communication. The communication of objects is difficult to test because in practice it is hard to isolate the interactions between classes. Object-oriented development leads to an object-oriented view of the system which makes it hard to isolate non-objects such as data transforms, communication, and temporal coupling.

Modular architecture is good because it limits the potential damage caused by changes, but just like encapsulation before, the contract to any module has to be unambiguous so as to reduce the chance of external reliance on unintended side effects of the implementation.

The reason object-oriented modular approach doesn't work as well is that the modules are defined by object boundary, not by a higher level concept. Good examples of modularity include stdio's FILE, the CRT's malloc/free, The NvTriStrip library's GenerateStrips. Each of these provides a solid, documented, narrow set of functions to access functionality that could otherwise be overwhelming and difficult to reason about.

Modularity in object-oriented development can offer protection from other programmers who don't understand the code. But why is a programmer that doesn't understand the code going to be safe even using a trivialised and simplified interface? An object's methods are often the instruction manual for an object in the eyes of someone new to the code, so writing all the important manipulation methods in one block can give clues to anyone using the class. The modularity is important here because game development objects are regularly large, offering a lot of functionality spread across their many different aspects. Rather than find a way to address cross-cutting concerns, game objects tend to fulfil all requirements rather than restrict themselves to their original design. Because of this bloating, the modular approach, that is, collecting methods by their concern in the source, can be beneficial to programmers coming at the object fresh. The obvious way to fix this would be to use a paradigm that supports cross-cutting concerns at a more fundamental level, but object-oriented development in C++ seems to be inefficient at representing this in code.

If object-oriented development doesn't increase modularity in such a way as it provides better results than explicitly modularising code, then what does it offer?

## 14.7  Reusable generic code

*Claim: Faster development time through reuse of generic code*

It is regarded as one of the holy grails of development to be
able to consistently reduce development overhead by reusing
old code. In order to stop wasting any of the investment in
time and effort, it's been assumed it will be possible to put
together an application from existing code and only have to
write some minor new features. The unfortunate truth is
any interesting new features you want to add will probably
be incompatible with your old code and old way of laying out
your data, and you will need to either rewrite the old code
to allow for the new feature, or rewrite the old code to allow
for the new data layout. If a software project can be built
from existing solutions, from objects invented to provide features for an old project, then it's probably not very complex.
Any project of significant complexity includes hundreds if
not thousands of special case objects that provide all particular needs of that project. For example, the vast majority of games will have a player class, but almost none share
a common core set of attributes. Is there a world position
member in a game of poker? Is there a hit point count member in the player of a racing game? Does the player have a
gamer tag in a purely offline game? Having a generic class
that can be reused doesn't make the game easier to create,
all it does is move the specialisation into somewhere else.
Some game toolkits do this by allowing script to extend the
basic classes. Some game engines limit the gameplay to a
certain genre and allow extension away from that through
data-driven means. No one has so far created a game API,
because to do so, it would have to be so generic it wouldn't
provide anything more than what we already have with our
languages we use for development.

Reuse, being hankered after by production, and thought
of so highly by anyone without much experience in making
games, has become an end in itself for many game developers. The pitfall of generics is a focus on keeping a class

generic enough to be reused or re-purposed without thought as to why, or how. The first, the why, is a major stumbling block and needs to be taught out of developers as quickly as possible. Making something generic, for the sake of generality, is not a valid goal. Making something generic in the first instance adds time to development without adding value. Some developers would cite this as short-sighted, however, it is the how that deflates this argument. How do you generalise a class if you only use it in one place? The implementation of a class is testable only so far as it can be tested, and if you only use a class in one place, you can only test that it works in one situation. The quality of a class's reusability is inherently untestable until there is something to reuse it, and the general rule of thumb is that it's not reusable unless there are at least three things using it. If you then generalise the class, yet don't have any other test cases than the first situation, then all you can test is that you didn't break the class when generalising it. So, if you cannot guarantee that the class works for other types or situations, all you have done by generalising the class is added more code for bugs to hide in. The resultant bugs are now hidden in code that *works*, possibly even tested in its isolation, which means any bugs introduced during this generalising have been stamped and approved, and are now trusted.

Test-driven development implicitly denies generic coding until the point where it is a good choice to do so. The only time when it is a good choice to move code to a more generic state, is when it reduces redundancy through reuse of common functionality.

Generic code has to fulfil more than just a basic set of features if it is to be used in many situations. If you write a templated array container, access to the array through the square bracket operators would be considered a basic feature, but you will also want to write iterators for it and possibly add an insert routine to take the headache out of shuffling the array up in memory. Little bugs can creep in if you rewrite these functions whenever you need them, and linked lists are notorious for having bugs in quick and dirty implementations. To be fit for use by all users, any generic container should provide a full set of methods for manipulation, and the STL does that. There are hundreds of different functions to understand before you can be considered an STL-expert, and you have to be an STL-expert before you can be sure you're writing efficient code with the STL. There is a large amount of documentation available for the various implementations of the STL. Most of the implementations of the STL are very similar if not functionally the same. Even so, it can take some time for a programmer to become a valuable STL programmer due to this need to learn another language. The programmer has to learn a new language, the language of the STL, with its own nouns verbs and adjectives. To limit this, many games companies have a much reduced feature set reinterpretation of the STL that optionally provides better memory handling (because of the awkward hardware), more choice for the containers (so you may choose a hash-map, trie, or b-tree directly, rather than just a map), or explicit implementations of simpler containers such as stack or singly linked lists and their intrusive brethren. These libraries are normally smaller in scope and are therefore easier to learn and hack than the STL variants, but they still need to be learnt and that takes some time. In the past this was a good compromise, but now the STL has extensive online documentation, there is no excuse not to use the STL except where memory overhead is very intrusive, such as in the embedded space where main memory is measured in kilobytes, or where compilation time is of massive concern[4].

The takeaway from this, however, is that generic code still needs to be learnt in order for the coder to be efficient, or not cause accidental performance bottlenecks. If you go with the STL, then at least you have a lot of documentation on your side. If your game company implements an amazingly complex template library, don't expect any coders to use it until they've had enough time to learn it, and that means,

---

[4]The STL is large, but not as large as some OS headers, so fight the right battle first

if you write generic code, expect people to not use it unless they come across it accidentally, or have been explicitly told to, as they won't know it's there, or won't trust it. In other words, starting out by writing generic code is a good way to write a lot of code quickly without adding any value to your development.

# Chapter 15

# Looking at hardware

The first thing a software engineer does when starting work on a new platform is to read the contents listings of all the hardware manuals they have access to. The second thing they usually do is try to get hello world up and running. It's uncommon for a game development software engineer to read all the documentation available. The return on investment doesn't generally look good. It usually turns out to be a valid call, as when it comes to developing a game, the amount of times you need that information is normally quite small, and by the time you need that information, you will likely have forgotten about it if you read it all up front. Software developers optimise their workload, even down to how much they learn in order to do their work. This isn't just game developers either, it's anyone working as a programmer now, as the CPUs and GPUs are too complex, or are black boxes to the developers, or don't exist in some cases, as the hardware is undocumented or the platform you are working on really is an abstraction, such as Javascript.

When developers read the manuals, they will be reading them out of necessity, and they will be taking them literally, and possibly not getting all the implied information. When it comes to understanding hardware, there are the theoretical restrictions implied by the comments and data sheets in the manuals, but there are also the practical restrictions which can only be found through working with the hardware at an intimate level.

As most of the contemporary hardware is now API driven, with hardware manuals only being presented to the engineers responsible for graphics, audio, and media subsystems, it's tempting to start programming on a new piece of hardware without thinking about the hardware at all. Most programmers working on big games in big studios don't really know what's going on at the lower levels of the game engines they're working with, and to some extent that's probably good as it frees their mind to write more code, but there comes a point in every developer's life when they have to bite the bullet and find out why their code is slow. Someday you're going to be five weeks from shipping and need to claw back five frames a second on one level of the game which has been optimised in every other area other than yours. When that day comes, you'd better know why your code is slow, and to do that, you have to have data and know what the hardware is doing when it's executing your code.

Some of the issues surrounding code performance are relevant to all hardware configurations. Some are only pertinent to configurations that have caches, or do write combining, or have branch prediction, but some hardware configurations have very special restrictions which can cause odd, but simple to fix performance glitches caused by decisions made during the chip's design process. These glitches are the gotchas of the hardware, and as such, need to be learnt in order to be avoided.

When it comes to the overall design of console CPUs, the vendors needed to make decisions about what to include. The XBox360 and the PS3 were RISC based, had low memory speed, but were multi-core machines. These machines had a set of considerations that remained somewhat misunderstood by mainstream game developers right up to the end of their lives. The current, and possibly future console generations are now based on the Intel CPU instruction set, and therefore also, the Intel approach to CPU layout. Understanding how your target device differs from the laptop or desktop x86 machines on which most programmers start their development life can be highly illuminating. Bedroom programmers aren't so much a thing these days, but even those programmers usually have access to mobile hardware, which gives them a taste of the difference between development hardware and target platform, both in power and in how they interact with the device. The future generations of consoles and other devices may change the hardware considerations again, but understanding that you need to consider the hardware can sometimes only be learned by looking at historical data.

## 15.1 Sequential data

When you process your data in a sequence, you have a much higher chance of a cache hit on reading in the data as it's often possible to predict loads. Making all your calculations run from and write to sequential data not only helps hardware with caches for reading but also when using hardware that does write combining, which is most hardware at the time of writing.

In theory, if you're reading one byte at a time to do something, then you can almost guarantee the next byte will already be in cache the next 63 times you look. For a list of floats, it works out as one memory load for 16 values. If you have an animation with less than 16 keys per bone, then you can guarantee you will only need to load as many cache lines as you have bones in order to find all the key indexes into your arrays of transforms.

In practice, you will find this only applies if the process you run doesn't load in lots of other data to help process your stream. That's not to say that trying to organise your data sequentially isn't important, but it's just as important to ensure the data being accessed is being accessed in patterns which allow the processors to leverage the benefits of that form. There is no point in making data sequential if all you are going to do is use it so slowly that the cache fills up between reads.

Sequential and independent data is also easier to split among different processors as there is little to no chance of evictions due to cache sharing. When your data is stored sequentially, rather than randomly, you know where in memory the data is, and so you can dispatch tasks to work on guaranteed unshared cache lines.

When multiple CPU cores compete to write to a particular cache line, the cache mechanism has to handle keeping the data consistent amongst all the cores. This is where a lot of people would refer to the dreaded cache-flush, but the cache-flush is a fallacy. What really happens is hardware dependent, but generally, the cache circuitry has to maintain coherence, so will have to do some heavy lifting to keep CPUs that write and read from the same lines all working without a broken memory model. Keeping things consistent is a big job and can cause calls out to main memory. If the data is randomly placed, such as when you allocate from a memory pool, or directly from the heap, you cannot be sure what order the data is in and can't even guarantee you're not asking two different CPUs to work on the same cache line of data. It's unlikely, but as we move to very large numbers of CPUs, that probability looks more like certainty.

The data-oriented approach, even when you don't use structs of arrays, still maintains that sequential data is better than random allocations. Not only is it good for the hardware, it's good for simplicity of code as it generally promotes transforms rather than object-oriented messaging.

## 15.2  Deep pipes

CPUs execute instructions in pipelines. This is true of all processors, however, the number of stages differs wildly. For game developers, it's important to remember that the pipelined execution model affects all the CPUs they work on, from the current generation of consoles such as Sony's PS4 and Microsoft's XBOX ONE, but also to handhelds such as the Nintendo 3DS, the iPhones and Androids, and other devices.

Pipelines provide a way for CPUs to trade gains in speed for latency and branch penalties. A non-pipelined CPU finishes every instruction before it begins the next, however, a pipelined CPU starts instructions and doesn't necessarily finish them until many cycles later.

You will find many CPUs will do a lot of work out of order if they can, and the possibility of doing things out of order is something worth striving for. Consider the well-known evil of a linked list. The reason why the linked list is worse than an array for lookups isn't just to do with all the jumping around in memory, but also the fact that it cannot start work on items many steps ahead. If it was all about jumping around in memory, then an array of pointers to objects would also be around the same cost, but in tests, it's shown that when accessing an array versus a linked list, the array of pointers to objects comes out closer to the array for performance than you would expect if it was the mere pointer dereferencing that was the cost. Instead, the cost stems from the fact that the next element cannot be deduced without loading in the current element. That is where the true cost lies. In the source code for linked lists 16.2, the array lookup is clearly the fastest, but on some hardware, the array of pointers approach, which offers some of the benefits of a linked list, cuts the time to process by more than 20%.

i5-4430 @ 3.00GHz

```
Average   24.35ms [Linked List Sum]
Average   19.03ms [Pointer Array Sum]
Average    4.37ms [Array Sum]
```

If you imagine a CPU as a factory, the idea is the equivalent of the production line, where each worker has one job, rather than each worker seeing and working on a product from start to finish. A CPU is better able to process more data faster this way because by increasing the latency, in well thought out programs, you only add a few cycles to any processing during prologue or epilogue. During the transform, latency can be mitigated by doing more work on non-related data while waiting for any dependencies. Because the CPUs have to do a lot less per cycle, the cycles take less time, which is what allows CPUs to get faster. What's happening is that it still takes just as long for a CPU to do an operation as it always has (give or take), but because the operation is split up into a lot of smaller stages, it is possible to do a lot more operations per second as all of the separate stages can operate in parallel, and any efficient code concentrates on doing this after all other optimisations have been made.

When pipelining, the CPU consists of a number of stages, firstly the fetch and decode stages, which in some hardware are the same stage, then an execute stage which does the actual calculation. This stage can take multiple cycles, but as long as the CPU has all the cycles covered by stages, it won't affect throughput. The CPU then finally stores the result in the last stage, dropping the value back into the output register or memory location.

With instructions having many stages, it can take many cycles for them to complete, but because only one part of the instruction is in use at each stage, a new instruction can be loaded as soon as the first instruction has got to the second stage. This pipelining allows us to issue many more instructions than we could otherwise, even though each instruction might have higher latency. This also saves on transistor count, as more transistors are being used at any one time.

There is less waste. In the beginning, the main reason for this was that the circuits would take a certain amount of time to stabilise. Logic gates, in practice, don't immediately switch from one logic state to another. If you add in noise, resonance, and manufacturing error, you can begin to see that CPUs would have to wait quite a while between cycles, massively reducing the CPU frequency. This is why FPGAs cannot easily run at GHz speeds, they are arrays of flexible gate systems, which means they suffer the most from stability problems, but amplified by the gates being located a long way from each other, in the sense that they are not physically close like logic circuits are inside an inflexible ASIC or production CPU.

Pipelines require that the instructions are ready. This can be problematic if the data the instruction is waiting on is not ready, or if the instruction is not loaded. If there is anything stopping the instruction from being issued it can cause a stall, or in the case of branching causing the instructions to be run, then trashed as the pipeline is flushed ready to begin processing the correct branch. If the instruction pointer is determined by some data value, it can mean a long wait while the next instruction is loaded from main memory. If the next instruction is based on a conditional branch, then the branch has to wait on the condition, thus causing a number of instructions to begin processing when the branch could invalidate all the work done so far. As well as instructions needing to be nearby, the registers must already be populated, otherwise, something will have to wait.

## 15.3 Microcode: virtually function calls.

Current hardware doesn't suffer from these issues, but something like it may come up again in the future, so it's included for posterity. It affected the generation of hardware in which data-oriented design got its name, and there may be new hardware with similar issues coming that we aren't aware, but it's unlikely, as hardware vendors appear to be acting with more caution.

To get around the limitations implicit in trying to increase throughput, some instructions on RISC chips weren't really there. Instead, these virtual instructions were like function calls, calls to macros that run a sequence of instructions. These instructions were said to be microcoded, and in order to run, they often need to commandeer the CPU for their entire duration to maintain atomicity. Some functions were microcoded due to their infrequent use or relative cost to implement as an intrinsic instruction, some because of the spec, and some because they don't fit well with the pipelined execution model. In all of these cases, a microcoded instruction caused a gap, called a bubble, in the pipeline, and that was wasted execution time. In almost all cases, these microcoded instructions could be avoided, sometimes by changing command line parameters, sometimes by adjusting how you solve a problem and sometimes by changing the problem completely.

## 15.4   Single Instruction Multiple Data

There are no current generation consoles that don't have SIMD of some sort. All commodity hardware now has some kind of vector unit, and to some extent, as long as you work within your boundaries, even hardware that doesn't have SIMD instructions, such as embedded microcontrollers, can operate on multiple data. The idea behind SIMD is simple: issue one command, and manipulate multiple pieces of data in the same way at the same time. The most commonly referenced implementation of this is the vector units inherent in all current generation hardware. With Intel CPUs, this is the SSE and AVX instruction sets. In the XBox360 and PS3, the AltiVec instructions on PPC, and the SPU instruction set contained many instructions that operated on multiple pieces of data at the same time, sometimes doing asym-

```
uint32_t CountBitsClever( uint32_t v ) {
  v = v - ((v >> 1) & 0x55555555);              // reuse
        input as temporary
  v = (v & 0x33333333) + ((v >> 2) & 0x33333333);   // temp
  c = ((v + (v >> 4) & 0xF0F0F0F) * 0x1010101) >> 24; // count
  return c;
}

uint32_t CountBitsDumb( uint32_t in ) {
  uint32_t numBits = 0;
  while( in ) {
    numBits += 1;
    in &= in-1;
  }
  return numBits;
}
```

Listing 15.1: Counting bits functions

metric operations such as rotating, splatting, or reconfiguring the vectors. On even older machines or simple machines such as microcontrollers, the explicit instructions may not exist, but in the world of bitwise logic, we've always had some SIMD instructions hanging around as all the bitwise ops run over multiple elements in a bit field of whatever native word length. Consider some of the winners of the quickest bit counting routines. My favourite is the purely SIMD style bit counter given in listing 15.1.

The sad thing is, these days, most compilers will build you a better bit counter if you write your code the dumb way, as on some CPUs there are instructions to count bits, which leaves all your clever code wasting time, while also being impenetrable to read. In this case, be aware of your target hardware, and the capabilities of your compiler, as you might be shooting yourself in the foot.

So, look to your types, and see if you can add a bit of SIMD to your development without even breaking out the vector intrinsics. Sometimes the compiler will beat you, other times you can beat it. Start simple, find performance issues, use your tools.

## 15.5   Predictable instructions

The biggest crime to commit in a deeply pipelined core is to tell it to do loads of instructions, then once it's almost done, change your mind and start on something completely different. This heinous crime is all too common, with control flow instructions doing just that when they're hard to predict, or impossible to predict in the case of entirely random data, or where the data pattern is known, but the architecture doesn't support that kind of pattern of branch predictions.

Most branch predictors will work great if you can provide a 99% chance of the branch being taken the same way as last time.

## 15.6   How your hardware actually works

The hardware you work on is what you work on. Whatever programming language you are using, the language is not the platform you are programming for. You do not run code on C++, you don't even run code on a Java Virtual Machine. The JVM is running on hardware, and being aware of the hardware will help you decide how to access your data.

Even in languages very far removed from the hardware, such as Python, considering the size of the cache, and what memory must be accessed to fulfil an operation, will help you formulate ideas to attempt in optimisation passes.

Your hardware doesn't just include your CPU. It also includes your hard drives, flash ram, network card, input devices and output devices. If you cannot handle the full payload of a motion controller, and end up sending choppy or incomplete data to a gesture recognition module, you're going to create a worse user experience than your competitor.

Learn how your hardware really works, how big each

cache is, what would cause memory to be dropped to disk, how long it takes to send data to another machine, how many hops on your protocol. Learn about the speed that information can, and must flow, for the user experience to be within tolerances.

In VR, these tolerances are tight, in web development, less so, but as mentioned in chapter 8 there is evidence to suggest that 100ms increase in page load times can amount to a very significant drop in sales. If every millisecond counts, why aren't you counting them?

In 2018, on a lot of CPUs, your lowest level cache is 32kb for data, 32kb for instructions. For mobile, you can estimate 16kb for each. On some other CPUs, the cache is shared. The next levels up vary considerably, but generally bump to 256kb, then 4mb or more. The largest and fastest CPUs do tend to have the largest caches, and the top of the range i9 series from Intel has over 20MB of cache in much of their offering.

# Chapter 16

# Sourcecode

In many academic texts, the sourcecode is hard to find, or just not available. In this book, much of the source is provided. You can get a copy of the full source from GitHub, or rebuild the tests yourself from the snippets provided in this chapter. I have tried to not waste pages with any of the unnecessary boilerplate that is required to run the tests, and include only the code that is different in each of the sources. In effect, providing you with what was meant to be tested in the first place.

https://github.com/raspofabs/dodbooksourcecode
This repository contains the tests performed, the supporting code, and the testing harness.

## 16.1　The basics

In this source, the idea is to test some of the straight forward cases such as memory accesses in different patterns.

```
void TestSummingSimple() {
  int sum = 0;
  for( int i = 0; i < ELEMENT_COUNT; ++i ) {
    sum += a[i];
  }
```

271

```
 6  | }
 7  | void TestSummingBackwards() {
 8  |    int sum = 0;
 9  |    for( int i = ELEMENT_COUNT-1; i >= 0; --i ) {
10  |       sum += b[i];
11  |    }
12  | }
13  | void TestSummingStrides() {
14  |    int sum = 0;
15  |    const int STRIDE = 16;
16  |    for( int offset = 0; offset < STRIDE; offset += 1 ) {
17  |       for( int i = offset; i < ELEMENT_COUNT; i += STRIDE ) {
18  |          sum += a[i];
19  |       }
20  |    }
21  | }
22  | template<int byte_limit>
23  | void TestWriteRangeLimited() {
24  |    int mask = (byte_limit / sizeof( c[0] ))-1;
25  |    for( int i = 0; i != ELEMENT_COUNT*16; i+= 16 ) {
26  |       c[i&mask] = i;
27  |    }
28  | }
29  | void TestWriteSimple() {
30  |    for( int i = 0; i != ELEMENT_COUNT; ++i ) {
31  |       c[i] = i;
32  |    }
33  | }
34  | void TestWriteBackwards() {
35  |    for( int i = ELEMENT_COUNT-1; i >= 0; --i ) {
36  |       c[i] = i;
37  |    }
38  | }
39  | void TestWriteStrides() {
40  |    const int STRIDE = 16;
41  |    for( int offset = 0; offset < STRIDE; offset += 1 ) {
42  |       for( int i = offset; i < ELEMENT_COUNT; i += STRIDE ) {
43  |          c[i] = i;
44  |       }
45  |    }
46  | }
47  | void TestSimpleCopy() {
48  |    for( int i = 0; i < ELEMENT_COUNT; ++i ) {
49  |       c[i] = a[i];
50  |    }
51  | }
52  | void TestMultiRead() {
53  |    for( int i = 0; i < ELEMENT_COUNT; ++i ) {
54  |       c[i] = a[i] + b[i];
55  |    }
56  | }
57  | void TestMultiWrite() {
58  |    for( int i = 0; i < ELEMENT_COUNT; ++i ) {
59  |       c[i] = a[i];
60  |       d[i] = a[i];
61  |    }
62  | }
63  | void TestMultiBoth() {
64  |    for( int i = 0; i < ELEMENT_COUNT; ++i ) {
65  |       c[i] = a[i] + b[i];
66  |       d[i] = a[i] - b[i];
67  |    }
68  | }
69  |
70  | void TestWriteAndModifyPaired() {
71  |    for( int i = 0; i < ELEMENT_COUNT; i+=2 ) {
72  |       c[i] = c[i] + b[i];
73  |       c[i+1] = b[i];
74  |    }
75  | }
76  | void TestWriteAndModifySeparate() {
77  |    const int HALF_ELEMENT_COUNT = ELEMENT_COUNT / 2;
78  |    for( int i = 0; i < HALF_ELEMENT_COUNT; ++i ) {
79  |       c[i] = c[i] + b[i];
80  |       c[i+HALF_ELEMENT_COUNT] = b[i];
81  |    }
82  | }
```

Listing 16.1: Basic theory

## 16.2 Linked lists

In this source, the idea is to test and prove that linked lists cost more than arrays because of the way they need memory loads to continue their work, as opposed to just being slow because of memory access.

```
struct A {
  int val;
  int pad1;
  int pad2;
  int pad3;
};
struct Alink {
  Alink *next;
  int val;
  int pad1;
  int pad2;
  int pad3;
};

A *aArray;
A **aPointerArray;
Alink *aLinkedList;

const int ELEMENT_COUNT = 4 * 1024 * 1024;

void TestSumArray() {
  int accumulator = 0;
  for( int i = 0; i < ELEMENT_COUNT; i+=1 ) {
    accumulator += aArray[i].val;
  }
}
void TestSumArrayPointer() {
  int accumulator = 0;
  for( int i = 0; i < ELEMENT_COUNT; i+=1 ) {
    accumulator += aPointerArray[i]->val;
  }
}
void TestSumLinkedList() {
  int accumulator = 0;
  Alink *link = aLinkedList;
  while( link != nullptr ) {
    accumulator += link->val;
    link = link->next;
  }
}
```

Listing 16.2: Linked Lists

## 16.3   Branch prediction

In this source, we're looking for the effect of branch prediction.

```
// a1 and b1 are random.
// a2 and b2 are paired the same, but are sorted by the values in
    a2

void TrivialRandomBranching() {
    int sum=0;
    for (int i = 0; i < ELEMENT_COUNT; i++) {
        if( a1[i] > 128 ) {
            sum += b1[i];
        }
    }
    output_buffer = sum;
}
void TrivialSortedBranching() {
    int sum=0;
    for (int i = 0; i < ELEMENT_COUNT; i++) {
        if( a2[i] > 128 ) {
            sum += b2[i];
        }
    }
    output_buffer = sum;
}
void RealisticRandomBranching() {
    int sum=0;
    for (int i = 0; i < ELEMENT_COUNT; i++) {
        if( a1[i] > 128 ) {
            sum += CalculateForHigh( a1[i], b1[i] );
        } else {
            sum += CalculateForLow( a1[i], b1[i] );
        }
    }
    output_buffer = sum;
}
void RealisticSortedBranching() {
    int sum=0;
    for (int i = 0; i < ELEMENT_COUNT; i++) {
        if( a2[i] > 128 ) {
            sum += CalculateForHigh( a2[i], b2[i] );
        } else {
            sum += CalculateForLow( a2[i], b2[i] );
        }
    }
    output_buffer = sum;
}
```

Listing 16.3: Branch prediction

## 16.4   Cache size effect

In this source, we're looking for how the size of the working set hits the size of the cache.

```
void TestSummingSimple() {
    int sum = 0;
    for( int i = 0; i < ELEMENT_COUNT; ++i ) {
        sum += a[i];
    }
}
```

```
7   void TestSummingBackwards() {
8     int sum = 0;
9     for( int i = ELEMENT_COUNT-1; i >= 0; --i ) {
10      sum += a[i];
11    }
12  }
13  void TestSummingStrides() {
14    int sum = 0;
15    const int STRIDE = 16;
16    for( int offset = 0; offset < STRIDE; offset += 1 ) {
17      for( int i = offset; i < ELEMENT_COUNT; i += STRIDE ) {
18        sum += a[i];
19      }
20    }
21  }
22  template<int byte_limit>
23  void TestWriteRangeLimited() {
24    int mask = (byte_limit / sizeof( c[0] ))-1;
25    for( int i = 0; i < ELEMENT_COUNT*16; i+= 16 ) {
26      c[i&mask] = i;
27    }
28  }
29  template<int byte_limit>
30  void TestModifyRangeLimited() {
31    int mask = (byte_limit / sizeof( c[0] ))-1;
32    for( int i = 0; i < ELEMENT_COUNT*16; i+= 16 ) {
33      c[i&mask] += 1;
34    }
35  }
```

Listing 16.4: Cache vs working set

## 16.5 False sharing

In this source, we're looking at the effect of false sharing.

```
1   template<int NUM_THREADS>
2   void TestFalseSharing() {
3     int sum=0;
4     int aligned_sum_store[NUM_THREADS] __attribute__((aligned(64)))
        ;
5
6   #pragma omp parallel num_threads(NUM_THREADS)
7     {
8       int me = omp_get_thread_num();
9       aligned_sum_store[me] = 0;
10
11  //#pragma omp for
12      for (int i = me; i < ELEMENT_COUNT; i += NUM_THREADS ) {
13        aligned_sum_store[me] += CalcValue( i );
14      }
15
16  #pragma omp atomic
17      sum += aligned_sum_store[me];
18    }
19    output_buffer = sum;
20  }
21
22
23  template<int NUM_THREADS>
24  void TestLocalAccumulator() {
25    int sum=0;
26
27  #pragma omp parallel num_threads(NUM_THREADS)
28    {
29      int me = omp_get_thread_num();
30      int local_accumulator = 0;
31
32  //#pragma omp for
```

```
33         for (int i = me; i < ELEMENT_COUNT; i += NUM_THREADS ) {
34             local_accumulator += CalcValue( i );
35         }
36
37 #pragma omp atomic
38         sum += local_accumulator;
39     }
40     output_buffer = sum;
41 }
42
43 template<int NUM_THREADS>
44 void TestSplitLoad() {
45     int sum=0;
46     const int WORK_LOAD = ELEMENT_COUNT / NUM_THREADS;
47
48 #pragma omp parallel num_threads(NUM_THREADS)
49     {
50         int me = omp_get_thread_num();
51         int local_accumulator = 0;
52
53         const int start = WORK_LOAD * me;
54         const int end = WORK_LOAD * (me+1);
55 //#pragma omp for
56         for (int i = start; i < end; ++i ) {
57             local_accumulator += CalcValue( i );
58         }
59
60 #pragma omp atomic
61         sum += local_accumulator;
62     }
63     output_buffer = sum;
64 }
65
66 void TestSinglethreaded() {
67     int sum=0;
68     // just one thread
69     {
70         int local_accumulator = 0;
71
72         for (int i = 0; i < ELEMENT_COUNT; i++) {
73             local_accumulator += CalcValue( i );
74         }
75
76         sum += local_accumulator;
77     }
78     output_buffer = sum;
79 }
```

Listing 16.5: False sharing

## 16.6   Hot, cold, access

In this source, we're looking at the effect of accessing hot and cold data.

```
1  const int NUM_PARTICLES = 10000;
2  const int FRAMES_PER_SECOND = 60;
3  const int NUM_UPDATES = FRAMES_PER_SECOND * 10; // ten seconds of
       particle updates at 60fps;
4  const float UPDATE_DELTA = 1000.0f / FRAMES_PER_SECOND; // delta
       in ms
5
6  struct particle_buffer_Simple {
7      struct particle {
8          Vec3 pos;
9          Vec3 velocity;
10         float lifetime;
11         uint32_t colour;
12         float size;
13         uint32_t materialOrUVLookupData;
```

```
14 |   };
15 |   particle *p;
16 | };
17 | struct particle_buffer_HotColdSplit {
18 |   struct particle_hot {
19 |     Vec3 pos;
20 |     Vec3 velocity;
21 |   };
22 |   struct particle_cold {
23 |     float lifetime;
24 |     uint32_t colour;
25 |     float size;
26 |     uint32_t materialOrUVLookupData;
27 |   };
28 |   particle_hot *ph;
29 |   particle_cold *pc;
30 | };
31 | struct particle_buffer_ReadWriteSplit {
32 |   struct particle_read {
33 |     Vec3 velocity;
34 |   };
35 |   struct particle_write {
36 |     Vec3 pos;
37 |   };
38 |   struct particle_cold {
39 |     float lifetime;
40 |     uint32_t colour;
41 |     float size;
42 |     uint32_t materialOrUVLookupData;
43 |   };
44 |   particle_read *pr;
45 |   particle_write *pw;
46 |   particle_cold *pc;
47 | };
48 |
49 | void TestUpdateParticles_Simple() {
50 |   particle_buffer_Simple *pb = &gData->pbSimple;
51 |   for( int u = 0; u < NUM_UPDATES; ++u ) {
52 |     float delta_time = pcg32_random_r_rangef(&rng, UPDATE_DELTA *
   |       0.9f, UPDATE_DELTA * 1.1f );
53 |     for( int i = 0; i < NUM_PARTICLES; ++i ) {
54 |       particle_buffer_Simple::particle *p = pb->p+i;
55 |       p->pos += p->velocity * delta_time;
56 |     }
57 |   }
58 | }
59 | void TestUpdateParticles_HotColdSplit() {
60 |   particle_buffer_HotColdSplit *pb = &gData->pbHotCold;
61 |   for( int u = 0; u < NUM_UPDATES; ++u ) {
62 |     float delta_time = pcg32_random_r_rangef(&rng, UPDATE_DELTA *
   |       0.9f, UPDATE_DELTA * 1.1f );
63 |     for( int i = 0; i < NUM_PARTICLES; ++i ) {
64 |       particle_buffer_HotColdSplit::particle_hot *p = pb->ph+i;
65 |       p->pos += p->velocity * delta_time;
66 |     }
67 |   }
68 | }
69 | void TestUpdateParticles_ReadWriteSplit() {
70 |   particle_buffer_ReadWriteSplit *pb = &gData->pbReadWrite;
71 |   for( int u = 0; u < NUM_UPDATES; ++u ) {
72 |     float delta_time = pcg32_random_r_rangef(&rng, UPDATE_DELTA *
   |       0.9f, UPDATE_DELTA * 1.1f );
73 |     for( int i = 0; i < NUM_PARTICLES; ++i ) {
74 |       particle_buffer_ReadWriteSplit::particle_read *pr = pb->pr+
   |         i;
75 |       particle_buffer_ReadWriteSplit::particle_write *pw = pb->pw
   |         +i;
76 |       pw->pos += pr->velocity * delta_time;
77 |     }
78 |   }
79 | }
```

Listing 16.6: Hot Cold

## 16.7   Key lookup

In this source, we're looking at how using cache lines more
effectively can improve something as fundamental as a
lookup by key.

```
int SECONDSOFANIMATION = 10;
static const int NUM_QUERIES = 1000;
static const int NUM_NODES = 145;
static int minFrameRate = 10;
static int maxFrameRate = 15;
static const float RATIO_OF_NON_SCALING = 0.85f;

// basic animation key lookup
struct FullAnimKey {
    float time;
    Vec3 translation;
    Vec3 scale;
    Vec4 rotation; // sijk quaternion
};
struct FullAnim {
    int numKeys;
    FullAnimKey *keys;
    FullAnimKey GetKeyAtTimeBinary( float t ) {
        int l = 0, h = numKeys-1;
        int m = (l+h) / 2;
        while( l < h ) {
            if( t < keys[m].time ) {
                h = m-1;
            } else {
                l = m;
            }
            m = (l+h+1) / 2;
        }
        return keys[m];
    }
    FullAnimKey GetKeyAtTimeLinear( float t ) {
        int i = 0;
        while( i < numKeys ) {
            if( keys[i].time > t ) {
                --i;
                break;
            }
            ++i;
        }
        if( i < 0 )
            return keys[0];
        return keys[i];
    }
};

// looking up keys by time
struct DataOnlyAnimKey {
    Vec3 translation;
    Vec3 scale;
    Vec4 rotation; // sijk quaternion
};
struct DataOnlyAnim {
    int numKeys;
    float *keyTime;
    DataOnlyAnimKey *keys;
    DataOnlyAnimKey GetKeyAtTimeBinary( float t ) {
        int l = 0, h = numKeys-1;
        int m = (l+h) / 2;
        while( l < h ) {
            if( t < keyTime[m] ) {
                h = m-1;
            } else {
                l = m;
            }
            m = (l+h+1) / 2;
        }
        return keys[m];
    }
    DataOnlyAnimKey GetKeyAtTimeLinear( float t ) {
```

```
       int i = 0;
       while( i < numKeys ) {
          if( keyTime[i] > t ) {
             --i;
             break;
          }
          ++i;
       }
       if( i < 0 )
          return keys[0];
       return keys[i];
    }
};
struct ClumpedAnim {
    int numKeys;
    float *keyTime;
    DataOnlyAnimKey *keys;
    static const int numPrefetchedKeyTimes = (64-sizeof(int)-sizeof
       (float*)-sizeof(DataOnlyAnimKey*))/sizeof(float);
    static const int keysPerLump = 64/sizeof(float);
    float firstStage[numPrefetchedKeyTimes];
    DataOnlyAnimKey GetKeyAtTimeBinary( float t ) {
       for( int start = 0; start < numPrefetchedKeyTimes; ++start )
          {
          if( firstStage[start] > t ) {
             int l = start*keysPerLump;
             int h = l + keysPerLump;
             h = h > numKeys ? numKeys : h;
             return GetKeyAtTimeBinary( t, l, h+1 );
          }
       }
       return GetKeyAtTimeBinary( t, numPrefetchedKeyTimes*
          keysPerLump, numKeys );
    }
    DataOnlyAnimKey GetKeyAtTimeBinary( float t, int l, int h ) {
       int m = (l+h) / 2;
       while( l < h ) {
          if( t < keyTime[m] ) {
             h = m-1;
          } else {
             l = m;
          }
          m = (l+h+1) / 2;
       }
       return keys[m];
    }
    DataOnlyAnimKey GetKeyAtTimeLinear( float t ) {
       for( int start = 0; start < numPrefetchedKeyTimes; ++start )
          {
          if( firstStage[start] > t ) {
             int l = start*keysPerLump;
             int h = l + keysPerLump;
             h = h > numKeys ? numKeys : h;
             return GetKeyAtTimeLinear( t, l );
          }
       }
       return GetKeyAtTimeLinear( t, numPrefetchedKeyTimes*
          keysPerLump );
    }
    DataOnlyAnimKey GetKeyAtTimeLinear( float t, int startIndex ) {
       int i = startIndex;
       while( i < numKeys ) {
          if( keyTime[i] > t ) {
             --i;
             break;
          }
          ++i;
       }
       if( i < 0 )
          return keys[0];
       return keys[i];
    }
};

struct HierarchyOutputData {
    struct NodeData {
       Vec3 translation;
       Vec3 scale;
       Vec4 rotation; // sijk quaternion
```

```
 144        };
 145        NodeData nodeData[NUM_NODES];
 146      };
 147      template<typename AnimType>
 148      struct TestHierarchy {
 149        AnimType animForNode[NUM_NODES];
 150        void SetupNode( int node, const AnimData &ad ) {
 151          FromData( animForNode[node], ad );
 152        }
 153        HierarchyOutputData GetAtTBinary( float t ) {
 154          HierarchyOutputData hod;
 155          for( int i = 0; i < NUM_NODES; ++i ) {
 156            auto keyData = animForNode[i].GetKeyAtTimeBinary( t );
 157            hod.nodeData[i].translation = keyData.translation;
 158            hod.nodeData[i].rotation = keyData.rotation;
 159            hod.nodeData[i].scale = keyData.scale;
 160          }
 161          return hod;
 162        }
 163        HierarchyOutputData GetAtTLinear( float t ) {
 164          HierarchyOutputData hod;
 165          for( int i = 0; i < NUM_NODES; ++i ) {
 166            auto keyData = animForNode[i].GetKeyAtTimeLinear( t );
 167            hod.nodeData[i].translation = keyData.translation;
 168            hod.nodeData[i].rotation = keyData.rotation;
 169            hod.nodeData[i].scale = keyData.scale;
 170          }
 171          return hod;
 172        }
 173      };
 174
 175      void TestFullAnimBinary() {
 176        for( auto t : gData->queries ) {
 177          HierarchyOutputData hod = gData->fullAnimHierarchy.
                  GetAtTBinary(t);
 178          memcpy( (void*)&output_data, &hod, sizeof( output_data ) );
 179        }
 180      }
 181      void TestFullAnimLinear() {
 182        for( auto t : gData->queries ) {
 183          HierarchyOutputData hod = gData->fullAnimHierarchy.
                  GetAtTLinear(t);
 184          memcpy( (void*)&output_data, &hod, sizeof( output_data ) );
 185        }
 186      }
 187      void TestDataOnlyBinary() {
 188        for( auto t : gData->queries ) {
 189          HierarchyOutputData hod = gData->dataOnlyHierarchy.
                  GetAtTBinary(t);
 190          memcpy( (void*)&output_data, &hod, sizeof( output_data ) );
 191        }
 192      }
 193      void TestDataOnlyLinear() {
 194        for( auto t : gData->queries ) {
 195          HierarchyOutputData hod = gData->dataOnlyHierarchy.
                  GetAtTLinear(t);
 196          memcpy( (void*)&output_data, &hod, sizeof( output_data ) );
 197        }
 198      }
 199      void TestClumpedBinary() {
 200        for( auto t : gData->queries ) {
 201          HierarchyOutputData hod = gData->clumpedHierarchy.
                  GetAtTBinary(t);
 202          memcpy( (void*)&output_data, &hod, sizeof( output_data ) );
 203        }
 204      }
 205      void TestClumpedLinear() {
 206        for( auto t : gData->queries ) {
 207          HierarchyOutputData hod = gData->clumpedHierarchy.
                  GetAtTLinear(t);
 208          memcpy( (void*)&output_data, &hod, sizeof( output_data ) );
 209        }
 210      }
```

Listing 16.7: Key lookup

# 16.8 Matrix transpose

In this source, we're looking at how you can improve memory throughput for an algorithm that has to touch memory in a bad pattern.

```
const int MATRIX_SIZE = 1024;
struct LargeMatrix {
    float m[MATRIX_SIZE * MATRIX_SIZE];
};
struct Data {
    LargeMatrix from, to;
};
Data *gData;

void TestTranspose_ReadRows() {
    float *in = &(gData->from.m[0]);
    float *out = &(gData->to.m[0]);
    for( int j = 0; j < MATRIX_SIZE; j++ ) {
        for( int i = 0; i < MATRIX_SIZE; i++ ) {
            out[i*MATRIX_SIZE+j]=in[j*MATRIX_SIZE+i];
        }
    }
}
void TestTranspose_ReadColumns() {
    float *in = &(gData->from.m[0]);
    float *out = &(gData->to.m[0]);
    for( int i = 0; i < MATRIX_SIZE; i++ ) {
        for( int j = 0; j < MATRIX_SIZE; j++ ) {
            out[i*MATRIX_SIZE+j]=in[j*MATRIX_SIZE+i];
        }
    }
}
template<int block_size>
void TestTranspose_RowBlock() {
    float *in = &(gData->from.m[0]);
    float *out = &(gData->to.m[0]);
    for (int bj = 0; bj < MATRIX_SIZE; bj += block_size) {
        for (int bi = 0; bi < MATRIX_SIZE; bi += block_size) {
            int imax = bi + block_size; imax = imax < MATRIX_SIZE ?
                imax : MATRIX_SIZE;
            int jmax = bj + block_size; jmax = jmax < MATRIX_SIZE ?
                jmax : MATRIX_SIZE;
            for (int j = bj; j < jmax; ++j) {
                for (int i = bi; i < imax; ++i) {
                    out[i*MATRIX_SIZE+j] = in[j*MATRIX_SIZE+i];
                }
            }
        }
    }
}
template<int block_size>
void TestTranspose_ColumnBlock() {
    float *in = &(gData->from.m[0]);
    float *out = &(gData->to.m[0]);
    for (int bi = 0; bi < MATRIX_SIZE; bi += block_size) {
        for (int bj = 0; bj < MATRIX_SIZE; bj += block_size) {
            int imax = bi + block_size;
            int jmax = bj + block_size;
            // these cause an overflow assumption warning on newer gcc
            //     compilers (found on 6.3.0)
            //imax = imax < MATRIX_SIZE ? imax : MATRIX_SIZE;
            //jmax = jmax < MATRIX_SIZE ? jmax : MATRIX_SIZE;
            for (int i = bi; i < imax; ++i) {
                for (int j = bj; j < jmax; ++j) {
                    out[i*MATRIX_SIZE+j] = in[j*MATRIX_SIZE+i];
                }
            }
        }
    }
}
template<int block_size>
void TestTranspose_WriteBlock() {
```

```
65      float *in = &(gData->from.m[0]);
66      float *out = &(gData->to.m[0]);
67      for (int bj = 0; bj < MATRIX_SIZE; bj += block_size) {
68          int jmax = bj + block_size; jmax = jmax < MATRIX_SIZE ? jmax
                : MATRIX_SIZE;
69          for (int i = 0; i < MATRIX_SIZE; ++i) {
70              for (int j = bj; j < jmax; ++j) {
71                  out[i*MATRIX_SIZE+j] = in[j*MATRIX_SIZE+i];
72              }
73          }
74      }
75  }
76  template<int read_block, int write_block>
77  void TestTranspose_RowBlock2() {
78      float *in = &(gData->from.m[0]);
79      float *out = &(gData->to.m[0]);
80      for (int bi = 0; bi < MATRIX_SIZE; bi += read_block) {
81          for (int bj = 0; bj < MATRIX_SIZE; bj += write_block) {
82              int imax = bi + read_block; imax = imax < MATRIX_SIZE ?
                    imax : MATRIX_SIZE;
83              int jmax = bj + write_block; jmax = jmax < MATRIX_SIZE ?
                    jmax : MATRIX_SIZE;
84              for (int i = bi; i < imax; ++i) {
85                  for (int j = bj; j < jmax; ++j) {
86                      out[i*MATRIX_SIZE+j] = in[j*MATRIX_SIZE+i];
87                  }
88              }
89          }
90      }
91  }
```

Listing 16.8: Matrix transpose

## 16.9   Modifying memory

In this source, we're looking at how the size of elements and
how many you affect at once, can affect the throughput of
your code.

```
1   const int BUFFER_SIZE = 1024 * 1024; // in bytes
2
3   template<typename T, size_t NumToParallelModify>
4   void TestParallelModifyTemplate() {
5       T *modify_buffer_ptr = (T*)(void*)c;
6       T temp[NumToParallelModify];
7       const size_t TOTAL_ELEMENTS = BUFFER_SIZE / sizeof(T);
8       for( size_t i = 0; i < TOTAL_ELEMENTS; i+=NumToParallelModify )
            {
9           for( size_t j = 0; j < NumToParallelModify; ++j ) {
10              temp[j] = modify_buffer_ptr[i+j];
11              temp[j] += i+j;
12              modify_buffer_ptr[i+j] = temp[j];
13          }
14      }
15  }
16  template<typename T, size_t NumToParallelModify>
17  void TestBatchModifyTemplate() {
18      T *modify_buffer_ptr = (T*)(void*)c;
19      T temp[NumToParallelModify];
20      const size_t TOTAL_ELEMENTS = BUFFER_SIZE / sizeof(T);
21      for( size_t i = 0; i < TOTAL_ELEMENTS; i+=NumToParallelModify )
            {
22          for( size_t j = 0; j < NumToParallelModify; ++j ) {
23              temp[j] = modify_buffer_ptr[i+j];
24          }
25          for( int j = 0; j < NumToParallelModify; ++j ) {
```

```
26 |       temp[j] += i+j;
27 |     }
28 |     for( int j = 0; j < NumToParallelModify; ++j ) {
29 |       modify_buffer_ptr[i+j] = temp[j];
30 |     }
31 |   }
32 | }
33 | void TestParallelModify64Bytes() {
34 |   uint8_t *modify_buffer_ptr = (uint8_t*)(void*)c;
35 |   uint8_t temp[64];
36 |   for( int i = 0; i < BUFFER_SIZE; i+=64 ) {
37 |     for( int j = 0; j < 64; ++j ) {
38 |       temp[j] = modify_buffer_ptr[i+j];
39 |       temp[j] += i+j;
40 |       modify_buffer_ptr[i+j] = temp[j];
41 |     }
42 |   }
43 | }
```

Listing 16.9: Modifying memory

# 16.10  SIMD

In this source, we're trialling some SIMD to solve a particle update.

```
 1 | const int NUM_PARTICLES = 10000;
 2 | const int FRAMES_PER_SECOND = 60;
 3 | const int NUM_UPDATES = FRAMES_PER_SECOND * 10; // ten seconds of
   |     particle updates at 60fps;
 4 |
 5 | const float UPDATE_DELTA = 1000.0f / FRAMES_PER_SECOND; // delta
   |     in ms
 6 |
 7 | struct particle_buffer_AoS {
 8 |   struct particle {
 9 |     float x,y,z,vx,vy,vz,t;
10 |   };
11 |   particle *p;
12 |   float gravity;
13 |   particle_buffer_AoS() {
14 |     p = (particle*)malloc( sizeof(particle) * NUM_PARTICLES );
15 |   }
16 | };
17 |
18 | struct particle_buffer {
19 |   float *posx, *posy, *posz;
20 |   float *vx, *vy, *vz;
21 |   float gravity;
22 |   particle_buffer() {
23 |     posx = (float*)aligned_alloc( 32, sizeof(float) *
   |         NUM_PARTICLES );
24 | // ...
25 |     vz = (float*)aligned_alloc( 32, sizeof(float) * NUM_PARTICLES
   |         );
26 |   }
27 | };
28 |
29 | void SimpleUpdateParticlesAoS( particle_buffer_AoS *pb, float
   |     delta_time ) {
30 |   float g = pb->gravity;
31 |   float gd2 = g * delta_time * delta_time * 0.5f;
32 |   float gd = g * delta_time;
33 |   for( int i = 0; i < NUM_PARTICLES; ++i ) {
34 |     particle_buffer_AoS::particle *p = pb->p+i;
35 |     p->x += p->vx * delta_time;
36 |     p->y += p->vy * delta_time + gd2;
37 |     p->z += p->vz * delta_time;
```

```
38  |        p->vy += gd;
39  |      }
40  |    }
41  |
42  |    void SimpleUpdateParticles( particle_buffer *pb, float delta_time
    |        ) {
43  |      float g = pb->gravity;
44  |      float gd2 = g * delta_time * delta_time * 0.5f;
45  |      float gd = g * delta_time;
46  |      for( int i = 0; i < NUM_PARTICLES; ++i ) {
47  |        pb->posx[i] += pb->vx[i] * delta_time;
48  |        pb->posy[i] += pb->vy[i] * delta_time + gd2;
49  |        pb->posz[i] += pb->vz[i] * delta_time;
50  |        pb->vy[i] += gd;
51  |      }
52  |    }
53  |    void SliceUpdateParticles( particle_buffer *pb, float delta_time
    |        ) {
54  |      float g = pb->gravity;
55  |      float gd2 = g * delta_time * delta_time * 0.5f;
56  |      float gd = g * delta_time;
57  |      for( int i = 0; i < NUM_PARTICLES; ++i ) {
58  |        pb->posx[i] += pb->vx[i] * delta_time;
59  |      }
60  |      for( int i = 0; i < NUM_PARTICLES; ++i ) {
61  |        pb->posy[i] += pb->vy[i] * delta_time + gd2;
62  |        pb->vy[i] += gd;
63  |      }
64  |      for( int i = 0; i < NUM_PARTICLES; ++i ) {
65  |        pb->posz[i] += pb->vz[i] * delta_time;
66  |      }
67  |    }
68  |    #if __SSE__
69  |    void SIMD_SSE_UpdateParticles( particle_buffer *pb, float
    |        delta_time ) {
70  |      float g = pb->gravity;
71  |      float f_gd = g * delta_time;
72  |      float f_gd2 = pb->gravity * delta_time * delta_time * 0.5f;
73  |
74  |      // delta_time
75  |      __m128 mmd = _mm_setr_ps( delta_time, delta_time, delta_time,
    |        delta_time );
76  |      // gravity * delta_time
77  |      __m128 mmgd = _mm_load1_ps( &f_gd );
78  |      // gravity * delta_time * delta_time * 0.5f
79  |      __m128 mmgd2 = _mm_load1_ps( &f_gd2 );
80  |
81  |      __m128 *px = (__m128*)pb->posx;
82  |      __m128 *py = (__m128*)pb->posx;
83  |      __m128 *pz = (__m128*)pb->posz;
84  |      __m128 *vx = (__m128*)pb->vx;
85  |      __m128 *vy = (__m128*)pb->vy;
86  |      __m128 *vz = (__m128*)pb->vz;
87  |
88  |      int iterationCount = NUM_PARTICLES / 4;
89  |      for( int i = 0; i < iterationCount; ++i ) {
90  |        __m128 dx = _mm_mul_ps(vx[i], mmd );
91  |        __m128 dy = _mm_add_ps( _mm_mul_ps(vy[i], mmd ), mmgd2 );
92  |        __m128 dz = _mm_mul_ps(vz[i], mmd );
93  |        __m128 newx = _mm_add_ps(px[i], dx);
94  |        __m128 newy = _mm_add_ps(py[i], dy);
95  |        __m128 newz = _mm_add_ps(pz[i], dz);
96  |        __m128 newvy = _mm_add_ps(vy[i], mmgd);
97  |        _mm_store_ps((float*)(px+i), newx);
98  |        _mm_store_ps((float*)(py+i), newy);
99  |        _mm_store_ps((float*)(pz+i), newz);
100 |        _mm_store_ps((float*)(vy+i), newvy);
101 |      }
102 |    }
103 |    void SIMD_SSE_UpdateParticlesSliced( particle_buffer *pb, float
    |        delta_time ) {
104 |      float g = pb->gravity;
105 |      float f_gd = g * delta_time;
106 |      float f_gd2 = pb->gravity * delta_time * delta_time * 0.5f;
107 |
108 |      // delta_time
109 |      __m128 mmd = _mm_setr_ps( delta_time, delta_time, delta_time,
    |        delta_time );
110 |      // gravity * delta_time
```

```
111  |    __m128 mmgd = _mm_load1_ps( &f_gd );
112  |    // gravity * delta_time * delta_time * 0.5f
113  |    __m128 mmgd2 = _mm_load1_ps( &f_gd2 );
114  |
115  |    __m128 *px = (__m128*)pb->posx;
116  |    __m128 *py = (__m128*)pb->posx;
117  |    __m128 *pz = (__m128*)pb->posz;
118  |    __m128 *vx = (__m128*)pb->vx;
119  |    __m128 *vy = (__m128*)pb->vy;
120  |    __m128 *vz = (__m128*)pb->vz;
121  |
122  |    int iterationCount = NUM_PARTICLES / 4;
123  |    for( int i = 0; i < iterationCount; ++i ) {
124  |      __m128 dx = _mm_mul_ps(vx[i], mmd );
125  |      __m128 newx = _mm_add_ps(px[i], dx);
126  |      _mm_store_ps((float*)(px+i), newx);
127  |    }
128  |    for( int i = 0; i < iterationCount; ++i ) {
129  |      __m128 dy = _mm_add_ps( _mm_mul_ps(vy[i], mmd ), mmgd2 );
130  |      __m128 newy = _mm_add_ps(py[i], dy);
131  |      __m128 newvy = _mm_add_ps(vy[i], mmgd);
132  |      _mm_store_ps((float*)(py+i), newy);
133  |      _mm_store_ps((float*)(vy+i), newvy);
134  |    }
135  |    for( int i = 0; i < iterationCount; ++i ) {
136  |      __m128 dz = _mm_mul_ps(vz[i], mmd );
137  |      __m128 newz = _mm_add_ps(pz[i], dz);
138  |      _mm_store_ps((float*)(pz+i), newz);
139  |    }
140  |  }
141  |  #endif
142  |
143  |  #if __AVX__
144  |  void SIMD_AVX_UpdateParticles( particle_buffer *pb, float
     |      delta_time ) {
145  |    float g = pb->gravity;
146  |    float f_gd = g * delta_time;
147  |    float f_gd2 = pb->gravity * delta_time * delta_time * 0.5f;
148  |
149  |    // delta_time
150  |    __m256 mm256d = _mm256_set1_ps( delta_time );
151  |    // gravity * delta_time
152  |    __m256 mm256gd = _mm256_set1_ps( f_gd );
153  |    // gravity * delta_time * delta_time * 0.5f
154  |    __m256 mm256gd2 = _mm256_set1_ps( f_gd2 );
155  |
156  |    __m256 *px = (__m256*)pb->posx;
157  |    __m256 *py = (__m256*)pb->posx;
158  |    __m256 *pz = (__m256*)pb->posz;
159  |    __m256 *vx = (__m256*)pb->vx;
160  |    __m256 *vy = (__m256*)pb->vy;
161  |    __m256 *vz = (__m256*)pb->vz;
162  |
163  |    int iterationCount = NUM_PARTICLES / 8;
164  |    for( int i = 0; i < iterationCount; ++i ) {
165  |      __m256 dx = _mm256_mul_ps(vx[i], mm256d );
166  |      __m256 dy = _mm256_add_ps( _mm256_mul_ps(vy[i], mm256d ),
     |          mm256gd2 );
167  |      __m256 dz = _mm256_mul_ps(vz[i], mm256d );
168  |      __m256 newx = _mm256_add_ps(px[i], dx);
169  |      __m256 newy = _mm256_add_ps(py[i], dy);
170  |      __m256 newz = _mm256_add_ps(pz[i], dz);
171  |      __m256 newvy = _mm256_add_ps(vy[i], mm256gd);
172  |      _mm256_store_ps((float*)(px+i), newx);
173  |      _mm256_store_ps((float*)(py+i), newy);
174  |      _mm256_store_ps((float*)(pz+i), newz);
175  |      _mm256_store_ps((float*)(vy+i), newvy);
176  |    }
177  |  }
178  |  #endif
```

Listing 16.10: SIMD particles

# 16.11   Speculative waste

In this source, we're looking at the effect of speculative reads
on performance.

```
 1   struct B {
 2     int height;
 3     bool isClockwise;
 4   };
 5   struct A {
 6     bool canStandOnOneLeg;
 7     bool hasTheirOwnHair;
 8     bool ownsADog;
 9     bool isOwnedByACat;
10
11     // cached "has B info"
12     bool isCached25 : 1;
13     bool isCached50 : 1;
14     bool isCached75 : 1;
15     bool isCached95 : 1;
16     bool isCached99 : 1;
17     bool hasBInfo;
18     bool isTall;
19   };
20   static std::map<int,B> BInfoMap;
21   static std::vector<A> AInfoVec;
22   static const int NUM_IN_TEST = 128 * 1024;
23   void Setup() {
24     Timer t;
25     for( int i = 0; i < NUM_IN_TEST; ++i ) {
26       A a;
27       a.canStandOnOneLeg = pcg32_random_r_probability(&rng, 0.99f);
28   //...
29       a.isOwnedByACat = pcg32_random_r_probability(&rng, 0.42f);
30       a.isCached25 = pcg32_random_r_probability(&rng, 0.25f);
31   // ...
32       a.isCached99 = pcg32_random_r_probability(&rng, 0.99f);
33       a.hasBInfo = pcg32_random_r_probability(&rng, 0.25f);
34       if( a.hasBInfo ) {
35         B b;
36         b.height = pcg32_random_r_range(&rng, 150, 200);
37         b.isClockwise = pcg32_random_r_probability(&rng, 0.5f);
38         BInfoMap[i] = b;
39         a.isTall = b.height > 185;
40       }
41       AInfoVec.push_back( a );
42     }
43   }
44
45   std::pair<int,int> Simple() {
46     int good = 0;
47     int taller = 0;
48     for( int i = 0; i < NUM_IN_TEST; ++i ) {
49       A &a = AInfoVec[i];
50       if( a.canStandOnOneLeg && a.hasTheirOwnHair ) {
51         good += 1;
52         if( BInfoMap.find( i ) != BInfoMap.end() ) {
53           if( BInfoMap[i].height > 185 ) {
54             taller += 1;
55           }
56         }
57       }
58     }
59     return std::pair<int,int>(good,taller);
60   }
61   std::pair<int,int> Bool() {
62     int good = 0;
63     int taller = 0;
64     for( int i = 0; i < NUM_IN_TEST; ++i ) {
65       A &a = AInfoVec[i];
66       if( a.canStandOnOneLeg && a.hasTheirOwnHair ) {
67         good += 1;
68         if( a.hasBInfo ) {
69           if( BInfoMap[i].height > 185 ) {
70             taller += 1;
71           }
```

```
 72 |       }
 73 |     }
 74 |   }
 75 |   return std::pair<int,int>(good,taller);
 76 | }
 77 | std::pair<int,int> CachedBool50() {
 78 |   int good = 0;
 79 |   int taller = 0;
 80 |   for( int i = 0; i < NUM_IN_TEST; ++i ) {
 81 |     A &a = AInfoVec[i];
 82 |     if( a.canStandOnOneLeg && a.hasTheirOwnHair ) {
 83 |       good += 1;
 84 |       if( a.isCached50 ) {
 85 |         if( a.hasBInfo ) {
 86 |           if( BInfoMap[i].height > 185 ) {
 87 |             taller += 1;
 88 |           }
 89 |         }
 90 |       } else {
 91 |         if( BInfoMap.find( i ) != BInfoMap.end() ) {
 92 |           if( BInfoMap[i].height > 185 ) {
 93 |             taller += 1;
 94 |           }
 95 |         }
 96 |       }
 97 |     }
 98 |   }
 99 |   return std::pair<int,int>(good,taller);
100 | }
101 | std::pair<int,int> Cached() {
102 |   int good = 0;
103 |   int taller = 0;
104 |   for( int i = 0; i < NUM_IN_TEST; ++i ) {
105 |     A &a = AInfoVec[i];
106 |     if( a.canStandOnOneLeg && a.hasTheirOwnHair ) {
107 |       good += 1;
108 |       if( a.hasBInfo && a.isTall ) {
109 |         taller += 1;
110 |       }
111 |     }
112 |   }
113 |   return std::pair<int,int>(good,taller);
114 | }
115 | std::pair<int,int> PartiallyCached25() {
116 |   int good = 0;
117 |   int taller = 0;
118 |   for( int i = 0; i < NUM_IN_TEST; ++i ) {
119 |     A &a = AInfoVec[i];
120 |     if( a.canStandOnOneLeg && a.hasTheirOwnHair ) {
121 |       good += 1;
122 |       if( a.isCached25 ) {
123 |         if( a.hasBInfo && a.isTall ) {
124 |           taller += 1;
125 |         }
126 |       } else {
127 |         if( BInfoMap.find( i ) != BInfoMap.end() ) {
128 |           if( BInfoMap[i].height > 185 ) {
129 |             taller += 1;
130 |           }
131 |         }
132 |       }
133 |     }
134 |   }
135 |   return std::pair<int,int>(good,taller);
136 | }
```

Listing 16.11: Speculative Waste

# 16.12   Finite State Machines

These are the source files for testing the finite state machine
variants.

```
namespace FSMSimple {
   enum State {
      S_sleeping,
      S_hunting,
      S_eating,
      S_exploring,
   };
   struct Machine {
      State state;
      float sleepiness;
      float hunger;
      float huntTimer;
      float eatTimer;
   };
   struct Data {
      Machine machine[NUM_MACHINES];
      Data() {
         pcg32_random_t rng;
         pcg32_srandom_r(&rng, 1234, 5678);
         for( int m = 0; m < NUM_MACHINES; ++m ) {
            Machine &M = machine[m];
            M.state = S_sleeping;
            M.sleepiness = pcg32_random_r_rangef(&rng, 0.0f, 0.2f );
            M.hunger = pcg32_random_r_rangef(&rng, 0.5f, 0.9f );
            M.huntTimer = HUNTING_TIME;
            M.eatTimer = 0.0f;
         }
      }
      void Update( float deltaTime ) {
         for( int m = 0; m < NUM_MACHINES; ++m ) {
            Machine &M = machine[m];
            switch( M.state ) {
               case S_sleeping:
               {
                  M.hunger += deltaTime * SLEEP_HUNGER;
                  M.sleepiness += deltaTime * SLEEP_SLEEP;
                  if( M.sleepiness <= 0.0f ) {
                     M.sleepiness = 0.0f;
                     if( M.eatTimer > 0.0f ) {
                        M.state = S_eating;
                     } else {
                        if( M.hunger > HUNGER_TRIGGER ) {
                           M.state = S_hunting;
                           M.huntTimer = HUNTING_TIME;
                        } else {
                           M.state = S_exploring;
                        }
                     }
                  }
               } break;
               case S_hunting:
               {
                  M.hunger += deltaTime * HUNT_HUNGER;
                  M.sleepiness += deltaTime * HUNT_SLEEP;
                  M.huntTimer -= deltaTime;
                  if( M.huntTimer <= 0.0f ) {
                     M.eatTimer = EATING_TIME;
                     if( M.sleepiness > SLEEP_TRIGGER ) {
                        M.state = S_sleeping;
                     } else {
                        M.state = S_eating;
                     }
                  } else {
                  }
               } break;
               case S_eating:
               {
                  M.hunger += deltaTime * EAT_HUNGER;
                  M.sleepiness += deltaTime * EAT_SLEEP;
                  M.eatTimer -= deltaTime;
                  if( M.sleepiness > SLEEP_TRIGGER ) {
```

```
72          M.state = S_sleeping;
73        } else {
74          if( M.eatTimer <= 0.0f ) {
75            if( M.hunger > HUNGER_TRIGGER ) {
76              M.state = S_hunting;
77              M.huntTimer = HUNTING_TIME;
78            } else {
79              M.state = S_exploring;
80            }
81          }
82        }
83      } break;
84      case S_exploring:
85      {
86        M.hunger += deltaTime * EXPLORE_HUNGER;
87        M.sleepiness += deltaTime * EXPLORE_SLEEP;
88        if( M.hunger > HUNGER_TRIGGER ) {
89          M.state = S_hunting;
90          M.huntTimer = HUNTING_TIME;
91        }
92        else {
93          if( M.sleepiness > SLEEP_TRIGGER ) {
94            M.state = S_sleeping;
95          }
96        }
97      } break;
98      }
99    }
100   }
101 };
102 }
```

Listing 16.12: Finite State Machine - Simple

```
1  namespace FSM00State {
2    struct State;
3    struct Machine {
4      State *state = nullptr;
5      float sleepiness;
6      float hunger;
7      float huntTimer;
8      float eatTimer;
9      inline void UpdateState( State *newState );
10     inline ~Machine();
11   };
12   struct State {
13     virtual State * Update( Machine &M, float deltaTime ) = 0;
14     virtual const char * GetName() { return "Base"; }
15   };
16   struct Sleeping final : public State {
17     State * Update( Machine &M, float deltaTime ) override;
18     const char * GetName() override { return "Sleeping"; }
19   };
20   struct Hunting final : public State {
21     State * Update( Machine &M, float deltaTime ) override;
22     const char * GetName() override { return "Hunting"; }
23   };
24   struct Eating final : public State {
25     State * Update( Machine &M, float deltaTime ) override;
26     virtual const char * GetName() override { return "Eating"; }
27   };
28   struct Exploring final : public State {
29     State * Update( Machine &M, float deltaTime ) override;
30     const char * GetName() override { return "Exploring"; }
31   };
32   Sleeping m_commonSleeping;
33   Hunting m_commonHunting;
34   Eating m_commonEating;
35   Exploring m_commonExploring;
36   struct Data {
37     Machine machine[NUM_MACHINES];
38     Data() {
39       pcg32_random_t rng;
40       pcg32_srandom_r(&rng, 1234, 5678);
41       for( int m = 0; m < NUM_MACHINES; ++m ) {
42         Machine &M = machine[m];
43         M.state = &m_commonSleeping;
44         M.sleepiness = pcg32_random_r_rangef(&rng, 0.0f, 0.2f );
```

```
45              M.hunger = pcg32_random_r_rangef(&rng, 0.5f, 0.9f );
46              M.huntTimer = HUNTING_TIME;
47              M.eatTimer = 0.0f;
48           }
49        }
50        void Update( float deltaTime ) {
51           for( int m = 0; m < NUM_MACHINES; ++m ) {
52              Machine &M = machine[m];
53              State *newState = M.state->Update( M, deltaTime );
54              M.UpdateState(newState);
55           }
56        }
57        int StateObjectToStateIndex( State *s ) {
58           if( strcmp( s->GetName(), m_commonSleeping.GetName() ) == 0
                 )
59              return 0;
60           if( strcmp( s->GetName(), m_commonHunting.GetName() ) == 0
                 )
61              return 1;
62           if( strcmp( s->GetName(), m_commonEating.GetName() ) == 0 )
63              return 2;
64           if( strcmp( s->GetName(), m_commonExploring.GetName() ) ==
                 0 )
65              return 3;
66           return -1;
67        }
68     };
69     // inlines
70     inline void Machine::UpdateState( State *newState ) {
71        if( newState ) {
72           state = newState;
73        }
74     }
75     inline Machine::~Machine() {
76        state = nullptr;
77     }
78     State * Sleeping::Update( Machine &M, float deltaTime ) {
79        M.hunger += deltaTime * SLEEP_HUNGER;
80        M.sleepiness += deltaTime * SLEEP_SLEEP;
81        if( M.sleepiness <= 0.0f ) {
82           M.sleepiness = 0.0f;
83           if( M.eatTimer > 0.0f ) {
84              return &m_commonEating;
85           } else {
86              if( M.hunger > HUNGER_TRIGGER ) {
87                 M.huntTimer = HUNTING_TIME;
88                 return &m_commonHunting;
89              } else {
90                 return &m_commonExploring;
91              }
92           }
93        }
94        return nullptr;
95     }
96     State * Hunting::Update( Machine &M, float deltaTime ) {
97        M.hunger += deltaTime * HUNT_HUNGER;
98        M.sleepiness += deltaTime * HUNT_SLEEP;
99        M.huntTimer -= deltaTime;
100       if( M.huntTimer <= 0.0f ) {
101          M.eatTimer = EATING_TIME;
102          if( M.sleepiness > SLEEP_TRIGGER ) {
103             return &m_commonSleeping;
104          } else {
105             return &m_commonEating;
106          }
107       }
108       return nullptr;
109    }
110    State * Eating::Update( Machine &M, float deltaTime ) {
111       M.hunger += deltaTime * EAT_HUNGER;
112       M.sleepiness += deltaTime * EAT_SLEEP;
113       M.eatTimer -= deltaTime;
114       if( M.sleepiness > SLEEP_TRIGGER ) {
115          return &m_commonSleeping;
116       } else {
117          if( M.eatTimer <= 0.0f ) {
118             if( M.hunger > HUNGER_TRIGGER ) {
119                M.huntTimer = HUNTING_TIME;
120                return &m_commonHunting;
121             } else {
```

```
122  |              return &m_commonExploring;
123  |            }
124  |          }
125  |        }
126  |        return nullptr;
127  |      }
128  |      State * Exploring::Update( Machine &M, float deltaTime ) {
129  |        M.hunger += deltaTime * EXPLORE_HUNGER;
130  |        M.sleepiness += deltaTime * EXPLORE_SLEEP;
131  |        if( M.hunger > HUNGER_TRIGGER ) {
132  |          M.huntTimer = HUNTING_TIME;
133  |          return &m_commonHunting;
134  |        } else {
135  |          if( M.sleepiness > SLEEP_TRIGGER ) {
136  |            return &m_commonSleeping;
137  |          }
138  |        }
139  |        return nullptr;
140  |      }
141  |  }
```

Listing 16.13: Finite State Machine - Object-oriented

```
 1  | namespace FSMTableState {
 2  |   struct Machine {
 3  |     float sleepiness;
 4  |     float hunger;
 5  |     float huntTimer;
 6  |     float eatTimer;
 7  |   };
 8  |   typedef std::vector<Machine> MachineVector;
 9  |   struct Data {
10  |     MachineVector sleeps;
11  |     MachineVector hunts;
12  |     MachineVector eats;
13  |     MachineVector explores;
14  |     Data() {
15  |       pcg32_random_t rng;
16  |       pcg32_srandom_r(&rng, 1234, 5678);
17  |       for( int m = 0; m < NUM_MACHINES; ++m ) {
18  |         Machine M;
19  |         M.sleepiness = pcg32_random_r_rangef(&rng, 0.0f, 0.2f );
20  |         M.hunger = pcg32_random_r_rangef(&rng, 0.5f, 0.9f );
21  |         M.huntTimer = HUNTING_TIME;
22  |         M.eatTimer = 0.0f;
23  |         sleeps.push_back( M );
24  |       }
25  |     }
26  |     void Update( float deltaTime ) {
27  |       MachineVector pendingSleep;
28  |       MachineVector pendingHunt;
29  |       MachineVector pendingEat;
30  |       MachineVector pendingExplore;
31  |       {
32  |         for( MachineVector::iterator iter = sleeps.begin(); iter
     |             != sleeps.end(); ) {
33  |           Machine &M = *iter;
34  |           M.hunger += deltaTime * SLEEP_HUNGER;
35  |           M.sleepiness += deltaTime * SLEEP_SLEEP;
36  |           if( M.sleepiness <= 0.0f ) {
37  |             M.sleepiness = 0.0f;
38  |             if( M.eatTimer > 0.0f ) {
39  |               pendingEat.push_back(M);
40  |             } else {
41  |               if( M.hunger > HUNGER_TRIGGER ) {
42  |                 M.huntTimer = HUNTING_TIME;
43  |                 pendingHunt.push_back(M);
44  |               } else {
45  |                 pendingExplore.push_back(M);
46  |               }
47  |             }
48  |             *iter = sleeps.back(); sleeps.pop_back();
49  |           } else {
50  |             ++iter;
51  |           }
52  |         }
53  |         for( MachineVector::iterator iter = hunts.begin(); iter
     |             != hunts.end(); ) {
```

```
54          Machine &M = *iter;
55          M.hunger += deltaTime * HUNT_HUNGER;
56          M.sleepiness += deltaTime * HUNT_SLEEP;
57          M.huntTimer -= deltaTime;
58          if( M.huntTimer <= 0.0f ) {
59            M.eatTimer = EATING_TIME;
60            if( M.sleepiness > SLEEP_TRIGGER ) {
61              pendingSleep.push_back(M);
62            } else {
63              pendingEat.push_back(M);
64            }
65            *iter = hunts.back(); hunts.pop_back();
66          } else {
67            ++iter;
68          }
69        }
70        for( MachineVector::iterator iter = eats.begin(); iter !=
              eats.end(); ) {
71          Machine &M = *iter;
72          M.hunger += deltaTime * EAT_HUNGER;
73          M.sleepiness += deltaTime * EAT_SLEEP;
74          M.eatTimer -= deltaTime;
75          if( M.sleepiness > SLEEP_TRIGGER ) {
76            pendingSleep.push_back(M);
77            *iter = eats.back(); eats.pop_back();
78          } else {
79            if( M.eatTimer <= 0.0f ) {
80              if( M.hunger > HUNGER_TRIGGER ) {
81                M.huntTimer = HUNTING_TIME;
82                pendingHunt.push_back(M);
83              } else {
84                pendingExplore.push_back(M);
85              }
86              *iter = eats.back(); eats.pop_back();
87            } else {
88              ++iter;
89            }
90          }
91        }
92        for( MachineVector::iterator iter = explores.begin();
              iter != explores.end(); ) {
93          Machine &M = *iter;
94          M.hunger += deltaTime * EXPLORE_HUNGER;
95          M.sleepiness += deltaTime * EXPLORE_SLEEP;
96          if( M.hunger > HUNGER_TRIGGER ) {
97            M.huntTimer = HUNTING_TIME;
98            pendingHunt.push_back(M);
99            *iter = explores.back(); explores.pop_back();
100         } else {
101           if( M.sleepiness > SLEEP_TRIGGER ) {
102             pendingSleep.push_back(M);
103             *iter = explores.back(); explores.pop_back();
104           } else {
105             ++iter;
106           }
107         }
108       }
109     }
110     sleeps.insert( sleeps.end(), pendingSleep.begin(),
            pendingSleep.end() );
111     hunts.insert( hunts.end(), pendingHunt.begin(), pendingHunt
            .end() );
112     eats.insert( eats.end(), pendingEat.begin(), pendingEat.end
            () );
113     explores.insert( explores.end(), pendingExplore.begin(),
            pendingExplore.end() );
114   }
115 };
116 }
```

Listing 16.14: Finite State Machine - Table based

# Bibliography

[1] Noel Llopis
*Data-Oriented Design (Or Why You Might Be Shooting Yourself in The Foot With OOP)*
http://gamesfromwithin.com/data-oriented-design

[2] John Lakos.
*Large-scale C++ Software Design*
Addison Wesley; 01 edition, 10 July 1996

[3] Peter Seibel
*Coders at Work, Reflections on the Craft of Programming*
Apress, 2009.

[4] Ben Moseley and Peter Marks
*Out of the Tar Pit*
February 6, 2006

[5] D. L. Parnas
*On the Criteria To Be Used in Decomposing Systems into Modules*
Communications of the ACM December 1972 Volume 15 Number 12

[6] David L. Parnas
in *Software Pioneers: Contributions to Software Engineering*
by Manfred Broy, Ernst Denert
Springer Science & Business Media 6 Dec 2012

[7] Codd, Edgar F.
    *A Relational Model of Data for Large Shared Data Banks*
    (June 1970). Communications of the ACM. 13 (6):
    377âĂŞ387. doi:10.1145/362384.362685.

[8] Codd, Edgar F.
    *Further Normalization of the Data Base Relational Model.*
    (Presented at Courant Computer Science Symposia Se-
    ries 6, "Data Base Systems," New York City, May
    24thâĂŞ25th, 1971.) IBM Research Report RJ909 (Au-
    gust 31st, 1971). Republished in Randall J. Rustin (ed.),
    Data Base Systems: Courant Computer Science Sym-
    posia Series 6. Prentice-Hall, 1972.

[9] Kent, William
    *A Simple Guide to Five Normal Forms in Relational
    Database Theory*
    (1983) Communications of the ACM, vol. 26, pp.
    120âĂŞ125
    http://www.bkent.net/Doc/simple5.htm

[10] Scott Bilas *A Data-Driven Game Object System* Gas Pow-
    ered Games, 2004 http://gamedevs.org/uploads/data-
    driven-game-object-system.pdf

[11] Valentin Simonov
    *10000 Update() calls*
    Unity3D, December 23, 2015
    https://blogs.unity3d.com/2015/12/23/1k-update-
    calls/

[12] Fay Chang, Jeffrey Dean, Sanjay Ghemawat, Wilson C.
    Hsieh, Deborah A. Wallach Mike Burrows, Tushar Chan-
    dra, Andrew Fikes, Robert E. Gruber
    *Bigtable: A Distributed Storage System for Structured
    Data*
    Google, Inc. 2006

[13] Daniel Kahneman.
    *Thinking, Fast and Slow*
    Farrar, Straus and Giroux, United States, 2011

[14] Albrecht, Tony
*Pitfalls of Object Oriented Programming*
Game Connect: Asia Pacific 2009
https://www.slideshare.net/EmanWebDev/pitfalls-of-object-oriented-programminggcap09

[15] Albrecht, Tony
*Pitfalls of Object Oriented Programming - Revisited*
Tehran Game Conference, July 2017
https://docs.google.com/presentation/d/1ST3mZgxmxqlpCFkdDhtgw116MQdCr2Fax2yjd8Az6zM/edit#slide=id.p

[16] Latency Numbers Every Programmer Should Know
https://people.eecs.berkeley.edu/~rcs/research/interactive_latency.html

[17] Carlos Bueno *Mature Optimization Handbook* Copyright
©2013 Facebook http://carlos.bueno.org/optimization/

[18] Drepper, Ulrich
*What Every Programmer Should Know About Memory*
2007        https://people.freebsd.org/        lstewart/articles/cpumemory.pdf

Made in United States
North Haven, CT
09 December 2023

45447207R00173